Garden Smarts

"A humdinger of a book . . . will help you to foresee and outwit the
various problems that you encounter in your garden, no matter
what they may be . . . engaging, easy to read, informative."
—BEVERLY (Mass.) TIMES

"By chatting with and quoting gardeners from all over the nation,
the book presents gardening tips, secrets and hints for the determined
gardener to gather, interpret, adapt and use in any garden situation.
A great idea and a tremendous help."
—THE TAB NEWSPAPERS (Boston, Mass.)

"Twenty–three chapters arranged by topic instruct,
enlighten and entertain."
—MAIL TRIBUNE, Medford, Oreg.

"You will enjoy this charming, folksy book, full of common sense
and hands–on information. . . ."
—THE FLORIDA GARDENER

"An ideal garden reference book . . . contains more than
a thousand invaluable tips from 200 leading amateur and
professional gardeners across the country."
—LAFAYETTE (Ind.) JOURNAL & COURIER

"A delightful book!"
—THE CHEYENNE (Wyo.) NEWSPAPERS

"It's like having a direct phone line to a whole lot of master gardeners."
—JOURNAL INQUIRER, Manchester, Conn.

Garden Smarts

A BOUNTY OF TIPS
FROM AMERICA'S BEST GARDENERS

SECOND EDITION

Shelley Goldbloom

The
Globe
Pequot
Press

OLD SAYBROOK, CONNECTICUT

Cover and text design by Nancy Freeborn

LIBRARY OF CONGRESS CATALOGING-IN-PUBLICATION DATA

Goldbloom, Shelley.
    Garden smarts : a bounty of tips from America's best gardeners / by Shelley Goldbloom. — 2nd. ed.
        p. cm.
    ISBN 1-56440-628-8
    1. Gardening. 2. Gardening—United States. I. Title.
SB453.G64 1995
    635—dc20   94-44272
                                      CIP

Manufactured in the United States of America
Second Edition/Second Printing

*This book is dedicated with great love to Josh,
who helped me raise my favorite crop of all:
three splendid Goldbloom daughters.*

Table of Contents

Civilization, for all its art, sophisticated technology
and many accomplishments, owes its existence
to a six-inch layer of topsoil,
and the fact that it rains.

—AUTHOR UNKNOWN

A Note on This Second Edition

When you read the garden advice that appears within these pages, I hope you will find much that is helpful. But please be aware that none of the tips are guaranteed, ironclad, foolproof, fail-safe formulas.

First, every garden is influenced by varying soil, light, temperature, wind, humidity, and other growing conditions. What works for one garden might not apply equally even to the garden next door.

Second, garden wisdom—gathered over generations, gleaned from personal experience, or even culled from current scientific research—is often speculative and sometimes wrong. Although I did my best to secure explanations and verify information, the answers were not always definitive. Sometimes even the authorities didn't agree. As with any advice, ultimately it's wise to trust your own judgment.

More than 230 gardeners throughout North America generously shared their knowledge with me for this book. In these pages are tips from leading national garden authorities, garden writers, and radio and television garden-show hosts. Horticulturists, botanists, soil and plant scientists, water quality and seed specialists, landscape designers, farmers, Extension agents, commercial growers, and home gardeners contributed hundreds of ideas, many from years of experience.

Some contributors are employed at major national gardens or till vast fields. Others cultivate just a few treasured plants on a postage-stamp lot or apartment windowsill. A few, like microbiologist Anne Johnson of NASA's Space Center, glean their knowledge in the most sophisticated facilities available, while some, like Amish farmers Mattie and Joe Borntreger, forgo entirely any form of mechanized equipment.

One of the nicest things about gardening is that if you want to try something new, you usually have to wait only until the next growing season. After writing a book, though, the moment it's published you start "Monday morning quarterbacking," wishing you'd included this and emphasized that, and feel a terrible sense of frustration because you're helpless to do anything about it. As my husband says, "Hindsight is 20/20 vision."

As a result, I'm grateful to Globe Pequot managing editor Bruce Markot for encouraging this revision. The new edition adds voices from regions of the United States and Canada previously underrepresented. It emphasizes more fundamentals on habitat and site considerations, landscape planning, lawns and turf alternatives, principles of plant nutrition, herb culture, and soil building, and it also adds super new secrets for successful growing.

Even in the relatively short time since the first edition appeared, there's been a growing public awareness of nature's complex and vital interconnectedness. Many of the new tips reflect this changed perception and strive for increasingly environmentally friendly gardening methods.

Researching *Garden Smarts* yielded an unexpected bonus for me: a link with so many enthusiastic and generous-spirited new gardening friends, both contributors and readers, who have become a continuing source of inspiration and expertise.

May the sun shine on your garden and on your life.

Acknowledgments

I owe a special debt of gratitude to Dr. Ernie Hartmann; retired county agent Jim Ness; nurserymen John Zoerb, Randy Baier, and Cy Klinkner; and arborist Jeff Davis for the time and knowledge they so generously shared throughout the process of evaluating and clarifying well over 1,200 garden tips. Thanks also to the reference staff of the La Crosse Public Library, Cooperative Extension Service agricultural agents Steve Rischette of the University of Wisconsin and Phil Smith of the University of Kentucky, and gardener extraordinaire Wendal Mitchell for cheerful patience with my zillion questions. University of Kentucky agronomy professor David Ditsch shed light on plant nutrition and gave pause to ponder the odds of a garden writer called Goldbloom consulting a soil expert called Ditsch in a town called Quicksand.

Any strengths in this book owe a large part of their existence to these kind folk. I alone, however, shoulder the blame for any misconceptions or errors.

I'm grateful also to Samantha Albert and Stefanie Goldbloom for helping locate sources; Kay Arenz, Hilda First, and Ingrid Goldbloom for interviewing several out-of-state gardeners on my behalf; my agent Elizabeth Pomada for wise counsel; and my dear friend and garden writer Kate Carter Frederick for all the hand-holding through both editions.

And my heartfelt thanks to the real creators of this book, the many gardeners throughout the United States and Canada listed hereafter, who so generously shared knowledge and garden wisdom:

Fe Abellera
Doc and Katy Abraham
Virgil Adams
George Allen
Odell Anderson
Jane Bahnsen

Randy Baier
Jeanette Baker
Ken Ball
Elmer Ballhagen
Karen and David Ballhagen
Cheryl Baskins

Lori Williams Bauer
Eugene Bauer
Keitha Cooper Baxa
Alec Berg
Lynn Biely
Scott Bjorge
Vern Bjorkquist
Tatiana Bodine
R. J. Bootzin
Joe and Mattie Borntreger
Ricardo Borrero
James W. Bricker
Josephine Broadhead
Professor Jan Harold Brunvand
LeeAnne Bulman
Richard Bunker
Mariel Carlisle
Vernon R. Carse
Mary Carter
Diane Cavis
Terri Clark
Jennifer Cohn
Chuck Comeau
Ruth Coombs
Sheila Coombs
Ralph Cramer
Jeff Davis
Ruth Ann Davis
Kathleen Deering
Mary Dempster
Joan Dolbier
Sr. Arita Dopkins
Josephine Drudick
Patti Emery
Mary Claire Fehring

Louis Ferris
Hilda First
Beverly Fortune
Kate Carter Frederick
Olga French
Mary Froegel
Pat and Steve Froegel
Donna Fuss
Dick Gagne
Professor James P. Gallagher
Annie Gardner
Mary Gehling
Mary Germann
Feroz Ghouse
Betty and John Gill
Charlet Givens
Anne Goldbloom
Margaret McFarlane Goldbloom
Kathy Guenther
Carol Hacker
Debbie Haldorson
Cyndi Hall
Kenneth Hall
Kathleen Halloran
Helen and Willard Halverson
Bill Hansen
Judy Hansen
Hank Harris
Ernie Hartmann
Pat Haugen
Roger Haynes
Cheri Hemker
Leah Hochart
Betty Holey
Tony Holt

Anne and Springer Hoskins
Carol Ignasik
Sharon Imes
Anne Johnson
Ken and Elinor Johnston
Carolyn Jones
John Kehoe
Clarence Kelly
Terry Kemp
Dale Kendrick
Wayne King
Cyril Klinkner
Gary Koller
Carl and Ann Korschgen
Manuel Lacks
Lyda Lanier
Eric Lautzenheiser
Vi and Jack Laws
Monica Lazere
Kathy Leslie
Lynne Leuthe
Meredyth Lillejord
Choua Lo
Jeanette Manske
Owen Marredeth
Tovah Martin
Robin Maxwell
Helen Mayville
Judith McCaslin
Cornelius McFarland, Jr.
Gary Menendez
Michelle Metrick
Fred Meyer
Susan Miller
Wendal Mitchell

Joseph Moos
Rosemary Muramoto
James K. Ness
Sally Nettleton
Bob Neuhaus
Jim Nichols
Ruby Nicks
Phil Normandy
Danny O'Deay
Linda George Olson
Pam Olson
Carolyn Ostrander
Pat Ostrander
Ruth Page
Milton Palmer
Deborah Paulson
Phil Pellitteri
Esther Pertzsch
Professor Arthur E. Peterson
Greg Philby
Elizabeth Pomada
Dona Popovic
Eleanor B. Potter
Sarah Price
Janet Raloff
Mary Jane Randolph
Steve Ranft
Bertha Reppert
Lisbeth Reynertson
Raymond Rice
Carol and Chuck Richlen
Conrad Richter
Yvonne Rickard
Jan Riggenbach
Kay Risberg

Lee Rodman
Mark Rogers
Joe Rusk
Kelly Ryan
Shirley Sauls
Judy and Stan Schabert
Martha Schams
Richard Schnall
Professor Emmett Schulte
Donna Schultz
Rita Schumacher
Larry Severeid
Luther Shaffer
Phyllis Shaudys
Pat Shedesky
Renee Shepherd
Mary Shriner
Herman Silver
Coya Silverlake
Eve Simon
Ruth Simons
Benny Simpson
Roberta Sladky
Ralph Snodsmith
Bill Snyder
Lillian and Bob Soules
Beatrice Sperling
Marvin Sperling
Richard Stelmach
Mona Stevens
Ruth Switzer
James M. Szynal
Hero Tamura

David Tarrant
Steve Taylor
Craig Thompson
Cherie Timming
Peter Tonge
Cathy Townsend
Anthony Tyznik
University of Alaska Cooperative
    Extension Service, Sitka, Alaska
May Vang
Gretchen Vetzner
Barbara Voight
Freek Vrugtman
Will Vultaggio
Iona Wabaunsee
Shirley Watterson
Stephen B. Webster, M.D.
Beth Weidner
Chris Weingand
Nick Wekseth
Kent Whealy
Bee Whirley
Deborah Whitehouse
Jan Scott Whiteway
Fred Wiche
Marianne Williams
Mary Witt
Ed and Irene Wojahn
Mary Wrodarczyk
Elsa Yeske
Dan Young
John Zoerb

Introduction

I t was November by the time the plans for this book jelled. "Could you have it done by early spring?" the editor asked.

"Sure," I replied, with what I hoped was a show of confidence. But all the time I was inwardly agonizing about whether I would be able to create a book with authentic trowel-in-hand flavor during months when nothing green was in sight and I was huddling indoors in long underwear.

Distracted by the winter's chill, I underestimated the powerful pull gardening can exert on us. Like an addiction, merely a whiff of fresh air and fresh soil draws us to the garden almost uncontrollably. This morning, for instance, dawns with an icy mist in the air. The ground is dusted with white, and the thermometer hovers near zero. Going out to replace the frozen water in the bucket in our poultry coop with warm water for our chicken flock, I shortcut through the rose bed, now bleak and bare.

Not quite bare. Brittle leaves still cling to their branches. Until now those leaves have been scarcely on the fringes of my consciousness—just a few dead leaves minding their own business, leaves that most likely would eventually have blown off in some winter storm, unnoticed.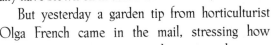

But yesterday a garden tip from horticulturist Olga French came in the mail, stressing how 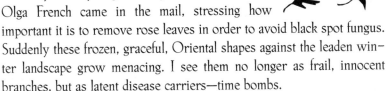 important it is to remove rose leaves in order to avoid black spot fungus. Suddenly these frozen, graceful, Oriental shapes against the leaden winter landscape grow menacing. I see them no longer as frail, innocent branches, but as latent disease carriers—time bombs.

Running to the garage, I grab my pruning shears and a basket in one hand, the snow shovel in the other. By the time I capture every last leaf clinging to each branch and poke around in the snow under the rosebushes to rout the fallen ones, my fingers are numb.

Too numb to get back to my word processor and type up gardening tips. But it doesn't matter. Because miraculously, it is garden season again—never mind what the calendar says. Maybe we can outwit fungi and get rid of beetles and aphids, but there is one bug we cannot dispel so easily: the Gardening Bug. Once it bites us, we're incurable—whatever the season.

If, dear readers, you have a favorite gardening tip you would like to share, I would love to hear from you. Please send your tips to me in care of the Globe Pequot Press, Inc., P.O. Box 833, Old Saybrook, CT 06475. Please include your name, address, telephone number, and anything else about yourself you would like to share.

CHAPTER ONE

Making Friends with Your Habitat

Desert winds are winds of war.
—KATHY LESLIE

When we stop to think about it, we realize with something like astonishment that our garden is far more than a simple plot of ground with plants and fertilizer. It's a complex alchemy powered by the sun, mingling a mind-boggling array of cosmic components, including tiny, invisible soil creatures; cloud fragments; winds that speed their way from across the world; elements trickling upward from the bedrock and hurled by lightning splitting the summer sky.

Our gardens are at the mercy of heat, cold, temperature variations, wind, storms, rain, humidity, frost, and snow. The plants are also affected by their soil, air and water quality, space, topography, weeds, disease, drainage, and the influences of nearby plants. Sunshine, moonlight, and even artificial light also wield power over our gardens. So do gravity, tidal pull, and myriad cosmic forces, some of which plant scientists as yet understand only dimly.

In this chapter gardeners from all over North America offer resourceful methods for coping with habitat challenges. You'll find counsel on plants that are more—or less—suitable for your climate and strategies to help plants thrive where you live.

It's no surprise that we who ignore the basic guidelines do so at our own peril. But despite occasional mishaps along the way, we ought not to become enslaved by rigid rules. It's easy for conscientious gardeners to get so caught up in our plants' needs that we neglect our own passions, forgetting that people are part of the environment too. We experience the greatest fulfillment when we take into account not only the external garden habitat but our own personal "climate" of aesthetics, lifestyle, temperament, and energy level.

And when all is said and done, even after 10,000 years of garden husbandry and our most sophisticated technoscience, we still have much to learn about what makes our gardens flourish.

As I gathered these tips, I was awed by the complex web of powerful natural forces interacting with everything that grows. These practical tips do more than help our gardens thrive. They are also a reminder of the bond that links all life—a reminder that ultimately, whether we're gardening in the mountains, the plains, the desert, or the rain forest, cultivating acres or simply tending a few potted plants on a windowsill, there is no boundary to our garden.

Recipe for a Greener Thumb

The only thing different about having a green thumb is that you don't get discouraged by failure—when something doesn't work, you try again.

—BETH WEIDNER, ASSISTANT PARK MANAGER,
ALFRED B. MACLAY STATE GARDENS IN TALLAHASSEE, FLORIDA

What's Your Zone?

Do you suffer from "numberitis"? If your Social Security number, tax-payer number, zip code, area code, driver's license number, and bank account number don't give you enough to remember, now you have a new one: Your garden address has changed, and you may not be where you used to be!

The U.S. Department of Agriculture has recently published new zone maps, and the zones have been revised. "So when you select plants according to a recommended hardiness zone, verify whether the new or the old zone is intended," says Beth Weidner, assistant park manager for Alfred B. Maclay State Gardens in Tallahassee, Florida.

AUTHOR'S NOTE: *And be aware that zone maps in garden catalogs are sometimes inaccurate.*

✳

Consider your official climate zones to be only a rule of thumb, recom-mends Eric Lautzenheiser, director of San Antonio Botanical Gardens. "San Antonio's climate, for instance, has horrendously erratic extremes. When temperatures plummet from 90 degrees to 20 degrees overnight, plants are not hardened off at all, so although it's officially considered Zone 8 and 9, even some Zone 7 plants may die."

Microclimates

As you gather garden advice for your climate zone, keep in mind that whether you live in California or Maine, your garden is influenced by not only your regional climate but its own little microclimate. "This can vary quite a lot even in the same community," says nurseryman Randy Baier of Baier Nursery in La Crosse, Wisconsin.

"For instance, if you live on a hilltop, it's likely to be windier. On the other hand, low-lying areas are subject to more frost. Land just a few miles inland will be less temperate than neighboring land in a river valley. These small differences within your immediate environment have an effect on your garden, too."

Terrestrial Aliens

"A lot of nurseries are serving very large areas in the nation. However, what's happy in California's climate maybe sulks and suffers in Texas. If we want good adaptability, we need to select plants from parent stock native within 100 miles of our garden," advises Eric Lautzenheiser. "This is especially important with trees, when you've got a huge investment and need long survival," he adds.

✳

When choosing native plants, realize they are native not to political boundaries but to biological boundaries. "'Native Texan' doesn't mean squat," scoffs Eric Lautzenheiser. "A lot of people have the misconception that because it's native, it will grow anywhere on your lot, but even a small yard may go from shade to full sun, to wet to dry, hard limestone to deep clay; a flower may thrive on one side of your yard and not the other."

✳

"Lots of us love to bring plants back from vacations. But when you import new strains from other climate zones," cautions arborist Jeff Davis of Davis Tree Service in Onalaska, Wisconsin, "be aware that they may have hitchhiking insects and fungus diseases that lack the natural controls of your native species, and so have the potential to be especially harmful."

Post-Traumatic Stress Syndrome

"If you live in areas where flash floods are common, as they are in Dallas, Texas, where I lived," warns Jan Scott, "do not use ground cover for entire lawns. Folks attracted to the modern landscape appeal of ground cover generally discover that it takes so long to take hold that violent storms wash the topsoil away, leaving the ground vulnerable to erosion. I suggest folks plant ground covers only as decorative borders, such as in rows along paths," Jan concludes.

✳

Cypress Gardens, owned and operated by the city of Charleston, South Carolina, is a remnant of a seventeenth-century rice plantation. The reflections of thousands of daffodils, snowflakes, bluebells, lilies, camellias, dogwoods, wisteria, tea olives, and magnolias shimmered in its black waters, delighting visitors who explored from flat-bottom boats—that is, until Hurricane Hugo struck in 1989.

"In the darkness of those two September days," says horticulturist Susan Miller, "centuries of work were viciously dashed. However, we are finding many ornamental shrubs broken but still thriving beneath the rubble. In the aftermath, as never before, we expect to learn some of nature's valuable lessons."

Cypress Gardens staffers share the following hints to help others whose plants suffer the ravages of storm damage.

- In many instances, drastic pruning is in order, horticulturist Susan Miller advises. In the long run the plants will be healthier and look lovelier than they did before the storm.

- "Even in cases where large trees fell on camellias and azaleas, the ornamentals escaped relatively intact. We carefully removed debris by hand, then pruned as necessary. Not only large limbs, but clumps of pine straw needles needed to be removed quickly to afford the plants as much sunlight as possible," she says.

- To help remove debris and undesirable vines and plants in the wake of storm damage, Cathy Townsend, superintendent of special facilities for the City of Charlston Department of Parks, recommends a mixture of one cup of Round Up and two pounds of Crisco shortening. Stir the ingredients with a stick and apply to the cut end of a vine.

- "With this method, the Round Up comes in contact with the problem plant without harming anything else. It also adheres to any awkward surface. It has kept our garden from turning into an uncontrollable jungle," she says.

AUTHOR'S NOTE: *Round Up is an extremely powerful herbicide manufactured by Monsanto.*

- "Many plants were uprooted in the storm," says Cheryl Baskins, head of public relations for Cypress Gardens, "but quite a few were successfully replanted. Even large bushes and small trees were uprighted and the roots covered back over."

- A come-along (wire stretcher) placed carefully around the padded trunk worked well, the South Carolina naturalist notes. For padding, wrap some resilient material, such as a few layers of burlap sacking or a folded blanket, between the trunk and the come-along; this prevents the wire from damaging the bark.

AUTHOR'S NOTE: *You might want to support such trees for at least one growing season until the roots reestablish. Tie a nylon rope around the trunk and tie it to a sturdy stake in the opposite direction from which the tree fell.*

- If shrubs are uprooted and cannot immediately be replanted in their appropriate places, it's possible to locate them temporarily in other parts of the garden until you are ready for them again, Cheryl says.

- "Give everything the benefit of the doubt," urges Cheryl. "We're waiting two seasons before we write a plant off our list. We are pruning the first spring. If after the second spring we see no signs of life, we will replant anew in that spot."

✹

Sooner or later almost every climate zone suffers a severe dip in temperature that leaves ornamental shrubs looking burned. "Technically it's desiccation," says John Gill, owner of Laurel Landscape in Keavy, Kentucky. "Freezing temperature dries all the moisture out of the leaves; the plant can't take up moisture from frozen ground and become 'freeze dried.'

"The biggest mistake people make is getting anxious and not waiting to see what is dead, and what will come back. If you've lost the top but the roots are intact, it's amazing how much will regenerate from the root system." If damage is severe enough, you may have to cut all the way back. But don't cut during dormancy, John warns. "Wait till growth starts and see how much is actually damaged. Prune, shape, water and feed. Coddle that growing season. And be patient; they'll look ugly until growth comes back, and may take two years to recover."

Coping with Mother Nature's Mood Swings

Do your winter temperatures have wide mood changes? "Here in Tallahassee, Florida, the temperature swings from the eighties to freezing from week to week," says Beth Weidner, assistant park manager for Alfred B. Maclay State Gardens, home to one of the South's most extensive camellia collections.

"In the warm spell, the sap starts to rise, and then the cold returns; sometimes camellia plants are damaged. You can minimize this problem (although not totally prevent it) by planting tolerant varieties," she advises.

✹

It doesn't seem fair, but skyrocketing summer temperatures don't give any immunity to winter freezes. Desert dweller Eve Simon laments, "During the last two winters we suffered from week-long freezes— enough to turn our desert garden into a brown devastation akin to what it might look like after a nuclear holocaust.

"What to do to prevent total brown-out of the bougainvillea, natal plum, hibiscus, ficus, young citrus, and all the other plants that are bravely blooming and green in what should be withering heat? You run around each night and cover the poor things with mattresspads, blankets, and—if you've had any foresight—burlap you have obtained at the garden stores. In the mornings, you gather up the frost-moistened, dirt-strewn coverings (of which you never have enough) and repeat the next night.

"Naturally," the Phoenix resident concedes, "laziness usually wins out, and you lose the battle. Then you are admonished not to prune the unsightly brown mess for at least six weeks, in case of another frost, since you mustn't expose anything tender that may still be alive underneath the frost-damaged blight."

Short Growing Season Strategies

In higher elevations you are often better off selecting shorter season varieties regardless of your official frost-free "allowance," advises Kathleen Halloran, associate editor of *Herb Companion* magazine. Kathleen lives in La Porte, Colorado, a nearly mile-high community along the front range of the Rockies.

"Technically we have a 120-day growing season," she says, but it's wise not to buy any seeds requiring more than 80 days. "If it says 80 days, plants may actually take 120 frost-free days to reach maturity at high altitudes because of the cold nights."

✳

In south-central Alaska, where Carolyn and Dennis Ostrander used to live, the short growing season and cold ground (so cold, in fact, that it doesn't support earthworms) present real challenges to gardeners.

To catch more sunshine, the Ostranders made sloping garden beds 10 to 12 inches high, "like little mountains," says Carolyn. As the sun hits the sloped sides, it warms the soil.

✳

Sometimes the oldest planting methods become the newest. In prehistoric times Native American gardeners also planted their garden rows in mounded beds with a trench on either side for temperature control.

Most recently, H'Mong families who fled political upheaval in Laos for asylum in the United States have been reintroducing a similar method.

"In the summer, we plant lower for cooler temperatures," says May Vang, now living in La Crosse, Wisconsin. "In the winter, we plant on flat beds, and in the fall, pile the soil higher to prevent frost damage."

✻

Ridged rows still offer many advantages to today's gardeners, says Dr. Jim Gallagher, director of the Mississippi Valley Archeology Center, just as they benefited Native Americans 500 years ago in the ancient gardens his archaeologists have excavated.

"If you have problems with excess moisture and frost where you garden, these are especially useful," counsels Dr. Gallagher. Some other advantages he notes are weed control, erosion control, fewer problems with wind and drought, and reduced compacting, allowing closer planting and accordingly higher yield.

✻

Here's yet another variation of the raised-bed gardening method. Gardening on a small city lot in Madison, Wisconsin, horticulturist Barbara Voight maintains nine flower and two vegetable gardens, growing enough to share the bounty with the families of her six grown children.

"To save space, make the garden more accessible, and to keep the soil drier in the spring so it warms up sooner, I garden on 4-by-4-foot mounds," says Barbara. The mounds need to be only 8 to 10 inches high and will hold their shape pretty well without side supports and without much erosion, she finds.

"The interstices are dug down two spade depths and filled with leaves, grasses, shredded newspaper, and the like, which gradually decompose," Barbara says. "Every second year, I move all the dirt over half a mound, so I'm gardening on the two-year-old compost."

✹

Any gardener finds climate a challenge, but for Ruth Ann Davis it's doubly so. Ruth Ann and her husband cope with heat and drought in Tucson, Arizona, for half the year and then commute to Eagle River, Wisconsin, where frost often comes in early September and lasts until Memorial Day. "To have good luck with a short growing season, buy seeds from a seed house that specializes in meeting the needs of cold climate gardening," she advises.

✹

If you have to gamble with a short growing season, it's especially hard to get a head start with corn, because you generally can't start seeds indoors and transplant them. Ruth Ann Davis offers a novel solution: "Buy a strip of the sod intended for lawns. Plant the kernels in the sod an inch apart. When the corn sprouts and is ready to go outdoors, simply cut the sod apart into individual plugs and space in the rows as you normally would," she says.

Frost, Ice, and Snow

"If spring frost hits after your strawberries are blooming," advises Jeanette Manske of Stoddard, Wisconsin, "hose them early in the morning to remove the ice. You might lose some, but you won't lose all. But if the sun hits, they freeze."

AUTHOR'S NOTE: *Interestingly, melting ice absorbs heat. If the frost crystals grab heat from the plants during the melting process, their delicate blossoms may freeze; however, hosing melts the ice so quickly that it has no chance to rob heat from the plants, taking it instead from the hose water.*

✱

You know that desperate feeling when the radio announces a frost warning and you run around frantically covering all of your roses, marigolds,
and mums with old bedspreads and tablecloths? Inevitably, there's a terrible wind howling that afternoon, and it's a hassle to keep the protective
covers from blowing away. Vern Bjorkquist of Mindoro, Wisconsin,
advises that they can be anchored easily and effectively by fastening them
in place with clothespins.

✱

Heavy snow damages some evergreens. Before it has a chance to turn to
ice, shake it from the boughs, advises Cheri Hemker of Onalaska, Wisconsin, who found this tip in an old post–World War I vintage garden
almanac. Don't shake vigorously, though, as icy branches are brittle and
vulnerable to breakage.

Wet Conditions

If your springs are rainy, it's hard to get an early start planting, as wet
soil is apt to form dense clumps when you try to tamp it around tender
transplants. You can solve this problem by plowing in the fall and protecting the fluffy, drier earth under plastic, suggests Wendal Mitchell, an
educator in Corbin, Kentucky.

✱

"Some plants have difficulty coming through in the spring," says nurseryman Randy Baier. "For example, baby's breath and chrysanthemums
can be a little touchy. When we lose them, most people assume that the
winter cold killed them. It's more likely, however, that the wet conditions
of early spring made them rot. You can prevent this by planting them on
a slight rise, instead of in a totally flat bed. A mound just an inch or so
high is enough to help drainage."

✱

"Don't consider mulch automatically the answer to everything," cautions research scientist Benny Simpson of Texas A&M's Texas Agricultural Experiment Station in Dallas. "I think a mulch in *most* cases helps, but if you get a cold, wet winter or a wet summer and there are root rot organisms in the soil, then it could set off some of these Mickey Mouse rots that you never knew you had."

✳

Saint John's wort does well as a ground cover in damp, mild climates, notes Jane Bahnsen of Seattle, Washington. "Ours is still green in late December. If a hard freeze turns it brown, it can be cut down with a lawn mower in the spring and will quickly grow new shoots."

✳

In rainy climates like that of Bellevue, Washington, where Carol and Chuck Richlen live, moss often becomes a slippery, unsightly nuisance on patios and paving stones. To remove it, apply a solution of three parts water to one part household bleach. Do it on a sunny day, and then keep pets (and kids) off for twenty-four hours. "It not only removes the moss; it also makes the paving stones clean and beautiful," Carol says.

✳

Lawns too tend to grow mossy in cool rainy climates with acid conditions. "I think we shouldn't worry about it too much," reassures David Tarrant, education coordinator for University of British Columbia's Botanical Garden in Vancouver, author of *David Tarrant's Pacific Gardening Guide* (Whitecap Books), and host of CBC-TV's "Canadian Gardener."

You'll have less moss, however, in a healthy lawn. To keep your lawn in top condition, add lime to sweeten acidic soil, aerate, and then apply a top dressing. An organic top dressing such as well-rotted manure or compost interferes less with the natural balance of your soil, advises David. Just brush it in with a broom after aerating.

✳

Sometimes fixing one problem creates another. Folks who live in the Pacific Northwest or other regions where soil is acidic commonly put lime on their lawns. Warns David Tarrant, "It's important you don't get any lime on rhododendrons, or they won't flower well, and will die eventually."

＊

"If the summers are wet where you live, don't bother to grow statice," counsels Ralph Cramer of Cramer's Posie Patch in Columbia, Pennsylvania. A national authority on everlastings, he cautions, "If you get rain during the last two weeks before harvest, the blooms turn brown."

Desert dwellers who have had problems growing everlastings should have good luck with statice, Ralph notes.

Desert Gardening

In the arid landscape of the Rio Grande Valley, where retired nurseryman Hero Tamura lives, you never have to worry about the sandy soil getting waterlogged. Instead, the challenge is wind and drought. Forty-mile-an-hour winds are commonplace, and 90-mile gusts are not unknown. And an average year yields only 8 to 10 inches of rainfall.

When planting trees in a desert climate, dig a reservoir around the base about 30 inches in diameter, depending upon the size of the tree, and about 4 to 6 inches deep, the New Mexico nurseryman advises.

Fill the reservoir with wood chips to hold water and prevent it from evaporating. "Use the large size chips so they don't blow away in the wind," he counsels.

＊

"Container gardening is a smart way to go for a desert gardener," advises Kathy Leslie of Thousand Oaks, California. "This allows you to conserve water, and to enjoy some plants which you couldn't otherwise grow in the hard alkaline soil.

"Many people resist the container approach at first, wanting a 'real' (in other words, English cottage) garden but after a few years and a few astronomical water bills, the containers start to make a lot of sense.

"When choosing containers, check out the new plastic terra–cotta colored pots. These are lighter and cheaper than clay, and conserve water far more efficiently. A plant in a traditional clay pot may need to be watered three times daily during the summer; plastic will give you a two- or three–day break between waterings. Best of all, plastic won't show the white crust that accumulates on clay after a few months from salts leaching out of the hard water," Kathy says.

*

"The desert soil is, as a rule, almost unbelievably alkaline (my own garden soil stays stubbornly at 8.5+ pH, in spite of many soil amendments)," Kathy observes.

"The best advice: Don't fight it. Go native instead. Your local nursery, newspaper gardening columnist, and a good book on desert gardening can advise you on the scores of plants that flourish in alkaline soil."

Some herbs that are lime lovers are aloe vera, fennel, artemisia, and lamb's ears. Mints don't mind it either.

*

"In a desert climate, the very best time to plant anything larger than a pony–pack of annuals is October or November and February and March," advises Californian Kathy Leslie. "Planting in the fall lets you take advantage of whatever amount of winter rain you may get, but the plants won't grow much until the summer. The spring planting is more encouraging, as longer and warmer days promote rapid growth, but you'll have to water more. Regardless of the month you choose to transplant, however, always do it when the sun is low in the sky, or you might just as well take the plants directly from container to the garbage."

One of the best transplant tools in a desert climate is a flat "soaker" hose, adds the California gardener. "After transplanting, cover the new babies with some type of mulch, place the flexible hose around each plant, turn it on low, and leave it in place for at least two hours. The need for adequate moisture in this climate cannot be overemphasized," she stresses. "I have not lost a single transplant since stumbling on this method by accident."

"Desert winds are winds of war, and they can be devastating, especially to tender young plants. A howling Santa Ana or other hot wind can permanently wilt a plant in a matter of hours," notes Kathy. "Keep all potted plants in a sheltered area, or, at the very least, be prepared to move them as soon as the winds come up."

✹

A good method of protection for young transplants, Kathy suggests, is a tomato cage lined with stiff paper. The sun is able to shine through the open top, but the wind cannot penetrate the paper. The plant is protected from moisture loss, and its young leaves cannot be stripped by the wind. Once the plant reaches a fair size, it can generally fend for itself, but the early protection can save a lot of plants and money the first year.

✹

For a low-growing ground cover around walkways and tree reservoirs, retired landscaper Hero Tamura of Albuquerque, New Mexico, likes dragon's blood (*Sedum spurium*), a hardy succulent that thrives even in heat and dry soil, producing a carpet of star-shaped wine-red flowers in midsummer and rich green foliage that turns bronze in the fall. "It's easy to propagate and care for. It doesn't spread like ivy and is easy to control," he says.

✹

For desert climates Albuquerque gardener Eileen Langner advises planting drought-tolerant perennials such as the hardy Mexican hat and prairie coneflower (*Ratibida pinnata*). "They'll bloom with cheer all summer long and then reseed like crazy," she says.

More on Drought

"In parts of Texas, it gets so dry that even the rocks need water," jokes Benny Simpson, a Dallas agricultural research scientist. If you too live in a dry climate, when planting woody, drought-tolerant plants, forget they're drought-tolerant the first year or two. You may need to water them quite often, depending on temperature, wind, and drainage. "Once you get them locked in the first couple of years, they're going to take much less water, but you may still have to help," he adds.

✳

Cultivate in times of drought, advises Amish farmer Joe Borntreger. "People think if you work the soil, it'll just dry out. But that's not the case. If it dries, it forms a hard crust, and the ground can't breathe. Cultivating keeps the soil loose and holds the moisture in," counsels the Missouri native.

AUTHOR'S NOTE: *Cultivation also aids in penetration when you water or it rains; a hard crust encourages runoff.*

Surviving Heat

"Fruit trees won't suffer sun scald from intense heat and sunshine if you paint their trunks white the first couple of years," advises Renee Shepherd of Shepherd's Garden Seeds in Felton, California.

"Citrus trees whose trunks are painted white seem odd the first time you see them," comments Arizonan Eve Simon. "Newcomers wonder whether this is due to an overeager decorating instinct, but its purpose is to deter sunburn.

"I have a much easier solution: I don't prune the trees, so the trunks aren't exposed. The only problem is that many of the ripening grapefruit are on the ground while still attached to the tree!"

❋

Some flowers can thrive in even the most torrid climate; others wilt when the temperature skyrockets. Suggests Rita Schumacher of Belleview, Florida, "Some flowers that tolerate our summer heat are vincas, Gerbera daisies, snapdragons, marigolds, canna lilies, mums, tiger lilies, and geraniums."

Hard-Bed Gardening: Outwitting Rocky Soil or Concrete

If your soil is horribly rocky or too steep to till, or even if you have nothing but a slab of concrete, you can still create a fine garden bed in bales of rotted hay.

"I first discovered this while working as a reporter in the United Kingdom," says Peter Tonge of Weymouth, Massachusetts, a director of the National Gardening Association. In areas where it was too cool to grow tomatoes outdoors, growers took rotting hay bales and planted the tomatoes directly in the hay. It was easier to haul hay than soil into the greenhouse.

Peter brought the method home. He explains, "Our Maine garden was on a rocky hillside. It was a pain to dig a conventional bed or haul soil for a raised bed, so I tried hay."

The method is simple. Lay one or more hay bales on the top of the bed in a single layer. Wrap the sides of the bales with plastic so water won't drain too quickly. If you're on a concrete slab, stand each bale in a tray 1 or 2 inches deep to hold the water.

Leave the bales intact; don't open them up. They will last for three years or more, although they'll gradually decrease in size. You can start with fresh hay, but if you can get it, start with spoiled hay. To help your hay rot during the first year, buy composting inoculant from a garden center and sprinkle it on the bales like you'd sprinkle sugar on a bowl of cereal. Water the bales well.

Plant directly into the top of the bale. In the first year stick to transplanting plants and sowing large seeds such as beans and squash. For each plant poke a long narrow hole in the hay. Insert the plant or seed and a couple of handfuls of soil. The first year especially, the bales are more susceptible to drying out, so keep them watered if it doesn't rain.

By the second year there's no need to add soil or composting inoculant, as the bales will be sufficiently rotted. By then you'll be able to broadcast fine seeds such as carrots and parsnips too. Just sprinkle a light covering of starter mix, peat moss, or garden soil over them.

Apartment Balcony Gardening

How do you transplant the experience of gardening in a sprawling hacienda in the Rio Grande Valley to living in a fourth-floor apartment?

"I fill my 6-by-12-foot balcony with potted plants—about twenty-two pots. With minimum care, they flower profusely all summer and I feel that I am in milady's bower," says Eileen Langner of Albuquerque, New Mexico.

The best way to do it, Eileen believes, is to "grow native." The more you go native with your choice of plants, the less you will have need for watering and chemicals.

✴

Often gardening on the balcony of a high-rise apartment means contending with high winds, points out ninety-year-old Anne Goldbloom of Vancouver, British Columbia. "To prevent the wind from knocking over the flowers, place them in larger, heavier pots," she suggests.

Protecting Habitat from Competing Species

If weeds from nearby habitats tend to invade your garden, suggests farmer LeeAnne Bulman of Independence, Wisconsin, "try growing a cover crop such as wheat, oats, or rye for a season. They have a natural weed suppressant in their root systems. Unless you want to harvest the crop, mow it three or four times during the season. If you're in the South, plant it in the fall for a winter cover crop."

AUTHOR'S NOTE: *To protect a tender new lawn from weeds and weather until it gets established, sow a fast-growing nurse crop such as annual rye or oats along with your grass seed.*

❋

"If your property borders on woods or other natural areas, you have more to think about than those who garden in an ordinary yard," points out Roberta Sladky, manager of the Como Conservatory in St. Paul, Minnesota.

In many areas invasive garden shrubs and plants such as Tatarian honeysuckle, buckthorn, and loosestrife can spread from home gardens via birds who eat the seeds, and soon they encroach on the natural sur-roundings, competing with the native species. To protect the native environment, Roberta Sladky urges, "Be very careful. Avoid plants that cause these problems."

Hindsight is 20/20 Vision

If the plant doesn't do well, it's not that it failed you—you failed to understand its environmental needs. Plants that fail to thrive are too often placed into the wrong growing situation. I know one keen gar-dener who, over a period of time, placed the same plant into twelve different sites in her garden before hitting the one just right for the plant.

—GARY KOLLER, MANAGING HORTICULTURIST, HARVARD UNIVERSITY'S ARNOLD ARBORETUM

CHAPTER TWO

Garden Design: People-Friendly, Earth-Friendly Landscaping

When you plant things with spring color and fall color and winter berries, you use them as your calendar.

—GARY MENENDEZ

M any years ago we had a neighbor who was such a perfectionist about his lawn that you'd walk by and there he'd be, crouching in the yard with an artist's paintbrush delicately poised in one hand and a single blade of problem grass gently clasped in the other as he applied some nostrum or other. I'd sort of shuffle by, hoping he didn't notice me, because our lawn, by contrast, was an embarrassment. Busy as I was raising toddlers in those days, the whole extent of my landscaping efforts was retrieving peanut butter sandwich crusts from the sandbox and cleaning up dog doo.

For most of us our landscapes are a product of far more than grand desires and horticultural considerations: They're a jumbled mishmash of culture and character bound by time constraints, energy levels, finances, and compromises; powered by inspiration and aesthetics; and nourished by dreams.

Whether you're a harried yuppie or a mellow retiree, a child of nature or a devotee of structured, formal design, whether you're struggling in the shadows of an overmature landscape or staring impatiently at barren ground, you'll meet kindred souls in this chapter. In the pages that follow, they share practical ideas for landscape planning: for saving water, money, labor, and time; for creating moods; and for achieving a more harmonious natural setting. You'll find solutions for common garden problems, guidelines for designing an authentic Victorian rose garden, earth-friendly suggestions for lawn care, and even a couple of creative options for more communal kinds of gardening that reach beyond your own garden's boundary.

And despite the above confession about my erstwhile low personal standards for landscaping, I too have been moved to doctor lawns when the occasion calls for drastic measures. During a snowstorm this past winter, my car slithered out of control down the drive and into a nearby yard—not the aforementioned gentleman's, but one belonging to an equally ardent lawn perfectionist. A kind young neighbor tried to back out the vehicle as I shoved and shouted useless directions and as the spinning wheels, flinging clumps of snow with churned-up sod, gouged deep, muddy ruts into the pristine surface.

Listening to Mother Nature

Don't be so tidy that you lose the beauty of the garden. Where nature has made the garden, nobody's worrying about insects and disease, nobody trims or rakes, and it never looks littered. We've become so obsessed that we've forgotten the real value: the harmony of nature.

—ANTHONY TYZNIK, ILLINOIS LANDSCAPE ARCHITECT

"He'll see where the tracks lead and know it was me—what am I going to do?" I wailed.

Surveying the mess, my neighbor shook his head doubtfully. Then his face brightened. "Don't worry," he said, "the lawn will look just fine. All it needs is a can of white spray paint."

Planning Basics

"Gardens are ephemeral. The herbaceous plants, the annuals, don't last long. What do last are the trees, the retaining walls, the pathway, the ponds. These strong physical structures need to be well thought about and placed, and relate to the surroundings. They are the elements that remain—the bones of the garden," advises Richard Schnall, vice-president for horticulture at the New York Botanical Garden.

✳

Be aware of the drawbacks of hiring a professional to design landscape plans, cautions arborist Jeff Davis of Davis Tree Service in Onalaska, Wisconsin. "Some landscapers are paid by the volume, and their work is overzealous. It can be costly for you, and your landscaping eventually can get out of control and become overcrowded as the shrubs and trees mature. By all means, consult with experts, but, ultimately, make your own decisions."

✳

To avoid overplanting, draw your landscape design on paper at the *mature* size of the plantings, counsels landscape architect Gary Menendez.

✳

Keep in mind that different varieties of the same plant may have radically disparate growth habits. "Research them well, and choose a low-growing cultivar for a typical home garden," cautions David Tarrant, education coordinator for the University of British Columbia's Botanical Garden in Vancouver. "A lot of people buy a cute little rhododendron in a gallon container and plant it near a driveway or window or path. Then it grows and grows—and grows, and takes over."

A Drop of Prevention Saves a Gallon of Cure

Like today's twelve-step programs for human fulfillment, Xeriscape, or water-efficient landscaping, preaches steps for success. For healthy landscapes that save water, labor, and money, here are seven fundamentals developed by Xeriscape Colorado! Inc. that Denver landscape architect Ken Ball, coauthor of Water Wise Gardening (Taylor Guide edition, Houghton Mifflin) and one of the nonprofit conservation group's founders, recommends:

1. Start with a plan: Solid groundwork, with input from water, plant, and design experts, can avoid costly problems.

2. Limit lawn size: Plant grasses that require less water, and consider turf alternatives, such as ground covers and decks.

3. Mulch to hold water, slow erosion, and reduce weeds.

4. Group plants with similar water and cultural needs.

5. Build up your soil for better absorption and water-holding capacity.

6. Irrigate efficiently: Water according to plant need, rather than by fixed schedule.

7. Practice regular maintenance: Water, prune, compost, fertilize, and weed before problems develop.

AUTHOR'S NOTE: *Xeriscape Colorado! Inc. offers a wonderful newsletter, workshops, and seminars. Its address is P.O. Box 4202, Denver, CO 80204-0202.*

$$$–Saving Strategy

Creating a perennial or wildflower garden on a shoestring budget is challenging. "It gets very pricey to use containerized plants," commiserates Denver landscape architect Ken Ball. "If you sink all your money into one or two large plants, you miss the flamboyant effect a mass planting can produce. Yet if you opt for tiny bedding plants, you have a long wait."

You can solve this dilemma by planting three levels of vegetation: First, plant a few well–established container plants that typically bloom the first year and are large enough to show in the landscape. Second, plant 2¼-inch or flat–size plants. "Those cost a tenth the price of a one gallon plant, but the second year they will catch up," Ken says. Last, sow seed (commercial or gathered) of the same varietal plants. This strategy stretches landscape dollars, gives instant results that prevent discouragement, and builds for the long term, counsels Ken.

Work–Saving Strategy

Be open to having wider foundation plantings of shrubs and reducing the size of your lawn area, suggests Roberta Sladky, manager of the Como Conservatory.

Shrubs require care, especially in their early stages, but they're more efficient over the long haul. You won't be so dependent on watering and on needing to fertilize and mow. Lawns are very energy demanding and inefficient.

States of Mind

This tremendous effort to have a perfect lawn is a total waste of effort. Why don't people devote that time to teaching people to read who can't, or feeding the hungry?

—MARY WITT, HORTICULTURE EXTENSION SPECIALIST, UNIVERSITY OF KENTUCKY

✻

If you feel pressured by gardening chores, double-sleeve landscaping can buy you time, advises Greg Philby, editor of Better Homes & Gardens's Special Interest Publication *Garden, Deck & Landscape Planner*. Here's how:

Buy stackable plastic pots. Sink some where you'll want annuals. Fill others with potting soil and plants, then slip them into the in-the-ground pots. You can move your annuals in seconds without raising a trowel. "Plastic pots are easier to stack and less likely to crack in the ground than clay pots," adds Greg.

"Drop and Run" Plants

For exceptionally low-maintenance landscaping, Betty Gill, co-owner of Laurel Gardens in Keavy, Kentucky, recommends the following plants. "They're so easy-care, I call them 'drop and run,' " says Betty.

1. Bishop's weed, also known as gout weed (*Aegopodium*): This ground cover has variegated light green and white leaves and thrives in shade.

2. Burning bush (*Euonymus alatus 'compacta'*): This shrub needs little trimming and has brilliant fall color.

3. Daylilies (*Hemerocallis*): There are more than one hundred popular varieties of this graceful, sun-loving flower, ranging from ½ foot to 8 feet tall.

4. Plantain lily (*Hosta*): Though its stalks of white or pale lilac bell-shaped flowers are pretty in bouquets, shade-loving hosta is mainly cultivated for its attractive foliage. (For more on hosta, see page 254.)

5. Lily-turf, sometimes called monkey grass (*Liriope*): This member of the lily family grows about 10 inches tall. Both dark green and variegated varieties make a pretty border.

6. Yew (*Taxus*): A landscape favorite since the time of the ancient Greeks, this evergreen is attractive year-round and is resistant to diseases and insects.

Going Native

Many of our woody ornamental plants are widely adapted to grow from coast to coast. Unfortunately, many have weak wood or lack drought tolerance, cautions research scientist Benny Simpson of Texas A&M's Texas Agricultural Experiment Station in Dallas.

For attractive, easy-to-grow plants that need less water and coddling, Benny advises planting native species. "Generally, every state has native plant societies that can advise you, as can reputable nurseries," he says.

AUTHOR'S NOTE: *There are many native plant conferences, and garden enthusiasts, as well as professionals, are welcome. Your college horticulture program can let you know about them, notes landscape architect Gary Menendez of Knoxville, Tennessee.*

Creating a Mood

"When you're looking at a painting or a landscape that you like and you really don't know why, then it's successful because it's created a mood," says landscape designer Yvonne Rickard of Shreveport, Louisiana. Here are some ways Yvonne uses shape, texture, and color to achieve a special feeling:

• If you want a stimulating mood, select plants with diverse textures, some with very big and others with very small leaves. Pick warm colors: bright reds, oranges, yellows. "But keep a focal point, so it's not too overwhelming. Group a color, instead of scattering it throughout, or you end up looking like you have a garden center," Yvonne warns.

For a soothing mood go with plants that have the same-size leaves and similar textures, whatever their height. Choose cool colors: whites, blues, purples, pale pink.

• For an especially tranquil feeling, include the sounds of running water and birdsong, Yvonne counsels. "Birds aren't only added ornaments in your landscape; they help with pollination. To attract birds, plant shrubbery such as American holly that has edible berries or fruit," she says.

AUTHOR'S NOTE: *The U.S. Soil Conservation Service has wonderful booklets recommending regional plantings that attract many species.*

Creating Natural Landscapes

At the University of Tennessee's Department of Ornamental Horticulture and Landscape Design, Gary Menendez teaches a natural landscaping concept he calls "Landscape Undesign." "Think of your house as a bull's eye," he advises. "The degree of maintenance goes down as you get farther away." Here's how to "undesign" your landscape for a more natural appearance:

• Go with the flow of seasons: Instead of skirting your foundation in rigid, never-changing evergreens, plant loose, floppy, deciduous shrubs such as spirea that add interesting texture, Blue Mist fothergilla for its fragrant bloom and yellow fall color, lilacs by a porch so you catch the fragrance. "When you plant things with spring color and fall color and winter berries, you use them as your calendar," says Gary.

• Nurture a mood of peaceful relaxation: "When I first did landscaping, I chose standbys such as rhododendron and dwarf globe blue spruce," says Gary. "Now I think it's more important to have a hammock with strawberries growing underneath to reach down and pick."

• No garden is complete without water, be it as simple as a birdbath or as elaborate as a pond with a recirculating pump.

- Scale down your lawn. Consider having an attractive free-form patch of grass, rather than a huge expanse to mow with a few amoeba-shaped beds floating in the middle without rhyme or reason.

- At the edge of your property line, maintain a natural buffer of plants such as chokeberry, witch hazel, and dogwood to provide privacy for you and food and shelter for wildlife.

- Last but not least, let nothing leave your site: Recycle. "We can't have that luxury anymore of putting our leaves at the curb to be hauled off and then buying commercially produced mulch at the garden center to replace them," says Gary.

Enchanting Walks, Inviting Entries

Even if it's only a simple mowed path or a gravel bed with fragrant pine needle overlay, a curved garden walk lends charm and creates an illusion of distance, counsels Anthony Tyznik, a landscape designer from Batavia, Illinois. Let your flowers drape over unedged borders for a more natural appearance, he adds. And to heighten the feeling of enchantment, let your garden have an entry portal, such as a climbing rose, a tall clump of grass, a graceful branch arching overhead, or an open rustic gate trailing bitter-sweet vine.

Garden Makeover

When garden editor Greg Philby and his wife, Jill, moved into their home in Ankeny, Iowa the corner lot had one big garden bed and mature trees. "It had a lot of plants, and a lot of color, but no real dimension, no structure—it wasn't interesting," recalls Greg. If you face similar challenges, here are Greg's three steps to a successful garden makeover:

1. Enclose your garden to create a backdrop. (The Philbys built a picket fence, with a jutting L-shaped corner section to lend interest.)

2. Vary plant heights and shapes for greater interest and balance. For example, replace spindly-stemmed poppies beneath towering trees with plants that have spreading foliage, such as baby's breath, to give shape and bulk.

3. Create small focal points, such as a concrete birdbath by a meandering flagstone path. "Before, the garden was just a jungle of plants, and we could only enjoy it at a distance. By curving the path," Greg says, "we're able to reach most of the areas of the flower beds, so we can maintain and sniff and touch everything."

Steep, Dark, Hard Challenges

If you're challenged by steep terrain, dense shade, heavy soil, and aggressive wild plants, Janet Raloff, senior editor for *Science News* in Washington, D.C., advises that you plant hosta.

"Once people find hosta, they grab it, because they need it," says Janet, who has sixty or more varieties in her Maryland landscape (there are literally hundreds to choose from). "It's not a plant of choice like roses. But you learn to love it and appreciate it. They can survive wet feet or drought. You can transplant any time of year, from 95-degree heat to near-frost conditions. They're indomitable," she says.

Root Problems

If you have mature trees near your flower beds, their big surface roots make it virtually impossible to till the soil. When Betty Gill of Laurel Gardens in Keavy, Kentucky, wanted to plant impatiens, she ran into that problem.

"Because I had no time to build raised beds, I just planted the flowers in 3-cubic-foot bags of potting soil. I formed a circle from several bags around the tree—they were beautiful."

Before planting, pierce the bottom of the bags with a pitchfork for drainage, Betty advises. After planting, mulch with shredded bark for a more natural look. Use a balanced fertilizer periodically. By the end of the season, the bags are filled with roots, so dump the soil into the garden and start fresh the next season.

Victorian Charm

You don't need to inherit a country estate to enjoy a traditional Victorian rose garden. Here are some design guidelines from Debbie Whitehouse, who is director of the Niagara Parks Botanical Gardens and School of Horticulture in Niagara Falls, Ontario, and whose Victorian rose garden is reputed to be the most outstanding in North America:

• Emphasize formal structure. The traditional Victorian garden is tightly controlled and organized, with flower beds in geometric shapes—"definitely not amoeba-shaped!" says Debbie.

• Confine each variety of rose in a separate bed. Plant brightly colored annuals in separately defined beds or in colored bands in straight rows, grouping tiers of tall flowers in back, short flowers in front. Space plants well apart.

• Let plantings be disciplined, with clipped forms. Grow a circular bed of coleus, for example, trimming plants to look like mounds.

• Let paths be straight and orderly, not curved and never meandering. Pave with brick or fine gravel.

• Include ornamental ironwork, such as painted wrought iron arbors. Other Victorian touches include lathe latticework for climbing roses, tile-paved pergolas, ornamental stone fountains, and rustic cedar lawn furniture.

• No Victorian rose garden would be complete without carpet bedding between the paths and island beds. Cultivate dense plants such as lavender cotton (*Santolina*), and keep them clipped to look like Oriental carpeting. "These are to admire, not to walk on," she admonishes.

Carry-Out Landscaping

Craig Thompson, a mixed-media artist in Berea, Kentucky, "grows" eye-catching instant gardens for his art fair booths. They're not only gorgeous but fun to create for special occasions. Here's how:

• Ignore basic landscaping considerations such as drainage and habitat, and mingle normally incompatible plants with impunity. Like a wonderful weekend romance, this is not destined to last, so all you need is enthusiasm, tenderness—and water.

• First "plant" three to five large rocks at your temporary site on each side of your entry. Bury them partially in the earth for a more natural look.

• Dig up clumps of plants with attractive foliage from your garden, and pot them. Bury the pots in the new site among the rocks, with rims at ground level. (If you keep the plants well watered, they can be replanted in a day or so, none the worse for their moves.)

• Next, add large potted plants of varying heights, such as ferns and philodendron, and flowering annual bedding plants (left in their little containers), but do not plant them.

• For the most natural, attractive feel, use odd-numbered groups, such as threes or fives. Group plants in clusters or triangles, not in a row. Abandon the normal rules of spacing: Plants will look better crowded together.

• Mulch thickly around plants and rocks to obscure the pots and give a natural appearance, using a lightweight, easy-to-clean-up mulch such as coarse cedar bark.

Easy Bed-Making

Have you ever wanted to convert lawn into garden beds, but quailed at the prospect of all that hard labor, digging up sod? Kate Carter Frederick, editor of *Garden, Deck & Landscape Planner* magazine recommends the easy no-dig alternative she used to transform her Des Moines, Iowa, yard into perennial and herb beds:

First, cover the turf with a layer of newspaper, twelve sheets thick. Next, cover the newspaper with a three-inch-thick layer of compost (Kate uses municipal compost) or a 50/50 blend of composted manure and topsoil. Wait six months, and all the layers, including the turf, completely decompose to create a beautiful six-inch layer of topsoil ready for planting.

"When I told people that I was building a new bed out in my front lawn," says Kate, amused, "they thought I was doing woodworking."

The Multicultural Lawn

"You'll have fewer problems if you refrain from a monocultural lawn," advises landscape architect Gary Menendez of Knoxville, Tennessee. "When you have only one kind of grass and that fails due to blight or fungus, it's all gone. So strive for species diversity, adding some tall grasses and clover to the mix.

And despite what many people believe, your lawn—as well as the environment—ultimately will do better if you avoid herbicides, Gary holds. "Herbicides kill the clover, which supplies your lawn with nitrogen and feeds plant-pollinating bees."

✱

Though she's a lawn specialist in the heart of Bluegrass Country, Mary Witt, University of Kentucky Extension horticulturist, is no great fan of bluegrass. "It's so shallow rooted," says Mary. She prefers fine-leaf fescue grasses because their deep root systems are better at surviving droughts and usually stay green even in tough, hot summers.

And for totally chemical-free lawn care, Mary suggests, simply keep the weeds mowed: "Its a healthy, environmentally friendly attitude," counsels Mary.

What Makes a Good Garden?

The only thing different about having a green thumb is that you don't get discouraged by failure—when something doesn't work, you try again.

—BETH WEIDNER, GROUNDSKEEPING SUPERVISOR,
ALFRED B. MACLAY STATE GARDENS IN TALLAHASSEE, FLORIDA

Lawn Care: Timing Makes the Difference

To save labor and hundreds of dollars on lawn chemicals, seed new lawns or renovate old ones with one of the newer and improved varieties of turf-type tall fescue, recommends turf management specialist and landscape contractor Steve Taylor of Corbin, Kentucky. "They're more disease and insect resistant, and aggressive enough to crowd out broad leaf weeds. Once you get a good, thick stand you'll have less crabgrass."

"Seed a new lawn or renovate an old one in fall," says Steve; you'll avoid competition from crabgrass, hard rains, and stress from dry, hot weather.

Fall is also the best time to fertilize lawns, as the top growth has slowed, but the grass roots are still growing and able to take in and store nutrients.

"Avoid spring fertilizing," Steve advises; "it only feeds the foliage. The top steals the nutrients due to fast growth and you'll have to mow twice as much."

Too Much of a Good Thing

"People put high nitrogen fertilizer on the lawn because it gets green quickly, and we've been brainwashed by national advertising," holds David Tarrant, host of CBC-TV's "Canadian Gardener" and author of *David Tarrant's Pacific Gardening Guide* and *Canadian Gardens* (Whitecap Books). "But too much nitrogen makes it more acidic. It's all top growth, and roots get weak; then you get weeds and moss coming in. It's better to use a fertilizer with a lower first number and higher middle number, such as 6–8–6," he counsels.

More on Lawns

When you mow, don't bother removing grass clippings, advises Batavia, Illinois, landscape architect Anthony Tyznik. "They're not harmful to the grass, and you reduce the need to fertilize by putting back the nitrogen, phosphorus, potassium, and trace elements that came from the land."

AUTHOR'S NOTE: *The nitrogen that clippings replenish also reduces the risk of lawn diseases such as red thread and rusts.*

✳

Permanent edging saves having to hand–edge your lawn or worry about grass encroachment. When putting in edging, don't economize, advises Anthony Tyznik. "The real cheap edging is usually not any bargain. The plastic kind is wavy, twisty, ugly, and hard to set back in the ground once it's pushed up by frost. Good quality aluminum or steel are longer–lasting. If they do have frost heave, you can hammer the top down and it won't break," he says.

Creative Alternative: Volunteer Gardening

Yes, you can experience the joys of gardening even if you lack adequate space or suitable habitat, maintains Richard Schnall, New York Botanical Garden's vice-president for horticulture: By becoming a volunteer gardener, you not only enjoy the pleasure without the expenses but have the opportunity to work with rare and endangered plants and learn from experts. "Almost all public gardens have a volunteer workforce; they can't survive without it," says Richard.

 AUTHOR'S NOTE: *Nursing homes, churches, schools, and libraries usually also welcome volunteer gardeners.*

Orphan Gardens

If you, like gardener Annie Gardner of Louisville, Kentucky, can't bear to throw plants away, what can you do with those that sprawl out of control or stay too spindly, haven't found the right niche to thrive in, or simply don't appeal?

The answer, counsels Annie, is a communal "Orphan Garden." In Annie's area problem plants go to a nurturing gardener with a green thumb and a large yard. As everybody in the neighborhood takes whatever he or she wants, sooner or later many of the plants find a welcome adoption.

What Makes a Good Garden?

Sometimes it can be disconcerting looking at pictures in garden magazines, because they're always in full bloom; real gardens are always in transition.

—STEVE RANFT, LEXINGTON, KENTUCKY, HORTICULTURIST

CHAPTER THREE

Touch the Earth: Tips on Preparing Soil

You couldn't raise an umbrella on that soil.
—OLD FOLK SAYING

In Greek mythology, after a great flood a voice commanded Pyrrha and Deucalion, the sole survivors, to cast away the bones of their mother. First they were horrified; then they realized that the Earth was their mother; her bones were the stones.

Earth's bones are the mother of us all. From bedrock comes all life on our planet. Rock crumbles to soil, supporting plant life, which in turn sustains the animals. Though bedrock may seem a pretty unyielding maternal breast, it is the basic source of all that nurtures us.

The soil of our "Mother Earth" is not just dirt; it is a balanced system of layers, each designed by nature to a specific purpose. Bedrock is the solid foundation for the surface materials that support plant life. Above bedrock are weathered rock fragments underlying the subsoil, a dense layer rich in minerals. Finally comes the topsoil layer, teeming with life.

Depending upon terrain and climate, the topsoil layer can be a couple of inches or a couple of feet deep. Here, where plant roots grow and gain their greatest nourishment (though roots of trees and larger shrubs may extend down to bedrock), tiny soil insects, earthworms, and microscopic organisms flourish. The greatest concentration of the soil's organic matter is in this layer, and as plants and animal debris break down into humus over time, they further enrich the soil, recycling over and over again in a spiral of life.

This near-magic, living topsoil is the layer gardeners strive to improve. The ideal soil—which good gardeners eventually achieve—is a loamy, humus-rich mixture that nurtures helpful earthworms and holds the sun's warmth. It absorbs enough water to bring needed nutrients and moisture to the plants, yet it drains quickly enough so as not to stay waterlogged and suffocate life in the soil. Its air spaces circulate vital oxygen to plants and soil bacteria. Loose and crumbly, it is easy to cultivate and is hospitable to roots.

Whether your soil is light, porous, and crumbly (commonly said to have good tilth) or is hard and lumpy hinges upon its texture, or relative balance of sand, silt, and clay. Other forces influence soil quality too, including existing vegetation, weather, freezing and thawing, the presence of earthworms, humus content, and acidity, or pH.

The differences between soils can be dramatic: a grain of coarse sand is at least 1,000 times larger than a particle of clay. If you've ever worked with sandy soil, you know how easy it is to cultivate and how smug you feel in spring when your garden warms up early and gives you a head start. On the other hand, it's dismaying to watch water and soluble fertilizers vanish into the earth and the air within the blink of an eye.

That's never your problem if you garden in clay soil, wherein water clings to the surface of all the tiny particles—and those particles cling to your tools, your hands, your clothes, your boots, and your floors. Clay soil stays too wet, cold, and lumpy in spring to allow an early start. Then, just when you rejoice that it's dry enough to plant, it gloms into a hard-packed crust that locks out water and air.

The tips in this chapter suggest numerous ways—often marvelously simple, sometimes quirkily innovative—to enrich your soil, understand it, protect it, and improve its structure. You'll find more ways to improve your soil, through manuring and composting, in the chapters ahead.

By the way, while interviewing a plant scientist for this edition I was taken to task for using the phrase "garden dirt." Dirt, he scolded, is grime to clean up and throw out, whereas soil is the medium used for growing things. I meekly apologized to keep the peace, although a dear friend has proved the case to be otherwise. When this harried mom neglected a bag of spilled grass seed strewn over the floor of her never-cleaned car, in no time flat she had a mobile lawn.

Soil Testing

AUTHOR'S NOTE: *Getting a soil test is the single most efficient, necessary, and money-saving step for better gardening. Of the more than 1,200 tips folks contributed to this book, this was the most common advice.*

✳

It's probably a good idea to test the soil in your flower gardens, as well as in your vegetable plots, advises Lori Bauer, a grower with Bauers Market and Nursery in La Crescent, Minnesota. She tests the soil for her commercial plants monthly, and for some crops every two weeks. "Once you get it to where it should be, it usually stays stable for several years," Lori says.

Where can you get your soil tested? "Ask your County Extension agent," says Lori. "Just about every County Extension office does soil testing or can tell you where to get it done for faster turnaround. Otherwise, your local nursery may test. Other sources would be a university department of horticulture or agriculture."

✳

The best time to test your garden soil is in late fall, Minnesota grower Eugene Bauer suggests. After you have your soil's profile, your county agent can suggest what to apply and when.

✻

"There are many soil tests available, but most home gardeners generally can find out what they ought to know with only a few basic ones," says Jim Ness, retired University of Wisconsin Extension agricultural agent.

"It's important to know your soil's pH, or acidity level, because your soil needs a balanced pH in order to take up nutrients and thrive. A pH of 7 indicates your soil is neutral; higher is basic (alkaline), and lower is acid. If your soil is alkaline, add sulphur; if it's acid, it's a sign that calcium is lacking. Adding lime increases the calcium.

"People commonly test for phosphorus and potassium. Your type of soil texture and amount of organic matter are also worth knowing. (The level of organic matter serves as a guide to whether there's enough nitrogen for the type of crops you want to grow.) Your Extension staff will make recommendations on improving the tilth, tailored to your soil.

"It's also possible to test for all the trace elements. But keep in mind," cautions Jim, "soil tests for micronutrients aren't generally necessary, and the more you check off, the more it costs. So talk it over with your Extension staff first."

Finding the Right Balance

AUTHOR'S NOTE: *Though garden writers seem practically obsessed with pH, a lot of folks are still pretty murky on the subject. Acid soils are often called sour, and alkaline ones called sweet. The pH scale describes the acid–alkaline balance on a scale of 1 to 14.*

Most garden plants thrive in a pH range of 6 to 7 but grow happily enough when the pH is between 5.5 and 7.2. (Not that you'd want to eat dirt, but by way of comparison the pH of orange juice is 4.0 and of baking soda 8.5.) Soils tend to be acid in rainy regions, whereas in desert regions they are often alkaline. Soils in the midcontinent tend to be neutral.

If soil, even when very fertile, is too acid or alkaline, plants can die of malnutrition, because some nutrients don't dissolve as well under acid or alkaline conditions. Nitrogen, phosphorus, and potassium are less available for plant uptake in acid soils; in alkaline soils phosphorus, manganese, and iron are less available. The presence of organic matter such as compost helps make soils at either end of the spectrum more neutral.

✳

If your soil is too acid and you need to add lime to raise the pH, the best time to do so is when your garden is dormant, after the crops are harvested, advises Eugene Bauer. The lime needs time to break down and neutralize the soil.

✳

If you need quicker results, Jim Ness advises that you apply quicklime or burnt lime. It demands extra care, though; to avoid burning the plants, put on the lime, till it in, water, and wait a couple of weeks to allow it to break down before planting.

✳

A no-cost way to neutralize the soil comes from horticulturist Barbara Voight of Madison, Wisconsin. When a neighbor is remodeling, collect cast-off plasterboard scraps. Soak, crush, and use the resulting solution on sour, mossy spots on the lawn or in the garden where the soil is too acidic. The lime in the plasterboard will lower the soil pH, increasing the alkalinity.

Plasterboard (also called Sheetrock) is nontoxic and won't burn plants. Before using it, however, dilute the mixture with water so it won't make chalky-looking spots. Shake as you pour to prevent the lime from settling.

✳

Drywall contracter Cornelius McFarland, Jr., of Corbin, Kentucky, doesn't bother to dissolve the plasterboard scraps, however; he just strews pieces in his garden and plows them in. "Most contractors would be glad to furnish you with a free supply," he says. "And if you have horses or cattle, lay the bigger scraps in the stalls. As the animals step on them, the pieces mash and mix with manure, which is even better," he adds.

✳

Many flowering plants, especially rhododendron, hydrangeas, ivy, holly, gardenias, and azaleas, produce their best growth when the soil is mildly acidic because it helps them take up soil nutrients," says nurseryman John Zoerb. One teaspoon of Sterns Miracid per gallon of water will keep the soil slightly acid, he advises.

AUTHOR'S NOTE: *For tips on pH and vegetable growing, see Chapter 14.*

Soil Transformation

"Most garden soils are low in organic matter, but you can overcome this by making compost. The humus helps the soil hold water, making it easier for gardens to survive dry periods. It will improve a heavy clay soil, or tighten up a loose, sandy soil. For building good soils, it's the greatest thing on earth," advise nationally syndicated garden columnists Doc and Katy Abraham ("The Green Thumb") of Naples, New York.

✳

"To soften and aerate my sandy–clay Dallas, Texas, soil," says Jan Scott, "I dug it all up to a depth of 4 feet and removed it. I mixed in grass clippings, cedar chips, and finely chopped leaves, and then mulched on top with salt marsh hay, cedar and cocoa chips to minimize evaporation."

✳

"Organic wastes are fine for a mulch but can't be a food source for plants until they're broken down," says former New Jersey landscaper Ernie Hartmann. "Microorganisms need a food source while they're breaking down organic material, but as they work, they temporarily deplete soil nutrients. So if you till organic material directly into the soil in its uncomposted state, you should also add nitrogen to feed the soil while the bacteria are feasting. If you compost first, however, the organic material is broken down and ready to release the nutrients immediately."

AUTHOR'S NOTE: *For more on nitrogen, see page 59.*

＊

When Ed Wojahn first started gardening thirty years ago in Galesburg, Illinois, his soil gave him lots of problems.

"It was black, greasy, and sticky. When it got wet, you came out of the garden with feet like an elephant. When it dried, it was just like cement. I tried to break it down with grass clippings and garden refuse. At that time, I wasn't very smart. I chopped and buried tomato vines. But if the vines are diseased, the disease goes right back in the soil!

＊

If your soil is heavy, impervious clay and very acidic, you might find that the best way to break it up is to research your local history. Up on Wills Mountain, where Jack Laws of Buffalo Mills, Pennsylvania, lives, lumbermen timbered the slopes back in the 1930s. Jack located the site of the old sawmill with a pile of well-aged sawdust close to 10 feet deep.

"It's been a good resource for us," says Jack. To counteract the nitrogen loss that occurs as the sawdust decomposes in the soil, he mixes 10-20-10 fertilizer with the sawdust when he applies it. Jack also adds manure, compost, lots of wood ashes, and topsoil to improve the pH and tilth of his land.

AUTHOR'S NOTE: *You'll find more on ashes on page 63.*

✸

To improve the sandy soil in her garden in Eagle River, Wisconsin, Ruth Ann Davis added seven truckloads of old hay. "It's best to compost this before applying it to kill weed seeds," she advises.

✸

Says Shirley Waterson of Morrow, Georgia, "The hard clay soils where I live must be loosened for better drainage. Ground pine bark is helpful. Spread 3 to 4 inches of bark on the soil surface and till it into the soil."

✸

"Compost should be added to your soil each year. Three inches spread over your garden plot will assist you in making 6 inches of workable, healthy soil," advises another Georgian, commercial compost manufacturer Bill Bricker of Augusta.

✸

"Don't spread peat moss on top of the ground. It blocks moisture, and it washes away," counsels retired nurseryman Cy Klinkner of La Crosse, Wisconsin. "Instead, work it into the soil. And be aware that all peats are not alike. The better quality peats have a higher acid content."

✸

"Well-prepared soil is loose and friable," notes John Zoerb of La Crosse Floral in La Crosse, Wisconsin. "Because it is porous, air can get to the roots, and moisture can permeate. This encourages plant roots to develop." John adds peat moss, manure, and chemical fertilizer to prepare his soil.

✸

Before you buy peat (and potting soils containing peat), insist upon knowing its origins, urges Ken Ball, a landscape architect with Denver Water. Unfortunately, much of this nonrenewable resource is plundered from pristine, fragile alpine environments that have existed for thousands of years. Several of the leading suppliers are the worst offenders, he says. Denver, Colorado, has outlawed the use of mountain peat, and informed communities, businesses, and individuals are following suit. Use compost, not peat, as a soil builder, Ken recommends.

✹

Would you like to make your garden soil more fertile, more absorbent, and better balanced with less work? Internationally renowned soil scientist Arthur Peterson, who has traveled around the globe helping Third World nations improve soil fertility, has found a way. Until now it was commonly held that leaves had to be composted to do any good; however, the University of Wisconsin–Madison professor emeritus's field tests have demonstrated that you can improve soil and produce high yields by mixing shredded leaves directly into the garden.

"You have to break up those leaves first," says Dr. Peterson. "The small crumbly leaf particles (about the texture of humus) break down rapidly once they're mingled with the soil bacteria," he explains. Though heavy farm rotary tillers can pulverize the leaves while plowing them into the soil, "a home tiller may not shred them finely enough unless the leaves are dry," he cautions. A small electric cone–shaped tub grinder should do the job, he says.

"Mix the leaves right into your garden, or use them as a mulch. There's no need to compost first. Assuming that you have kept your soil in a good state of fertility in the past, I feel you definitely would not have to broadcast extra nitrogen."

More Ways to Improve Soil Structure

If you've ever eaten a huge, heavy meal of meat, potatoes, and gravy and then topped it off with two pieces of pie, you know how lethargic you feel. Do you suppose plants feel sluggish too, when they're dragged down in soggy, dense clay soil?

"If you have heavy clay soil, there are a couple of things you can do to alleviate problems," suggests nurseryman Randy Baier of Baier Nursery in

La Crosse, Wisconsin. "One is to elevate the bed so that water drains away. The elevated bed need not have a flat surface, though. Mounding the soil even just a few inches high under each cluster of plants gives an undulating look, making the garden more interesting."

Your second choice, suggests Randy, is to amend the soil by adding organic matter such as peat, compost, pine needles, or grass clippings. Just stir this into the soil.

It might seem reasonable to assume that adding sand would help, since sand itself drains so well, but don't do it. "It will make matters worse," cautions Randy. "If you add sand to clay, the clay fills in the air spaces between the sand granules and gets hard and dense, almost like concrete," he warns.

Although sandy soil doesn't get waterlogged, it has the opposite problem: Water passes right through it. So if your soil is sandy, add organic matter to increase its moisture-holding capacity, Randy advises.

✳

Don't be so quick to rake up autumn leaves, advises Batavia, Illinois, landscape architect Anthony Tyznik: "Where the rake is spared, a new kind of soil results. Fallen leaves decompose and encourage earthworms to burrow freely beneath their cover. The worms permeate the soil with countless channels, advancing the movement of water, roots, air, and nutrients," he says.

How to Be a Soil Farmer

Most home gardeners grow quality vegetables. Longtime Illinois gardener Ed Wojahn also grows quality soil. Here's how:

- In the spring when the frost has left the ground, fetch a trailerload (about 1 cubic yard) of cow or horse manure from a farmer. Pile this in a wooden box about 2 feet wide by 4 feet long by 20 inches high.

- Add to this about 2,000 red worms, which are sold through fishing magazines for about $10 per 1,000. "Earthworms won't do," Ed advises. "They won't eat the manure—they prefer dirt and coffee grounds. But red worms eat the manure and deposit their waste. It's the richest soil that you can get."

• "It's important to remember that manure generates heat," Ed cautions. "Wait till it's generated, or it will kill your worms." Generally, though, manure you get from a farmer has been mixed with straw or corn cob bedding and has sat piled up all winter. By mid-April the heat has usually dissipated. (The heat also kills most of the weed seeds, so you won't get a lot of weeds, as you will in raw manure.)

• You don't have to mix, add, or do anything: Just leave the manure pile alone until the fall. By then it will have turned into wonderful loamy soil and be ready to till into your garden.

Green Manure

"Having dealt with manure," says Tony Holt, a gardener in Grants Pass, Oregon, "I have very little good to say about it. The back-breaking labor of spreading, the high weed seed content, and the stench (not well accepted by the neighbors) are all good reasons to use alternatives. I use sheet composting. All organic material from our yard: leaves, lawn clippings, prunings, and the like are scattered in the garden during the summer, and plowed under in the fall.

"Then I broadcast a mix of winter oats, cowpeas, and crimson clover as well as a green manure winter crop," Tony adds. It takes less than an hour to broadcast and rake in and provides more tilth and nitrogen than two truckloads of manure.

Tony's method is also prettier than manure. "Right now in midwinter, a 6-inch-high velvet green carpet covers the garden. By springtime, it will be 18 inches high, and when the crimson clover flowers, the heads are an inch long and bright scarlet. The honeybees love it, too."

If you need convincing that plants such as winter rye pack power, consider this: One single rye plant grows more than 3 miles of roots daily. In a single season its root length measures 387 miles, and its root hairs an incredible 6,603 miles!

AUTHOR'S NOTE: *Green manure improves your soil's texture and water-holding capacity. It also curtails weeds and helps prevent erosion. It can flourish even in regions with severe winters. Winter rye, for instance, stays green under the snow and starts to grow again as soon as the temperature reaches forty degrees Fahrenheit. Your County Extension agent can recommend the best cover crop for your area.*

Soil and Climate

"When preparing garden beds, add organic matter in the fall, so your garden will be all ready in the spring," advises John Kehoe, park services supervisor for Colt Park in Hartford, Connecticut.

If you wait until the spring, you may do some damage, because your wheelbarrow (or any other piece of equipment) may sink in the wet soil and leave ruts, he warns.

✳

"Turning over the topsoil in the spring gives your plants a better start," counsels nurseryman John Zoerb of La Crosse Floral in La Crosse, Wisconsin. John goes one step further than most gardeners by checking out soil temperatures with a probe thermometer.

Soil heats from the top down; when you turn it over, you mix warm soil with the cold lower soil and raise the garden's temperature. If you don't turn the soil and the roots are cold, the roots won't bring up moisture and the plant becomes dehydrated, John explains.

✳

"Don't expect your plants to do much of anything until the ground warms up. Below 50 degrees Fahrenheit, virtually all plant activity comes to a standstill," says soil scientist Arthur Peterson.

But if you garden in a cold climate, don't waste too much envy on gardeners in more torrid zones. Notes Dr. Peterson, who has worked with soils in such places as Thailand, Egypt, Syria, and Indonesia, organic matter decomposes so rapidly in heat and humidity that tropical soils can't hold humus and so are actually very poor.

Crop Rotation

"I learned the hard way that you have to rotate," says retired railroad man Ed Wojahn. "You can't plant the same crops in the same spot year after year—that's where diseases come in. Now I plant in a different place each year, rotating back to the original spot over a four-year cycle."

❉

"As they decompose, different plants leave different nutrients in the soil that can be used by another plant the next growing season. For example, peas are nitrogen-producing, leaving more nitrogen in the soil than they take out of it. This can be used by sweet corn the next year," says farmer LeeAnne Bulman of Independence, Wisconsin.

"So check a plant chart to find out what nutrients each plant gives and which ones it requires. That way you'll get the most benefit out of crop rotation," advises LeeAnne.

❉

"Many home gardeners recognize the benefits of crop rotation in the vegetable plot but leave their flowers in the same place year after year," says grower Eugene Bauer of La Crescent, Minnesota. "Sooner or later, if you don't rotate your bulbs—geraniums, iris, and the like—they'll have eaten up a particular nutrient, and then the fertilizer you've always used won't work anymore."

Every flower needs a balance of nutrients, and this requirement varies from plant to plant, he explains. "For instance, if there's no longer enough nitrogen to meet the plant's needs, and you use a 10-10-10 fertilizer, the plant takes up the nitrogen while the unneeded potassium and calcium build up. The pH goes out of whack, and nothing you throw at it works."

Clean Dirt: Soil Sterilizing

If you bring garden soil indoors to use as potting soil, you take the risk that the soil has hitchhiking insects and weed seeds. Generally, these aren't major problems, but you can run into difficulties with damping off, a disease caused by soil fungi that kills seedlings just before or after they emerge. (See page 99 for more discussion on damping-off disease.)

You can avoid damping off, as well as weed and bug problems, by heat-treating the soil in your oven. Although folks generally call this "sterilizing" the soil, "pasteurizing" would probably be more accurate, believes nationally syndicated garden columnist Jan Riggenbach of Glenwood, Iowa. Here's Jan's recipe:

Spread about a gallon of dirt into a shallow baking pan. (A three-pound coffee can holds about a gallon of dirt.) If you measure more than that amount, it may not get hot enough. Add a cup of water and bake it forty-five minutes at 180 degrees. Or put a small potato in the center of the soil. When the potato gets tender enough to be pierced with a fork but not yet as soft as a baked potato, you can take the soil out of the oven.

✳

Be careful not to leave your soil in the oven too long, cautions horticulturist Randy Baier. "Sterilizing kills not only the fungi but also the good soil organisms, and heat might alter elements. If you heat to 180 degrees and hold the temperature for a half hour, that seems to take care of weed seeds, insects, and harmful pathogens but apparently doesn't kill good organisms."

Potting Soil: What's Best for Container Gardening?

It's generally best to repot container plants every year and a half to two years, counsels nurseryman John Zoerb. "By then the peat moss in the soil has decomposed, leaving nothing but compacted mineral soil with improper drainage."

✳

"Often people call me, upset and asking what went wrong. They've just repotted and the plants are dying. Almost always, it's poor soil that's to blame," says Cyndi Hall, a plantscape consultant in La Crosse, Wisconsin.

"Never buy the prepackaged soil sold in department and discount stores; go to a flower shop or garden center that makes their own. You'll pay a little more, but it's worth it. The cheaper soils are not your best soils. They usually contain a black peat moss, which isn't as good as the brown kind."

What Makes a Good Garden?

Many people think that, like parenting, gardening is in your bones, or they figure it's complicated and technical. If you're not experienced, it's really helpful to get a basic gardening book. A good garden center also can help answer your questions and give good advice. Remember, too, that some of the best sources for information in your area are the older gardeners who know the ropes.

—RENEE SHEPHERD, SHEPHERD'S GARDEN SEEDS

CHAPTER FOUR

Understanding Fertilizer

How would you like to live on just water?
—ALEC BERG

onsidering that gardeners lavish such fortunes on fertilizers, it's surprising that the seventeenth, most recently discovered essential plant
nutrient turns out to be not gold but nickel. Avid gardeners fuss as much
over their garden's nutrition as they do over their own. Do our plants lack
nutrients, we fret, and if so, which ones and in what form? How much
should we add, and when? Can too much fertilizer be toxic to plants, the
way vitamin overdoses can be toxic to humans? Are organic fertilizers
really superior to inorganic ones, or just more politically correct?

The six essential elements plants use in large amounts, called major elements, are carbon, hydrogen, oxygen, nitrogen, phosphorus, and potassium.
Plants take in the first three from air and water; the others, in dissolved form
in the soil through their root hairs (or through leaves via foliar feeding). The
most common boosters needed by cultivated plants are nitrogen, phosphorus, and potassium.

Plants also use three elements, called intermediate nutrients, in moderate amounts: calcium, magnesium, and sulphur. They also need just a trace of eight other minerals, called micronutrients: iron, manganese, boron, zinc, copper, chloride, molybdenum, and nickel.

Often folks go overboard with fertilizers, figuring that if one is good, ten are ten times better. But before you go flinging small change around, consider this: The amount of nickel present on a seed's coat before it even germinates is *enough to last it for the rest of its lifetime.*

Unless your soil has a particular deficiency, adding any given nutrient is like throwing your money on the ground. Moreover, excessive amounts can cause toxic buildups, block the absorption of other nutrients, and discourage beneficial soil organisms. Even when a given nutrient is ample in the soil, plants may be unable to use it if the soil pH is too far from the neutral range. As contributors to this chapter point out, these are solid reasons for getting soil tests.

Organic versus Inorganic

It's a common belief that synthetic fertilizers are toxic to soil microorganisms, but applied at the recommended rates, they are not. Many gardeners extol organic fertilizers as more natural than organic ones. To plants, though, all foods "taste" alike, as their roots can't absorb *any* food before it's converted into specific ionic forms.

Plant nutrients derived from organic fertilizers (animal and plant origin) are typically less concentrated than inorganic fertilizers on a per weight basis and are less likely to cause "burning" from salt injury. They gradually decompose into an inorganic form in the soil that plants can take up, acting as slow-release fertilizers. Organic fertilizers aren't intended as last-minute, gulp-and-run fast-food suppers, though, for then they may not release nutrients quickly enough to meet immediate plant demands.

Inorganic fertilizers, both manufactured chemicals and mined minerals, tend to be more concentrated. They dissolve quickly in water, making them available for plant use right away. On the downside it's a little trickier to match up plant need with application rate, and dumping a lot on at once can be more wasteful if the plant doesn't need it right away.

You might say that organic fertilizers are like a nanny that spoon-feeds a baby tiny portions whenever it's hungry throughout the day. The inorganics are more like a lunch line where you go through and pile all kinds of stuff on your plate whether or not you're going to consume it.

In the tips that follow, you'll find pros and cons of these various options, in addition to helpful hints on timing, sound advice on nutrition, and innovative techniques for delivery. If you want to feed your plants a varied diet, you'll find recipes for low-cost down-home potluck as well as the plant's equivalent of nouvelle cuisine. And the best part of feeding plants is—no dirty dishes.

Hindsight Is 20/20 Vision

Whether you're using fertilizer, weed killers, insecticides, fungicides, or mixing soil, READ THE LABEL and follow the manufacturer's recommendations! So many times people don't bother to read the label, until it fails.
—RALPH SNODSMITH, RADIO HOST, "GARDEN HOTLINE,"
AND GARDEN EDITOR, ABC TV'S "GOOD MORNING AMERICA"

How Often Is Mealtime?
And What's for Dinner?

Your garden plants, especially the fruiting ones such as melons, tomatoes, and berries, need fertilizing for top yields, says mail-order seed merchant Renee Shepherd of Shepherd's Garden Seeds in Felton, California.

"We're asking our vegetables to produce artificially, probably more than they normally would. Also, a lot of the hybrids need extra food to produce their best. Fertilize monthly until the first fruit appears and then stop," she advises.

✱

"Organic nutrients generally don't give a big hit all at once, but commercial ones with a high nitrogen content tend to promote lots of leafy growth rather than abundant fruiting," Renee Shepherd notes. Some good organic fertilizers are fish emulsion, liquid kelp, blood meal, cottonseed meal, manure, and compost, advises the California seed specialist. "If you use commercial fertilizers, look for well-balanced ones such as Miracle-Gro and Rapid-Gro."

✱

Manuel Lacks has a wonderful vegetable garden that makes him the envy of his Keysville, Virginia, neighbors. He credits his success to his style of three-times-a-season fertilizing. Here's how to do it his way:

First, sprinkle a little fertilizer in the row when planting. Second, sprinkle a little around each plant the first time you hoe or cultivate, and water it in. Then the next time you cultivate, repeat. "By directing it close to the plants, you don't waste fertilizer or feed the weeds," he says.

✱

Years ago Alec Berg of Onalaska, Wisconsin, wondered why his flowers remained nearly as he had planted them even as the growing season progressed.

"Why don't they get fuller?" he asked a nurseryman. "How would you like to live on just water?" came the reply. "He told me that plants are no different than you or me: They need food like we do," recalls Alec.

Since then Alec has fed his annuals almost daily from the first day he transplants them into his garden. He uses a very dilute solution of Rapid-Gro. As a result, he says, "the impatiens measured 4 feet tall this year and the little old petunias got just like bushes!"

Alec believes his sandy soil needs all the help it can get. "Maybe if you have richer soil, plants need less feeding."

The problem with daily feeding and watering is that your plants grow so profusely that they end up fertilizer junkies. "If I go somewhere for the weekend, the first thing I have to do when we come home, even if it's ten at night, is water them," Alec observes.

"But you can kill with kindness, too. Don't overfeed," he cautions. "Before I knew better, I overfed the flowers and they all started browning. They almost looked like they were dying." (About a half–teaspoon of Rapid–Gro to two gallons of water is ample, he advises.)

✳

Because container–grown plants can't grow deeper or spread out in search of food, you must compensate by feeding them more frequently, Renee Shepherd of Shepherd's Garden Seeds in Felton, California, counsels. "Container plants thrive on a constant supply of nutrients in small but regular feedings of a weak fertilizer solution. Use about one half the strength called for on the label every ten days to two weeks. Or premix into a one–fifth strength solution and use it at every other watering. Organic gardeners will have fine results with a combination of manure tea or fish emulsion and liquid kelp (seaweed extract)," she advises.

AUTHOR'S NOTE: *"Complete"* fertilizers contain nitrogen (N), phosphorus (P), and potassium (K). The three numbers, such as 5–10–5, on their labels are not some cryptic cult code like 666 but merely the percentages of nitrogen, phosphorus (as P_2O_5) and potash (as K_2O), always in that order. A soil test before planting will take the guesswork out of determining fertilizer needs.

For Gradual Feeding

In the dry desert areas of Pakistan and northern India, gardeners reduce evaporation through controlled irrigation by sinking unglazed clay jugs into the ground around plants. When the jugs are filled with water, moisture slowly seeps out into the ground.

"I heard of this and decided to try it with plastic milk jugs," says Peter Tonge, author of *Growing Your Garden the Earth Friendly Way* (Christian Science Publishing Society). "They do not work quite as well as clay jugs for watering, but they do a pretty good job of fertilizing by allowing the fertilizer to trickle into the ground very slowly over several days." This can be an advantage in very sandy soil like Peter's, he says, where water quickly drains right past the roots, as well as in heavy soils that tend to get water-logged. "And if suddenly a thunderstorm rolls by, the fertilizer isn't all washed away.

"For each plant, take a plastic, one-gallon milk jug. With an awl or knit-ting needle, punch about twelve to fifteen fine holes into the bottom. Place the jug upright at the base of the plants. If you wish, sink it an inch or so into the soil for stability. (There is no need to bury the jug except for aes-thetic reasons; if you do, punch holes in the sides of the bottom half and put the jug up to its neck in the ground.

"Fill the jug with liquid fertilizer. (My preference is Seamix, an organic fish emulsion and seaweed solution.) To control the time it takes to empty the jug, adjust the screw-on cap; the looser it is and the larger the holes in the bottom are, the faster the solution will seep out. If the jug has a snap-on lid, punch a hole in the top. If you find you want the fertilizer to flow faster, enlarge the hole.

"It may take one to ten days to empty. Experiment, adjusting the flow to suit the needs of your garden environment. You can, for instance, let the fertilizer slowly seep out and then refill the jug every two weeks, or you might use a very dilute solution and refill whenever the jug empties. Because of my sandy soil, if the solution drips too quickly, nutrients flow away before plants get enough, so I tighten the cap so they can feed gradually over several days."

The solution also collects heat from the sun, which is a bonus for heat-loving crops, Peter adds.

Nitrogen

AUTHOR'S NOTE: *Nitrogen serves many functions, including chlorophyll and protein synthesis. Although 78 percent of our planet's atmosphere is nitrogen, your garden can't utilize this element until it's converted to a soluble form. Nature's myriad ways of accomplishing this alchemy are nothing short of astonishing.*

During thunderstorms lightning zaps the atmosphere, liberating nitrogen and hurling it earthward in the pelting rain. This fanfare delivers instantly available nitrogen, though it's only a fraction of the amount your plants need.

A less dramatic but far more significant converter is the microscopic soil organisms that digest organic matter and recycle the nitrogen back to the soil in a form available for plant life.

Legumes, such as peas and beans, are other exceptional power plants, as they're able to pull nitrogen from the air and change it to a form available to the host plant with the help of nitrogen-fixing bacteria in their root nodules. As legumes grow, nitrogen trickles from the their roots to neighboring plants; as legumes die off and decompose, the entire plant becomes a rich source of nitrogen.

When your garden needs extra nitrogen, "carry out" meals are available in many forms: Inorganics such as nitrate of soda, calcium nitrate, ammonium sulphate, urea, ammonium phosphate, and ammonium nitrate supply nitrogen in forms plants can immediately absorb. They're most effective in early spring when soil is cold and organic sources decompose slowly, or for a quick boost when your plants start looking pale.

Urea-form is a newer synthetic fertilizer that slowly releases its nitrogen over months and won't burn. It can supply a whole season's nitrogen needs in one application.

Organic nitrogen sources, such as dried blood, cottonseed meal, and fish meal, provide slow release throughout the growing season but have a slower start, because organic nitrogen must first decompose to an inorganic form to become available. The soil bacteria required for this process need warmth and a near–neutral soil (6.4 to 7.0 pH) to be active and accomplish this.

Caution: Nitrogen fertilizers, especially the inorganics, can burn plants upon contact; contact with seed can prevent germination.

When sending a soil sample to be tested, keep in mind that nitrogen levels can alter in a short period, points out retired agricultural agent Jim Ness. Climatic conditions often cause nitrogen depletion. "Nitrogen is normally used up quickly, and it may leach even more rapidly if it rains, so you may need to add nitrogen even if your test levels come out okay. Just use common sense," he advises.

✳

When it comes to adding nitrogen, more gardeners overfertilize than underfertilize, holds nationally renowned soil scientist Dr. Arthur Peterson, professor emeritus of the University of Wisconsin–Madison.

"If you have a problem with too much vegetative growth, or your tomatoes are not setting fruit, the likelihood is that your soil's getting too much nitrogen. Adding shredded (uncomposted) leaves will improve the soil's tilth and set nitrogen in balance."

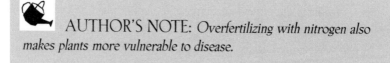

AUTHOR'S NOTE: *Overfertilizing with nitrogen also makes plants more vulnerable to disease.*

✳

Chemical fertilizers such as 10–10–10 are best applied after your crop is planted, advises Minnesota grower Eugene Bauer. If you apply this kind of fertilizer when no crop is growing, the nitrogen in it gets leached by moisture or burned by sunshine.

> 🪣 AUTHOR'S NOTE: *Keep in mind that if you don't need a particular element, a balanced fertilizer is not in your best interest; unused nitrogen dissipates, whereas phosphorus and potassium build up and harm the soil.*

Lime

> 🪣 AUTHOR'S NOTE: *I used to think lime was something to be served with tequila and salt, not a chalky white grit to strew on the ground that supplies calcium and magnesium, sweetens the soil, accelerates the action of beneficial soil organisms, helps free other plant nutrients so they're in an availabe form, and speeds the break-down of organic material. Often even experienced gardeners are unclear about the distinctions between various kinds of lime and have questions about their respective benefits and disadvantages.*

Wisconsin horticulturist Ernie Hartmann notes, "Generally it's fine to use whatever is locally available. Lime is slow-acting, but the more finely it is crushed the quicker it will work." Dr. Hartmann demystifies garden lime with some easy guidelines:

- Agricultural lime, or calcium carbonate, is sometimes called "ground lime." This form is the most common kind for gardens. It is the coarsest lime, but it's safer than others and generally won't burn. Still, it's best not to put even this directly on plants.

- Dolomite lime is quarried and crushed. This form supplies the two major acid-lowering chemicals: calcium and magnesium.

- Burnt or hydrated (quicklime) lime will act more rapidly than the others, but be careful, as it especially can burn.

- It's best to add lime in the fall or early spring before plants are vigorous.

- "Regardless of which type of lime or fertilizer you're using, if it gets on the leaves, wash it off," Dr. Hartmann advises.

- Never mix lime with nitrogen in ammonium nitrate form. When you water this combination, you will release toxic gases that are harmful to plants. To avoid this, spread lime two weeks before adding ammonium nitrate to your garden. Says Dr. Hartmann, "This reaction is especially intense with burnt lime, so it's safer to stick to agricultural or dolomite lime."

＊

"Barn lime is a very good thing for your garden," says organic gardener Jeanette Manske. Jeanette scatters barn lime down the row just after the soil in her onion beds has been prepared. "Cover it lightly with a hoe so the onion sets don't have direct contact with the lime, and you'll get big, healthy onions."

AUTHOR'S NOTE: *Barn lime is slower to release and longer lasting than agricultural lime because it is so coarse. Though it is used primarily to keep floors dry in dairy barns, it's also a boon to any cold-climate gardener because of the fantastic traction it provides on icy driveways and walks. Its use for this purpose has the added advantage of being beneficial to plants as it washes off the walkways.*

Smart Shopping

"Bonemeal is a good source of phosphorus, and blood meal not only supplies nutrients such as nitrogen, but deters rabbits," notes horticulturist Barbara Voight of Madison, Wisconsin. "However, they are fairly expensive if you buy them in small quantities at a garden center. But you can buy them in fifty pound sacks at a feed mill much cheaper and have enough to last for several years," she advises.

AUTHOR'S NOTE: *By the same token, buying other fertilizers in bulk at farm supply stores yields incredible savings. Five pounds of fertilizer may commonly sell for $3.95, for instance, whereas at a farm supply store, another nickel can buy you a 50-pound bag.*

Ashes

Radishes, carrots, and other root crops need potash. "Instead of getting the commercial fertilizer, I mix a lot of wood ashes into the soil," says Ed Wojahn, who gardened in Galesburg, Illinois, for many years.

AUTHOR'S NOTE: *Ashes have long been a popular natural source of potassium and calcium and a means of insect control. Who would have imagined they'd become controversial? Just after* Garden Smarts *first came out in 1991, it was discovered that many trees contain radioactive minerals from nuclear fallout as a result of the 1958–63 Cold War weapons testing. When burned, their ash concentrates those minerals a hundredfold.*

Are ashes hazardous to crops? It's a complex question. No one to date has answers, although the level of radioactive minerals that end up on our table from this source is believed to be extremely low. Interestingly, the ash's potassium has a potentially *protective* effect that may actually block radioactive uptake. To complicate things still more, another popular source of natural potassium, mined potash, is inherently radioactive. The jury is still out—stay tuned for further developments.

Phosphorus and Potassium

The tips that follow talk about two nutrients that commonly need supplementing: phosphorus and potassium. Plants take up both of these elements from the soil. Unlike nitrogen, they don't leach and (barring erosion) stay put until used, but they need to be applied within reach of a plant's roots. If, however, you place high rates near a seed or a plant, salt injury may occur, so take caution.

Phosphorus promotes stem and root development and stimulates fruiting. Superphosphate, which is phosphate rock treated with sulfuric acid, supplies quick benefits. Bonemeal is a good slow-release, nonburning source. Nonetheless, since it's common to underfertilize plants when using organic phosphorous sources because of their low nutrient content, you might want to consult a county agent or organic growers' organizations for guidelines.

Potassium fosters vigorous plants, disease resistance, and flower color intensity. Kelp meal and greensand are natural sources of potassium, as are wood ashes, although the latter can create serious imbalances. Other potassium fertilizers are potassium chloride (muriate of potash), potassium sulphate, and potassium nitrate.

Iron

Even plants can become anemic. One of the more common problems in azaleas is iron chlorosis, notes Beth Weidner, assistant park manager of Alfred B. Maclay State Gardens in Tallahassee, Florida. If the leaves yellow while the veins stay green, your azalea may have iron deficiency.

Iron is usually plentiful in soil but is unavailable to plants. Tied up with other elements, it doesn't go into solution, and plant roots can't absorb it. Luckily, iron deficiency in azaleas can be corrected by a foliar spray or direct application to the soil. Iron sulfate and chelated iron are the two most commonly used solutions.

Iron sulfate works well for foliar applications but binds quickly to other elements in the soil so that roots can't absorb it. Chelated iron is better for soil application; it remains in a condition that's available to the plants for a long time, concludes Beth.

Keep this in mind too: Phosphorus is one of the elements that bind to iron and prevent it from going into solution so that plants can use it, notes Beth. Overfertilizing with phosphorus can create iron deficiency in plants, she warns.

To correct iron deficiency in your soil, check its pH; either too high or too low a pH ties up the iron.

✳

Have you ever noticed fabulous geraniums blooming in an old coffee can? They flourish thanks to the rust coming from the can's interior, says horticulturist Barbara Voight. Though the plants take up this form of iron less quickly than the chelated form in commercial iron fertilizers, Barbara has tried comparison plots in her home garden and believes the rust does wonders for geraniums and other iron-hungry plants. "Now I keep a rust bucket going all the time for a cheap source of iron fertilizer."

Here's how: Fill a bucket with water and keep it in a sunny place to speed up the oxidizing process. Throw in rusty nails, broken tools, pieces of wire, paper-coated twisters, and any other iron scraps. Continue to add iron as you find it, and add enough water to cover the contents. When watering plants, add one-fourth of a cup of rusty water to each gallon of fresh water.

✳

Medicine Shelf Fertilizers

One of the world's most extravagant garden tips comes from an acquaintance of mine who has been a surgical patient. "I was so ill I couldn't eat, so my doctor put me on Total Parenteral Nutrition intravenous feeding. When I was finally ready to go home, a partially used bottle of the fluid was left and a nurse suggested that I bring it home for houseplants. Since then, I've stored it in the refrigerator, adding a minute amount to the weekly watering. The plants have really flourished."

It must be the plants' equivalent of beluga caviar: "My pharmacy bill was $5,000!" she reports.

She adds a word of caution: "It is only T.P.N. intravenous fluids that can be used in this way—a saline and glucose solution used routinely for patient hydration would be disastrous if used as a plant fertilizer."

❋

A couple of generations back, there was scarcely a medicine cabinet in the land that didn't have a supply of Epsom salts. Whether or not you'd ever dose yourself with this old-time laxative made from magnesium sulfate, it can be valuable for doctoring your garden. Retired veterinarian Ken Johnston of West Salem, Wisconsin, sprinkles a small handful of Epsom salts around the base of his pepper plants as soon as they are well established and again when they blossom.

❋

Many a novice gardener in southern Oregon has harvested lavish quantities of tomatoes, thanks to similar advice from octogenarian Joseph Moos, master gardener at Oregon State University Extension Service. The retired professor advocates sprinkling a generous handful of Epsom salts around each plant when it starts to bud.

AUTHOR'S NOTE: *If your soil tests deficient in magnesium (most common in the highly weathered and sandy soils of the southern and eastern United States), Epsom salts can be beneficial. An occasional light sprinkling of Epsom salts also encourages African violets to flower.*

❋

"Many crops have their greatest demand for nutrients when the fruit is setting," explains Emmett Schulte, a professor emeritus of soil science at the University of Wisconsin–Madison. "Because magnesium is a constituent of chlorophyll and necessary for continued growth, a shortage in the soil causes some of the magnesium in the plant to translocate (it moves upward), and the lower leaves start to break down."

Kitchen Fertilizers

Jeanette Baker's fisherman husband provided food for more than the dinner table. When the fish were cleaned, the Bakers buried the innards in their Onalaska, Wisconsin, vegetable bed to add rich nutrients. "Dig them in 6 to 8 inches," Jeanette advises, "so raccoons won't dig them out."

Fish aren't the only kind of leftovers that will nourish your garden. "If you bury a banana peel with every plant you set out, you'll be adding potassium," Jeanette advises.

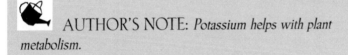

AUTHOR'S NOTE: *Potassium helps with plant metabolism.*

✳

In Manchuria, where Tatiana K. Bodine grew up, it was common practice to fertilize with egg whites. In her Iowa home Tatiana uses a method similar to that used in her homeland.

"I put the eggshells in a jar of water, cover the jar, and shake it to rinse the egg whites into the water. I let it stand for an hour, or overnight," she says, "and I use the water for my houseplants. Just throw away the shells."

✳

Philippine-born Fe Abellera once enjoyed a career as an elite international caterer in Cleveland, Ohio. Since then she's devoted countless hours to raising money for charitable causes by selling her homemade Philippine delicacies and organizing fund-raising dinners. It's only natural, then, that even when Fe is gardening, food is seldom far from her mind.

One of Fe's favorite tips came from a Filipino priest, who advised her to crush leftover eggshells and add them to her soil. "I was cooking one day and needed an egg yolk for a wine sauce, but not the white. So I dumped the whole egg white into my favorite houseplant.

"It bloomed well, but it started to stink. For weeks, I couldn't figure out where the smell was coming from. I thought it was my dog or possibly my garbage can. Then I followed it with my nose and realized it was the egg. So just the shells are okay, but don't overdo it with the whites," Fe says ruefully.

 AUTHOR'S NOTE: *Crushed eggshells contain calcium. Professor Schulte, an authority on plant nutrition, says, "They could help if the soil is acid; if it's alkaline, they won't hurt." Eggshells may have indirect effects too. For instance, they may loosen up the soil and allow aeration.*

Egg whites and the matrix of the shell have protein, which yields nitrogen. "Plants cannot use protein until it breaks down to nitrogen. They take up the nitrogen and make their own protein," Dr. Schulte says. Egg whites also have enzymes that could possibly be beneficial to plants, he speculates.

Utility Shelf Fertilizers

Ivy grows lush and rampant when you add a drop of household ammonia to each quart of water when watering the plant, notes horticulturist Barbara Voight.

 AUTHOR'S NOTE: *Ammonia supplies nitrogen.*

✳

Eggplants grow well in volcanic environments such as Greece and Pakistan because of the sulphur in the soil. If your garden plot has a less fiery history, you can help your eggplants flourish by sticking about a half-dozen unburned wooden matches, head side down, around each plant, says Dale Kendrick, a native of Wichita, Kansas.

✳

Jeanette Manske, an organic gardener from Stoddard, Wisconsin, advocates fertilizing pepper plants the same way.

Listening to Mother Nature

Mother nature is continually giving us new conditions. There are things happening that both professional growers and horticulturists don't fully understand though we study every day of our life. Sometimes it's baffling.

—EUGENE BAUER, MINNESOTA NURSERYMAN

CHAPTER FIVE

The Scoop on Manure

*Rabbit pellets . . . last all summer. But "llama beans"
break down easily in the soil."*

—DIANE CAVIS

One year we invited a Southeast Asian refugee family to share our garden plot, with the understanding that they would use only organic fertilizers. "Okay, I go ask a farmer for some cow s——," Lu, the father, said.

I explained to Lu that the word to use in polite company was manure.

"Manure? But isn't that a military term?" Lu replied in bewilderment. Eventually it dawned on me that he had confused it with maneuver.

Manure can be a confusing substance for the gardener, as well as for the recent immigrant grappling with the English language. Though gardeners have used it successfully for thousands of years, it usually comes without labels, sizes, or exact instructions.

Manure is nothing more than the polite term for animal–dung fertilizer (although in Victorian times even the word *dung* was taboo around lady gardeners). This humble substance with almost miraculous power is rich in the major elements that plants need to grow: nitrogen, phosphorus, and potassium. Manure also contains other trace elements that are valuable to plant nutrition.

Does a plant "know" the difference between nourishment it receives from manure and nourishment it receives from chemical fertilizers? The prevailing view among plant scientists is that it does not. Once elements are released from manure, they are reduced to their pure chemical form regardless of their source.

Like the differences between organic and inorganic fertilizers, the differences between chemicals and manure are ones of quality. In a sense, chemical fertilizers are the chocolate bars of the plant world. They give plants a quick feeding of specific amounts of chemicals but add nothing of long-term value to the soil.

The nutrients in manure, on the other hand, are slowly released and remain active longer. Manure stimulates the crops and improves soil quality as its partially decomposed vegetable matter boosts the soil's moisture-holding ability. Horse and cattle manure also contains a fair amount of the animals' bedding material (straw, sawdust, etc.). This rapidly decomposes in the heat generated by the manure, adding an extra source of nutrition and humus.

The greatest benefit manure bestows, however, is its power to improve the soil. Truly dedicated gardeners are wise enough to seize any opportunity they can—in *any* form: Wildlife biologist George Schaller, for example, while living at a research station on the plains of East Africa, not only gathered zebra dung but also collected elephant droppings to augment his hard garden soil.

This chapter considers ways to use manure fertilizers to the best advantage, offers tips for avoiding potential problems, and describes novel methods of applying manure.

When you use manures, you don't have to worry about precise measurements or stringent rules. One rule of thumb generally agreed upon is that it's best to age manure for a couple of months before use to reduce the risk of burning the plants.

As a common guideline, the clumpy, wet manures from cows and horses are spread on the soil surface and plowed in at planting time. Poultry and sheep manures are easier to handle and can be sprinkled between the rows even after the plants are up. Work them into the soil with a cultivator, but avoid close proximity to plants and seed furrows, as burning is possible (observe this precaution with all fresh manure as well).

Traditionally, we think of cow, horse, sheep, and chicken dung as the most common manure fertilizers (in terms of nutrition, pig dung is excellent too, but its odor is horrendous). An account of possible manure animals would read like a medieval bestiary, however, for the variety is nothing short of marvelous. Immigrant Southeast Asian gardeners extoll the virtues of buffalo to me, and in many areas a much-valued manure is guano, gathered from wild seabirds.

Although this chapter offers no tips for collecting elephant droppings, buffalo dung, or guano, it provides ideas for common sources that are often overlooked (some possibly even in your own household), as well as others that are far more exotic, from wild beasts to crickets. No matter which "maneuver" you opt for, with just a little bit of care you're bound to have a victory garden.

What Makes a Good Garden?

*The best thing to put on a garden to make it grow is saline solution—
the kind that comes off your face.*
—WENDAL MITCHELL, CORBIN, KENTUCKY

The Pros and Cons of Manure

One of the best fertilizers for the home gardener is a truckload of manure, says grower Eugene Bauer, of Bauers Market and Nursery in La Crescent, Minnesota. To be efficient, dump it on the garden in the fall so it can age over the winter. Snow, frost, and rain take it into the ground, where it improves both soil fertility and tilth.

✳

Unfortunately, manure introduces not only nutrition but also lots of weed seeds to the garden. That won't become a problem if you apply it mainly to large row crops like sweet corn, where you'll be tilling the weeds mechanically with a minimum of hand-weeding, says wildlife biologist Carl Korschgen, who gardened for many years in Bangor, Maine.

✳

"Don't use manure to fertilize gladiolus," cautions Jeanette Manske of Stoddard, Wisconsin. Her son raises them commercially, putting in 30,000 or more bulbs a year. "If you do, they get thrips [a very small, juice-sucking insect] and turn brown."

✳

A mixture of sheep manure, bonemeal, and alfalfa meal works well as an organic fertilizer, finds Ruth Coombs, a native of Kansas City, Missouri. The most economical source for the meals is farm supply stores, Ruth notes.

✳

Especially in the spring, manure tea is second to none for an early nitrogen boost, maintains horticulturist Barbara Voight of Madison, Wisconsin.

Put a large dollop of manure in a bucket, add water, and let it sit to dissolve. To keep from burning tender seedlings, dilute this manure tea so that the water is barely colored.

"If you can get it, chicken manure is especially beneficial because it's more balanced and has more lime," Barbara adds.

Another Reason to Own a Pet

"I have two cats and I dump their dirty kitty litter on my garden all winter, says Ruth Switzer of Nehawka, Nebraska. "It's a good fertilizer—I have raised sweet potatoes so big that you can't get them in a three-pound coffee can."

✳

Man's best friend is also a friend to the garden. Veterinarian Richard Stelmach has a bountiful supply of dog droppings from the boarding kennel at his Onalaska, Wisconsin, Central Animal Hospital. He brings the droppings home to fertilize his evergreens and tomato plants.

Dick digs a foot-deep hole to bury the droppings, covers them with soil, and then plants the tomatoes on top. "It made a big difference," he notes. "Also, it's probably better for the environment if it doesn't go to the dump."

Many pet owners aren't sure if dog and cat droppings are safe for the garden. Dr. Stelmach cautions that common internal parasites in dogs and cats may pass to humans through handling, kneeling, or going barefoot in garden soil.

"As long as you don't handle it (or if you know it's parasite-free), you have no problem." If you live in a cold climate, spread the pet manure on the garden only in the winter, as freezing kills any parasite eggs that might be present. Still, Dr. Stelmach warns, "Don't ever touch it!"

It's safest to keep pet droppings out of your compost pile, cautions veterinarian Stelmach. Even in warm months the compost may not get hot enough to destroy all the parasite eggs, and in the winter the pile may not freeze hard enough to kill them.

Something Worth Crowing About

Cow, horse, and sheep manure are well known as fertilizers, but Bill Hansen, who raises prize chickens at his Bangor, Wisconsin, farm, has another "brand" he recommends. Bill produces fabulous raspberry and strawberry crops with the help of chicken manure.

Once the berries have finished bearing, spread the manure between the rows thickly enough to keep the weeds down and the moisture in. Since most of the manure has been mixed with the poultry-bedding material of sawdust, wood shavings, or corn cobs, you don't have to worry about it burning the plants.

Teaming Up: Horse versus Cow

For ready access to a lot of good free manure, go to your local riding stable. "They like to have you come help," says Ruth Ann Davis of Tucson, Arizona. Ruth Ann's enthusiasm for this product is so great, she confesses, that sometimes she's there shoveling right out of the stalls, shooing away the horses to get elbow room. "With manure as fresh as that, it's best to pile it somewhere first to age before spreading it on your garden," she advises.

✳

In the communities where Amish farmer Joe Borntreger has lived, horse-drawn vehicles are a common sight, as the Amish religion shuns mechanized transportation. For them horse manure is in plentiful supply. With this simple tip from Joe, it would be worth your while to find a manure supply in order to try his Amish planting method.

In the fall plow and get the garden all ready to plant. Cover it with a 4-inch layer of horse manure. In the spring make a trench in the manure for each row and just drop the seeds in. Cover and let grow.

✳

Be leery of horse manure, which heats up and is apt to burn plants, cautions Wisconsin octogenarian Bob Neuhaus, from experience gleaned during sixty-seven years of gardening. "I wouldn't use it at all," says the strict cow-manure advocate.

✳

In fact, in the old days cow manure was commonly called a "cold manure" and horse manure was a "hot manure," notes retired University of Wisconsin Extension agricultural agent Jim Ness. Horse manure is more likely to burn than cow manure because it has more nitrogen.

To dissipate the nitrogen, advises Jim, mix the manure with a little dirt so the soil bacteria can help it break down. Then let it age six to eight weeks before applying it.

AUTHOR'S NOTE: *To conserve nutrients and prevent the pile from smelling or attracting flies, keep it covered. (A leaf mulch is good, because you can plow that in with the manure, whereas a tarp leaves you with yet another messy item to handle.)*

If you opt for packaged dried manure, you pay a sacrifice for being so dainty, as dried manure has less nitrogen.

Scooping the Best Bargains

The best bargains in town aren't always in the shopping malls. If you're looking for a good source of free manure, compost manufacturer Bill Bricker of Augusta, Georgia, recommends a visit to a local slaughterhouse.

AUTHOR'S NOTE: *If you live in an urban area, you may think it's impossible to locate chicken manure for your garden, but you'd be surprised. Even large cities have small-scale breeders. We realized this after discovering that for years our neighbor had kept a flock of bantam chickens in his garage so discreetly that the other people on the block had no inkling.*

Most of these folks would be delighted to swap manure for some help cleaning the poultry coop. To find poultry owners, check health food shops selling organic farm eggs, feed stores, classified ads for farm produce, and even racing-pigeon clubs.

Llama Beans

Perhaps you've heard gardeners hotly debating the relative merits of fertilizers: chemical supplements versus cow manure, sheep dung versus chicken manure. Well, llama breeder Diane Cavis of Holmen, Wisconsin, waxes enthusiastic about the virtues of llama manure. "I've had rabbit pellets, and they last all summer. But 'llama beans' break down easily in the soil. And it's nicely piled for you, always in the same corner of the yard."

AUTHOR'S NOTE: *Don't expect to save money by raising your own supply, though. The price for one llama is roughly equivalent to that of a new car.*

Where the Wild Things Are

"Zoo Doo from the San Francisco Zoo's lions, tigers, and hoof stock was a popular fertilizer in our area," recalls California gardener Elizabeth Pomada. The company that produced Zoo Doo is no longer in business, but other zoos or animal refuges may have similar programs.

Zoo Doo was safe because it was dried and composted, says a spokeswoman for the San Francisco Zoo. But beware, she warns: If you do find a source of this kind, avoid raw manure, which might have parasites.

AUTHOR'S NOTE: *My veterinarian agrees that wild cat droppings might be a hazard but believes there's no risk from elephant manure—unless you get stepped on.*

✹

"My grandma lives on a two-hundred-acre farm with lots of pines, which attract deer," says Linda George Olson of Ettrick, Wisconsin. "Grandma gathers the deer pellets and mixes them with water for fertilizer."

The Best Things Come in Small Packages

Large animals aren't the only ones whose manure can benefit the garden. Georgia garden writer Virgil Adams, is lavish in his praise of the benefits to be gleaned from far-smaller creatures: crickets. Intrigued by Virgil's enthusiasm for such an unconventional prize ingredient, I queried him, and he put me in touch with Bill Bricker of Augusta, Georgia, manufacturer of Kricket Krap.

After retiring from the military, Colonel Bricker decided to parlay his love of organic gardening into a new career. Now he has a work force of about two billion crickets helping him produce his product.

Kricket Krap is an extremely rich organic fertilizer resulting from the high-protein diet of the commercial fish-bait crickets that produce this manure. Unlike the majority of other fresh animal manures, Bricker's product is weed-free and nonburning. (Available from Bricker's Organic Farms, Inc., 824-K Sandbar Ferry Road, Augusta, Georgia 30901.)

Gardens Grow Gardeners Too

Have fun! People keep telling what you should and shouldn't do: map, dig, spray—the heck with it! You can take advice, but the keystone is, if you're happy with what you're doing, you're successful.

—ERIC LAUTZENHEISER, DIRECTOR, SAN ANTONIO BOTANICAL GARDENS

CHAPTER SIX

Composting the Easy Way

Most people . . . think compost is just a polite word for manure.

—BILL BRICKER

Many gardeners talk about composting with such rapture that you'd think they didn't have merely a decomposing pile of debris but the wonder-working relics of a saint. For nature's ability to recycle once-living substance into life anew does seem magical. As bacteria that live in the soil digest organic matter, this plant and animal debris converts into humus, which holds essential nutrients, boosts the soil's absorption and water-holding capacity, improves tilth and aeration, fosters the growth of helpful soil organisms, and reduces erosion. No wonder compost is sometimes called "black gold"! Because gardeners seldom have the time to wait for natural breakdown, they hasten the course of nature by composting. Like most recipes, composting lends itself to variations: You can fiddle with the process to suit your particular circumstances and temperament. To produce wonderful compost, all you need is air, soil, water, and plant and (if you wish) animal matter. As you'll see in the tips that follow, the organic materials you can use are nearly infinite, but to avoid attracting animals, it's best not to use meat or fish scraps unless they're buried deeply in the pile.

Generally, for every 6 to 12 inches of organic material, add a high-nitrogen fertilizer or three or four shovelfuls of manure to feed the bacteria, then cover the pile with an inch or so of soil. Moisten the entire mound with water, and then begin a new layer of organic debris on top. There's no precise rule you have to follow—after all, this isn't a recipe for French pastry—and a little more or a little less fertilizer, water, or soil isn't going to hurt anything.

If you build your compost pile 3 to 4 feet high, it will be tall enough to hold moisture, yet low enough for convenience. You can contain the pile in bins made of wire, wood slats, or concrete block, or you can simply heap everything up with no enclosure at all. Unless you live in a very cool climate such as Alaska, you can even put it in a pit. (I confess that lately I've been so busy with this book that I've settled for just flinging kitchen scraps over the porch railing and kicking a little dirt over everything once in a while.)

Keep the pile moist but not soggy; it will decompose faster. If the compost dries out or gets too wet, the process slows down, but it is not in serious jeopardy. It is much harder to ruin compost than it is to ruin houseplants, for instance, by over- or underwatering.

The aerobic bacteria work quickly to convert the organic material into compost, provided that you turn the pile over frequently to supply them with the oxygen they need in order to live. If the pile isn't turned, the anaerobic bacteria, which thrive in airless environments, temporarily take over. Don't worry if this happens; the anaerobic bacteria also decompose the pile, though they're pokier. The pile will get smelly and slimy, but nothing fatal happens to it, and when eventually you aerate the pile, aerobic bacteria appear again.

How long does composting take? A dark, crumbly humus will be ready in as little time as a few weeks or as much as a year, depending upon the ingredients you add, the temperature and humidity of your location, and the frequency with which you turn the pile. You don't have to schedule compost pile turning like a chore, though. Whenever you have some energy or aggression to work off, get out there with a shovel or fork and flip that heap around—it's marvelous therapy. And should you find yourself not in the mood, don't force yourself to do it.

In this chapter you'll discover imaginative yet practical labor-saving shortcuts and ecologically sound recycling hints. Granted, they're not quite faith healing, but they do cure many a garden ill and promote a healthy planet.

Listening to Mother Nature

If everybody composted their garbage, we'd really cut down on the garbage disposal problem.

—RUTH ANN DAVIS, RETIRED RESORT OWNER

A Heavy Task Made Easy

At Bricker's Organic Farms, Inc., in Augusta, Georgia, Bill Bricker produces up to fifty tons a day of an organic compost called Compost Toast. "Most people in the South don't know the difference between compost and manure—they think compost is just a polite word for manure. If we'd known, we'd probably never have called it that," Bill reflects.

"A good compost pile won't smell bad; if it does, it's probably because it needs more air. When too much water goes in, air goes out, and the compost pickles and putrefies," he cautions.

Too much dirt can also weigh down a compost pile and make it airless. Instead of dirt, you can substitute a thin layer of old compost. "If you use dirt, just sprinkle it like you were salt-and-peppering an egg or a steak," the Georgia compostmaker recommends.

✳

It's easy to get in the habit of composting if you locate your compost pile close to the back door and keep a long-tined pitchfork in it, advises *Lexington Herald Leader* garden writer Beverly Fortune (she uses an old-fashioned hay fork).

"The key to having your compost break down is keeping it turned and aerated. We're all lazy and if it's out of sight, it's out of mind. Because the pitchfork is right at your fingertips, if you have an extra few minutes, you can turn it a couple of times. It's less of a chore," she says.

✳

To keep your compost pile aerated without backbreaking labor and to keep your hands and clothes clean while you're doing it, take a hint from Judy and Stan Schabert of La Crosse, Wisconsin. They use a large rotating drum called a Kemp Compos Tumbler. Just five turns a day converts kitchen waste and garden debris into good compost in short order (about two weeks). The manually operated drum stands about 2 feet off the ground, so that a wheelbarrow can catch the finished compost and transfer it to the garden easily.

"The only drawback," notes Judy, "is that if you add fresh waste continuously, the compost is always mingled with uncomposted material. Occasionally you have to call a temporary halt and let the entire drumful decompose before you empty it."

Keeping Compost Healthy

"Whenever you add a layer of garden or kitchen waste to your compost pile, sprinkle about 2 inches of soil on top. This inoculates the pile with soil bacteria, which are needed to break down the compost," advises horticulturist Ernie Hartmann. "The soil also helps keep odors down. However, you needn't waste your best soil—use the worst soil in your garden."

Definitely don't put sick plants in your compost pile, or any leaves that show any signs of disease, Dr. Hartmann warns.

AUTHOR'S NOTE: *Because they're prone to disease, it's safest to refrain from composting tomato or cucumber vines.*

✳

Green leaves are a boon to composting. "If you're pruning or have access to the debris pile of a local tree surgeon, green leaves are a wonderful addition to a compost pile. But avoid black walnut, sycamore, and locust leaves because they have a growth retardant," notes Bill Bricker of Augusta, Georgia.

✳

"To keep odors down, put household ammonia in the kitchen compost container," suggests horticulturist Barbara Voight of Madison, Wisconsin. For indoor containers Barbara adds about one fourth of a cup of ammonia to a gallon compost container. "You can pour a little ammonia over the outdoor compost, also. It adds nitrogen to the heap," she says.

✳

Make the top of your compost heap dish-shaped so that rainwater will collect, advises the University of Alaska Cooperative Extension Service in Sitka, Alaska.

To speed up the breakdown of organic matter and keep optimum moisture levels in your compost heap, the service suggests, cover it with clear (milky) plastic polyvinylchloride. The plastic helps retain heat but still allows sunlight to penetrate. It also prevents evaporation and protects the pile from heavy rainfall that might add too much water.

✳

"You may want to add dolomitic limestone to raise the pH and sweeten your compost pile," suggests commercial compostmaker Bill Bricker of Augusta, Georgia. The dolomitic lime contains calcium and magnesium. "But don't do this if the compost is going to be used on acid-loving plants."

Compost Pile Architecture

To make compost on a small city lot, writer Lynne Leuthe of La Crosse, Wisconsin, recommends an assembly–line approach. "If you don't have a lot of room for big piles in one place, this method lets you turn the material over as it composts in three bins. To make the most of your space, place the bins in separate areas in the yard," she says. Here's how to build Lynne's "dirt factories":

* Make wood–framed bins any size you desire (Lynne's are 3 feet square and 30 inches high) with three sides of half–inch–mesh hardware cloth, and the fourth side of removable wood slats.

* In the first bin, pile green organic materials such as grass clippings, spent flower blossoms, weeds, and leaves. A thickness of 5 to 10 inches is sufficient for the first layer.

* Sprinkle a little lime, commercial fertilizer, or manure to add nitrogen. Add a few handfuls of garden soil for bacteria. (The soil also helps the compost retain moisture and reduces odor.) Continue layering.

* As the compost in the first bin decomposes, lift the slats off the side of the bin and, with a pitchfork, remove the more decomposed bottom material. Use a wheelbarrow to move that partially decomposed material to the second bin, and move bottom matter from the second bin to the third. The whole process can take as little as six weeks or as much as a year, depending on the warmth of the season. In the meantime, start the process again in the first bin.

✳

Dr. Ernie Hartmann of La Crosse, Wisconsin, has been a forester and a landscape contractor, a garden radio–show host, a professor, and a horticulture professor. He credits his immigrant German mother with selling him on pit composting.

"When I was a child, she had a circular pit into which she threw kitchen garbage such as vegetable peelings, fish heads, and bones for a rich compost. To keep down odor and neutralize acids, she sprinkled soil and a few handfuls of ground agricultural lime (not quick or hydrated lime) over the garbage."

Composting without Compost Piles

"In Galesburg, Illinois, where we gardened for sixteen years," recall Ed and Irene Wojahn, "the sticky clay soil was terrible. And when it was dry, it split open into crevices so wide that we had to watch the little kids to make sure their feet didn't catch in the ground."

To improve the soil's tilth, the Wojahns set about composting right in the garden. Ed believes in using not only table scraps such as vegetable peelings but also fish heads and meat scraps. "I never have garbage," he comments. "Just dig a little hole here and there and put the scraps between the plants—use a different hole every day. Cover them with about 6 inches of dirt, so dogs won't dig them up, and in just a few weeks they'll decompose."

*

If you have limited space, as Ruth Ann Davis does at her mobile home in Tucson, Arizona, try her style of blender composting, which works like a miniature shredder–composter:

"Take kitchen leavings such as carrot tops, melon rinds, and potato peels (but not meat scraps or fibrous, coarse material like corn cobs) and grind them with a little water in your blender. For a small household, you can accumulate these in a jug for a few meals and then do a batch before it starts to spoil. It's surprising how much you can produce in a blender," notes Ruth Ann.

"When you pour this around your outdoor plants, you're watering them and feeding them nutrients at the same time. And even if your soil is poor, like Tucson's cementlike caliche, the organic material helps retain moisture. To work it in, merely loosen the earth a bit with a hand cultivator."

For a mini–compost pile, you can also pour the blender mixture into a hole, she adds. "If I happen to have a bag of dried ground steer manure around, I add a little to help it decompose a little faster. Then I kick in a little soil, just so it doesn't look like a garbage heap."

"One spring, cherry tomato seeds from the blender compost sprouted. Little plants were already coming up when my husband and I were leaving Tucson for the resort we used to operate," Ruth Ann recalls. "I didn't want to waste them, so I brought them along and planted them. The tiny tomatoes reseeded themselves, coming up again the following summer. Melon seeds will come up that way, as volunteers, too."

AUTHOR'S NOTE: *The resilience of tomato seeds is almost legendary. One upstate New York community spread compost made from treated sewage on parkland. Before long, the community had a park full of tomato plants.*

Garbage Can Composting

You don't need carefully engineered pits or elaborate contraptions to make wonderful compost. Doc and Katy Abraham, authors of seven garden books and hosts of "The Green Thumb" radio program on WHAM in Rochester, New York, offer their popular (as well as simple and convenient) strategy for garbage can composting:

- Choose a galvanized or plastic garbage can with a tight-fitting lid—any size will work.

- Punch four nail holes in the bottom of the can, closer to the center than to the edge and equidistant from each other.

- Keep the garbage can in a garage or cellar where it won't freeze. If space is limited, you can even put a five-gallon can in the kitchen. (Rubbermaid cans are sturdy and pretty.)

- Place it on a platform of bricks or cement blocks, and place a pie pan underneath it to catch any liquid that drains out. This liquid is odorless and can be used on houseplants to add nutrients.

+ Put a starting layer of 3 inches of good soil (either garden or potting soil) in the bottom of the can. Sawdust is okay too.

AUTHOR'S NOTE: *Do not use sawdust or woodchips from wood that has been chemically treated with preservatives or insecticides.*

+ To help the organic refuse break down faster and also to enrich the compost, include some red worms or "manure worms" if you can get them. (They are often advertised in fishing magazines.) If you buy them, purchase the minimum amount offered. One hundred worms is plenty. If a friend has some, ask for a couple of handfuls—the worms will multiply. If none are available, forget it.

+ Add some chopped leaves or a few sheets of shredded newspaper.

+ Toss in just about any plant or food matter from the kitchen. Potato skins, corn husks and cobs, vegetable leaves, coffee grounds, melon rinds, and fruit peelings (worms tolerate citrus skins in moderate amounts) are perfect. Table scraps such as cooked vegetables, leftover egg, and bread crusts are okay.

+ Avoid meat scraps; they attract rodents. Bones won't break down, so leave them out.

+ Avoid onions or other highly acidic materials. Worms don't like them and will crawl out of the can if they are added. (If you don't use worms, then you can add onion peels.)

+ Add other organic household debris, including dog hair, untreated sawdust and wood chips, eggshells (a good source of calcium), nut shucks, even dust from the vacuum cleaner bag.

+ Cover each addition of fresh garbage with a sprinkling of garden soil, grass clippings, or shredded leaves. Don't worry about odors or flies—compost cans are usually pest-free and odorless. If you notice an unpleasant odor, a fresh layer of shredded newspapers, tea leaves, or coffee grounds will solve the problem almost immediately.

- One large can is able to handle the debris from a family of four, if the children are young. Some families start one can in the fall, then add another as the first one becomes nearly full. The fall one is usually ready to dump on the garden in the spring. You might need to add it to the outdoor pile if it's not completely decomposed.

- If you use worms, you can save them to reuse in your next compost can. Since the worms prefer darkness, leave the lid off for a short time before you get ready to dump the can; the worms will go to the bottom, and the composted material can be shoveled off the top. You can also shine a flashlight on top of the compost in the can to accomplish the same purpose.

- Completely converted garbage can be worked into the soil immediately. You can fortify your composted material with any kind of plant food, plus a light scattering of lime or wood ashes. Sand scattered on the compost helps make a looser mixture but isn't necessary.

Living Fire

"The heat which a compost pile generates is not necessarily high enough to kill weed seeds," notes horticulturist Dr. Ernie Hartmann. "Some seeds, such as maple seeds, actually thrive under such conditions, and that's why you get so many 'volunteers.'"

AUTHOR'S NOTE: *An actively working compost pile may reach 150 to 170 degrees Fahrenheit, but the material on the outer edges doesn't get as hot.*

90

Many gardeners wonder if you can compost in cold weather. "Once the temperature drops below 45 degrees Fahrenheit, the heating and decomposing process becomes inactive," Dr. Hartmann says. "Though the compost won't keep breaking down, it doesn't hurt at all to keep adding your kitchen wastes. They'll supply a good reserve to start up decomposing action in the spring."

Spreading the Rewards

"Put a shovelful of finished compost at the bottom of the hole when you plant tomatoes, perennials, trees, or bushes, and your plants will thrive," suggests garden writer Lynne Leuthe. "Spread the rest (there's never enough) over your flower beds for top-dressing, or dig it into your vegetable garden in the spring."

❋

"Compost is good to mix with garden soil for houseplants. Use one part each of coarse sand, compost, and garden soil for a good potting mixture," recommend nationally syndicated garden columnists Doc and Katy Abraham of Naples, New York. "We don't sterilize our soil and have never had any problems, but if you have any doubt that your soil may have harmful organisms, sterilize it," they say.

States of Mind

Composting is not faith healing.

—BRUCE MARKOT, MIDDLETOWN, CONNECTICUT

CHAPTER SEVEN

Starting with Seeds

*If you want seeds that will germinate reliably and prove true
to promise, steer clear of cheap brands.*

—DR. ANN KORSCHGEN

very dormant seed holds inside its drab outer husk the complete script
necessary to create a uniquely beautiful plant. All the genetic instructions that determine the adult plant's potential, its appearance, and its
behavior are already programmed. In addition, even the most nondescript
seed packs just the right combination of enzymes, fat, carbohydrate, and
protein to nourish the seedling in its first weeks of life.

Inside the seed waits an embryo plant, complete with stem and its first
leaves. Even while still dormant, the seed takes in oxygen and water from
the air and gives off carbon dioxide. So though a dormant seed looks dry
and lifeless, it's actually very much alive. Place this tiny kernel into a growing medium, give it warmth, water, and air, and soon it burgeons forth,
vibrant and green.

In this chapter you'll find tips on selecting quality seeds, regional seeds that are especially suitable for your locale, and heirloom seeds. There are helpful hints for germinating, getting an early start with indoor sowing, maintaining seed health, transplanting, and saving leftover seed, as well as an admonition about what happens when plants, like people, opt for "love on the wild side."

Speaking of recklessness, a nineteenth-century tip on soaking seeds in boiling water (which appears later in this chapter) intrigued me, so I gave it a try. I tried modernizing this suggestion by carrying the seeds to the garden in a thermos bottle. Alas, it kept them hot too long and cooked them.

Hopefully, the advice herein will help you avoid such mishaps. But should Murphy's Law ("If things can go wrong, they will") crop up from time to time, you'll be able to take them more in stride if you keep some historical perspective. For instance, my thermos disaster made me feel I was in good company, right up there with James Morrow, the naturalist who collected seeds on Commodore Perry's expedition to Asia. Morrow never got a chance to worry about hail or cutworm destroying his seed—hostile natives boiled them.

Smart Shopping: "Seeds, Sex, and Lies"

"Call this tip "Seeds, Sex, and Lies," says Dr. Ann Korschgen of Onalaska, Wisconsin. "If you want seeds that will germinate reliably and prove true to promise, steer clear of cheap brands. Last year we bought nickel-a-package seeds from a discount store. The germination was terrible. And when they came up, some weren't even what the seed packet claimed they were. So this year we ordered all our seeds from Burpee."

✱

Seed packets from retail stores include helpful information such as planting depth, whether or not to cover the seeds, and days to maturity. Mail-order seed packets, however, may have none of this, cautions *Lexington Herald Leader* garden writer Beverly Fortune. "So save your catalog for planting instructions."

*

AUTHOR'S NOTE: *This warning comes from the sad experience of growing sweet corn, popcorn, and decorative miniature Indian corn and having them all interbreed: If you grow more than one variety of corn, be sure to select ones that mature at different times, or stagger the plantings to prevent them from cross-pollinating.*

Also, if your neighbors' gardens are near your own, the wind can cause their corn and yours to cross-pollinate. It's a good idea in such cases to plant the same variety as your neighbor does. Otherwise, talk over your planting schedules, or choose varieties with different maturing dates to avoid this problem.

More on Choosing: Seeds, Home, and History

"Good seeds make good plants," declares gardener Tony Holt of Grants Pass, Oregon. "Many of us buy our seeds from major national seed catalogues and are hardly aware that smaller houses catering especially to our particular habitat may exist.

"I have gone almost exclusively to using seeds from the Territorial Seed Company of Lorane, Oregon," says Tony. "Their seeds are specially hybridized for the climate and conditions of the Willamette Valley. The Rogue River Valley where we live is close enough, and I've had good success with their material."

*

Would you like to grow heirloom seeds that have been passed down in families for generations, seeds you'll never see sold in commercial nurseries?

You can buy a bean that came over on the Mayflower, the legendary and once nearly extinct Moon and Stars watermelon, and tomatoes that are pink, white, yellow, orange, purplish, or striped. These and thousands of other rare, flavorful, and hardy seed varieties are available through Seed Savers.

A nationwide nonprofit access network for backyard gardeners, Seed Savers includes members who "adopt" endangered seeds, sharing them with others and saving them for future generations. The seeds they safeguard and perpetuate are treasure troves of plant genetic material that in many instances would otherwise be lost to humanity.

For a free brochure detailing Seed Savers' projects and publications, director Kent Whealy invites you to send $1.00 and a long self-addressed, stamped envelope to Seed Savers Exchange, 3076 North Winn Road, Decorah, IA 52101.

AUTHOR'S NOTE: *You'll have the best success with legume crops such as beans and peas with seeds that have been inoculated prior to planting with nitrogen-fixing bacteria. (For more on nitrogen-fixing bacteria, see page 59). When buying pretreated seeds, plant soon after purchase, as the active bacteria may break down the seed shell.*

If you plan to hold extra legume seeds over for future plantings, avoid the above-mentioned possibility of breakdown by buying untreated seed; apply dry inoculant instead (one that's specific for your crop) when you're ready to plant.

Moistening your seeds in a solution of water and Pepsi or other soda pop helps the inoculant powder adhere. Just a half-teaspoon of soda per gallon of water is ample, because if the solution is too sticky, seeds clump.

Starting Seeds Indoors

Before starting annuals indoors, note the recommended planting time for your area, as well as the number of days it will take for the seeds to germinate and mature to transplanting size. Don't sow seeds too early, or they will be ready to go outdoors before it's warm enough, cautions John Kehoe, park services supervisor of Hartford, Connecticut's Colt Park.

"If it's still too early to transplant them outdoors when they're big enough, they become root-bound and don't do as well when they finally go outdoors," John says.

✳

"Because of our short growing season, starting certain plants indoors can be helpful, and with some, even necessary," says Tony Holt, a gardener in Grants Pass, Oregon. "With watermelons, cantaloupe, cucumbers, zucchini, and pumpkins, you can place the seeds in wet newspaper. Roll the paper up and place it in a plastic bag for three to five days. Then plant the already germinated seeds in plastic pots filled with potting soil and place them in a cold frame outdoors. (I can do this by mid-April, generally waiting until late May to transplant to the open garden because of possible late frosts.)

"The wet newspaper/plastic bag germination technique works well for sweet corn, too," Tony adds.

AUTHOR'S NOTE: *This technique has several advantages. Unlike seeds planted directly in the field, 100 percent of the seeds in your garden will be germinated (because, obviously, you'll toss any that don't germinate). Also, there should be less predation from birds that pilfer kernels before they have time to come up.*

"Plant vegetable seeds in 6-inch pots rather than the more common 2- to 4-inch pots," advises Tony. "This allows for freer, more exuberant root growth, and there seems to be little or no transplant shock."

✳

Herb grower Terry Kemp of God's Green Acres in Onalaska, Wisconsin, offers this advice on starting flowers, vegetables, or herbs indoors from seed. Recycle Styrofoam cups and plastic sandwich bags into individual minigreenhouses. These fit perfectly on windowsills and don't need a tray, as the water collects in the bag. The cups make nice pots for the plants to grow in until ready for transplanting.

For each greenhouse poke three holes into the bottom of the cup for drainage and tuck the cup into a plastic bag. Put 2 inches of potting soil mixture into the cup. Plant three seeds in each cup, and mist lightly. Then cover the seeds with ¼-inch of dirt, or according to the seed package directions (some seeds require no dirt).

Mist again to make sure the soil is moist enough for germination. Close the bag over the cup (with fold or twister) and keep moist until the seeds germinate.

After they germinate, pull the bags down for better light and ventilation; leave the bags in place to catch the water. Provide at least six hours of sunlight daily.

Once the plants get their first true leaves, remove the two weakest plants from each cup. Add more dirt, and fertilize. Pinch back as needed to keep the seedlings from getting leggy.

✴

"If you're starting your plants from seeds, here's a hint for keeping the seed trays from drying out," says farmer Jeanette Manske of Stoddard, Wisconsin. "Use an old cake pan or tray. Put a couple of handfuls of gravel on the bottom and add water. Set the seed trays on the gravel. The water wicks into the drainage holes and moistens the soil without letting it get waterlogged.

"When starting seeds outside in my hotbed, I work the ground up, put down the seed, and then sprinkle a good quality commercial potting soil to cover the seeds. The potting soil spreads evenly, and doesn't lump (the way cold garden soil is apt to do in the early spring). I get a better start this way," says Jeanette.

✴

Most gardeners can allow themselves to be laggards once in a while. But Lynne Leuthe can't grant herself that luxury. Lynne has to get her Midwest garden in early and select crops that won't mature until August, as she and her husband commute to Alaska every summer to do commercial salmon fishing.

She makes up for those weeks of lost gardening pleasure by starting her seeds way back when snow is still on the ground. Lynne shares these tips for sprouting from scratch:

Make sure that young seedlings get fourteen to sixteen hours of sunlight daily; keep them close to the source of the light so that they become sturdy, with straight stems and many leaves. If your seedlings "grow tall and spindly and look like prairie grass blowing in the wind," Lynne reminds you to correct this by placing them in direct sunlight "as soon as they sprout . . . the more the better."

If you want to sprout seeds (such as petunias) that take several months to reach transplanting size, start the seeds in winter. "Because daylight is in short supply, a grow light is especially useful for this type of seed," advises Lynne.

Avoiding Damping-Off Disease

AUTHOR'S NOTE: *Damping-off disease is a fungus that attacks seedlings. The young plants seem to be flourishing, when suddenly they flop over and drop dead. These three tips may prevent this affliction.*

The risk of damping-off fungus was an ever-present problem (especially with lavender and sweet marjoram) for herb grower Chris Weingand, in Kalaheo, Hawaii, until she discovered this solution:

"Knowing that chamomile has antiseptic properties as well as tonic action, I started using chamomile tea to water my seed flats. I used the annual sweet false chamomile (*Matricaria recutita*), but Roman chamomile (*Anthemis nobilis* or *Chamaemelum nobile*) would also work. It has eliminated my problem with damping off!

"Pour a pint of boiling water over each ounce of chamomile flowers. Steep them for ten or fifteen minutes, and cool before using. Water the emerging seedlings with this infusion."

✳

Caution: If you want healthy seedlings, "do not use compost for starting seeds," warn two of America's most popular garden experts, Doc and Katy Abraham of "The Green Thumb" radio show. They suggest that you "use one of the sterile 'soil–less' mixes on the market such as commercial growers use. These contain sphagnum peat moss, perlite, and vermiculite; some also contain added nutrients. Many brands are readily available."

✳

"Do your little seedlings fall on their faces and wither away right after they sprout?" asks Lynne Leuthe. This common complaint indicates damping–off disease. (See page 99.)

"If you use soil as a sprouting medium, don't be frugal—open a new bag of sterilized soil, available at any garden center, when you plant your seeds, and it will totally eliminate the problem."

Lynne cautions that an old, opened bag of soil picks up fungi. "It's still okay to use for repotting houseplants," says Lynne, "but not for starting 'babies.'"

AUTHOR'S NOTE: *If compost and old soil can cause damping off in seeds started indoors, you may wonder why this is not a problem in plain soil in the garden. Although it occasionally happens, damping–off disease is less likely in the outdoors because sunshine, fresh air, and natural soil offer healthier growing conditions and are less conducive to the growth of pathogens.*

Go for Good Germination

If you hold seeds over one year to the next and aren't sure they're still good, test before you sow, suggests Beverly Fortune, garden writer for the *Lexington Herald Leader*. Press a half-dozen seeds on two to three layers of soggy-wet paper toweling; keep the towel moist until the seeds sprout. If only half germinate, take that into account and sow two times as thickly.

✳

Gardeners can get seeds to sprout much sooner by following the advice of *Facts for Farmers*, first published in 1865: "Quicken the powers" of black, hard-shelled seeds such as melon and sunflower by soaking for half a minute in boiling water, then planting while still hot and moist."

AUTHOR'S NOTE: *If you do try this, remove the water from the heat before adding seed, and be forewarned that this won't work for all black, hard-shelled seeds—for example, woody legumes.*

✳

Just soaking those tough, woody, hard-shelled seeds overnight in tepid water will also do the trick, notes horticulturist Ernie Hartmann.

✳

"Parsley seed germinates poorly sometimes. Here's my secret for getting it to germinate," says retired nurseryman Vernon R. Carse, of Central Point, Oregon: "Place seeds on a sheet of sandpaper and rub them with another piece of sandpaper as vigorously as possible (without losing the seed). Then freeze the seeds for a week. Just before planting, pour boiling water over the seed."

✳

"Peas need a period of cold temperature before they sprout. If the soil can't be worked because it's still frozen, store the peas in a refrigerator or freeze them in ice cubes until they can be planted," advises Raymond Rice of Kutztown, Pennsylvania.

✳

Manuel Lacks is famous for the beauty of his garden, say his rural Keysville, Virginia, neighbors. The key to success, he believes, is freezing his seed before sowing it. Then when you put it in the warm ground, the condensation from the freezing speeds up the sprouting, Manuel says.

✳

"If you don't plant perennial seeds in the fall, you can imitate the natural cold period they need to germinate by freezing them in an ice-cube tray and planting them, ice cube and all, in the spring," suggests horticulturist Barbara Voight of Madison, Wisconsin. "This fools the seeds into thinking they were out all winter. Self-seeding annual seeds needing a cold spell to germinate, such as love-in-a-mist (*Nigella damascena*), benefit also."

✳

"Wound seeds with a fine file before planting to stimulate growth and to help moisture reach the seed," advises eighty-eight-year-old gardener Nick Wekseth of Onalaska, Wisconsin.

✳

Having trouble getting carrot seed to germinate? Try this, suggests long-time Oregon nurseryman Vernon R. Carse: Chill seed in refrigerator for a day or two. Soak seed for an hour in warm (not hot) water. Prepare soil with generous applications of compost-manure combination. Rake carefully to make a very fine seed bed. Draw a very shallow furrow and plant seed sparingly.

Cutting the Apron Strings: Transplanting Seedlings

"Less-experienced gardeners need the most help with the fortitude and resolve to thin," observes Renee Shepherd of the Felton, California, mail-order seed house Shepherd's Garden Seeds. "I find a lot of gardeners are so pleased when their plants come up, they're loath to pull them out. But thinning is crucial for proper spacing, for circulation, and for disease-free growth. If you can't bear to throw away the extra seedlings, transplant them."

✳

Little kids can usually visit their new kindergarten to familiarize themselves with the surroundings before they actually start school. Your juvenile plants, coaxed from seeds indoors or in a hothouse, also need a chance to get used to the outside world before you leave them in the garden for good.

Wisconsin melon growers Bill and Helen Halverson put their seed pots outdoors for a few days to acclimate them to the fresh air and sunlight before they are transplanted in the garden. "Bring them indoors at night if the temperature drops," they suggest.

"Plant tender new plants on a shady day. If it's possible, plant them just before a rain, so you won't need to water them," suggests Helen Halverson.

✳

"If you can't transplant on a cloudy day, wait until after four o'clock," advises former Illinois gardener Dona Popovic.

AUTHOR'S NOTE: *Be sure to protect seedlings from wind as well as bright sunlight.*

✳

If you start your plants from seeds, they won't necessarily be ready to transplant into the garden at the same time, observes farmer Jeanette Manske of Stoddard, Wisconsin. If you use a trowel to dig them from the seed flat, take care not to injure the less mature plants. Jeanette advises that you wet the soil and pull them gently from the seed flat one at a time as they become ready to transplant.

Getting Seeds off to a Good Start: Outdoor Sowing

"Many people don't have a cold-frame, but do have outdoor flower-boxes. You can use these for getting a head start on cold weather crops, such as spinach, cabbage, and broccoli," suggests Wendal Mitchell, a gardener in Corbin, Kentucky. To avoid risk of damping-off disease, play it safe and fill the boxes with sterile potting soil. Then sow, and cover with clear plastic for warmth. The vegetables will be ready to transplant into the garden by the time it's warm enough to plant your flower-box annuals.

❋

To plant seed sparingly, advises longtime nurseryman Vernon R. Carse, "mix one part of seed in a container with at least ten parts of dry sand or vermiculite. Lightly scatter the mixture directly into the garden soil. Cover the seed with one quarter of an inch of vermiculite and press firmly with a wooden block."

❋

"You weaken your plants a bit when you transplant because you injure roots," maintains Ruth Switzer of Nehawka, Nebraska. So if you have enough space, she advises sowing directly into the garden. Plant only two seeds in each grouping; when they come up, keep only the strongest one.

"Many times," says Ruth Switzer, "I plant twelve to fifteen seeds in a little circle that fits under a gallon milk jug with the bottom cut out. Use the jug as a hot bed. Keep the lid on if it's cold, and pop it off when it's warm. I do this to start tomatoes, cauliflower, and cabbage in my garden."

Saving Seeds for Future Plantings

Stories have been told of ancient Egyptian seeds, long entombed but still bearing life. Although the pyramid wheat tale may be just legendary, there is documented proof of a lotus seed from Manchuria that germinated after about 700 years.

So what about our seeds forgotten on a garage shelf: How long do they retain their vital power?

"Even without special care, tomato and bean seeds left unused in a shed or drawer generally will live four to five years," says Seed Savers Exchange founder and director Kent Whealy. "But they'll stay vigorous ten times that long—forty years or more—by drying them and freezing them in heat-sealed plastic bags," he says. Kent's suggestions for drying and storing make it easy to preserve your favorite seeds.

First, never dry seeds in an oven; temperatures above ninety-five degrees Fahrenheit will damage them. Just put them on a paper plate in a warm place, such as a shelf over a furnace register, and let them air-dry. "This will probably take a few days. You can tell when seeds are dry enough; they break instead of bending," Kent notes.

"Some people think that powdered milk is a good drying agent for seeds, but it isn't," says the Iowa seed saver. "We use silica gel. It's a drying agent with a color-indicating chemical that changes from blue to pink as it picks up more moisture." Here's how to use it:

Take paper envelopes of seed and weigh out an equal amount of silica gel. Seal together in an airtight container such as a large jar with a lid. The moisture goes down to optimum levels for storage in a week. Remove the seed envelopes from the jar and seal the envelopes in heat-sealable foil packages. Now you can freeze them with no damage.

Do not store your seeds in silica gel, Kent cautions. "Those little plastic BBs suck moisture out of the seeds and can prevent them from sprouting."

Once the seeds are dried, you can also freeze them for as long as you want in airtight jars. "Use something like a peanut butter jar that screws tight, with a good amount of rubber under the lid," Kent advises. "It's okay to store several varieties of seed in one jar—just separate them in paper envelopes."

Southern Exposure Seed Exchange sells silica gel and heat–sealable foil packages and offers a wonderful, detailed free catalog of heirloom seeds. You can reach the company at P.O. Box 170, Earlysville, VA 22936; telephone (804) 973–4703.

✳

If the plants in your garden are hybrid varieties, don't bother to save the seeds, as they won't breed true, advises Seed Savers Exchange director Kent Whealy of Decorah, Iowa.

"The non–hybrid varieties, on the other hand, will breed true year after year," he says.

AUTHOR'S NOTE: *Interestingly, though, even non–hybrid self-pollinating plants such as peppers and tomatoes sometimes prove to be untrustworthy parents. In many cases they, too, yield hybrid seeds, due to cross-pollination by bees.*

Many folks like to save seeds from favorite squash and pumpkins to replant the next year. But don't be too surprised if the next generation come out lacking the shape, taste, or other desirable qualities of the parent, cautions Bangor, Wisconsin, farmer Bill Hansen. During the previous summer a bit of forbidden romance may have gone unnoticed on your part. These vegetables often cross–pollinate with other squashes and pumpkins in your garden, resulting in some pretty odd specimens such as a pumpkin –spaghetti squash cross.

AUTHOR'S NOTE: *Bill's tip could have saved me disappointment. A few years ago I set out to grow a jack-o'-lantern for every child in our neighborhood with seeds I'd saved from pumpkins we had grown in our garden the previous year. The vines yielded abundantly, and I watched the swelling pumpkins with delight, anticipating the happiness they'd bring. Alas, they never turned orange; Halloween came and went, but every pumpkin remained green. (Come to think of it, what would be more appropriate for Halloween than a pumpkin disguised as a squash?)*

CHAPTER EIGHT

Smart Planting and Cultivating

*If you always plant the same way, it's like wearing
the same clothes every year.*

—BILL HANSEN

Our silver maple sapling was so small when we first planted it by the edge of our garden that we never gave a thought to its future growth. Unfortunately, by the time a few years had passed and we'd built the garden bed up to ideal tilth and fertility, the tree had huge branches blocking most of the sunshine and spreading roots that dominated the soil.

By then the maple was so magnificent we didn't have the heart to destroy it. So we're back to cultivating less level, less convenient land.

Dona Popovic's tip in this chapter on choosing a garden site is intended for beginners, she says. But something terribly obvious can be the downfall of even experienced gardeners. We'd never have planted that silver maple where we did if we'd had Dona's tip as a reminder.

In this chapter gardeners across the land share their best vegetable-growing tips. They talk about garden sites, basic planting strategies, and succession planting.

The chapter includes a section on companion planting, an intriguing gardening system that, despite its devoted following, remains controversial. Just like kids, plants may have a good or bad influence on their companions. They won't tempt them to skip school, but they can expose them to other harm: hormones, insects, and diseases. Contrariwise, some plant companions help to control insects and disease and foster better growth. Unfortunately, the numerous rules of "which–like–which" and "what's–taboo–with–that" are as convoluted as those in high society. It's almost impossible to keep in mind the almost infinite combinations of dos and don'ts, which is possibly why very few of the 1,000–plus tips that gardeners shared in this book touch on plant compatibility. If any of you are computer wizards, you could make a fortune writing companion planting software to help the rest of us remember.

Hindsight is 20/20 Vision

Failures are but stepping–stones. Remember that all growers lose plants to disease, injury, pests, or improper growing conditions. By working at this hobby and weathering the difficult times, you will succeed.

—WAYNE A. KING, PRESIDENT, ORCHID GROWERS' GUILD

Site Seeing: The Garden Environment

Until his retirement as director of the National Fisheries Research Laboratory, fish pathologist Fred Meyer traveled around the globe on behalf of a global food crop: fish. In his La Crescent, Minnesota, garden, his scope is on a far more modest scale. Fred specializes in growing as much as possible in a small area and ignores the recommended spacing when he plants.

Instead, Fred lays out his garden so the plants will just touch each other.

Not only does he get more plants in a relatively small plot, but he believes that the shading of the nearby plants restricts the growth of weeds.

✳

"My grandfather, Chris Schmitz of Bonnots Mill, Missouri, was a lifelong farmer. He was fond of saying 'You can crowd the rows, but don't crowd in the row,'" says U.S. Department of the Interior wildlife biologist Carl Korschgen.

✳

"When choosing your garden site, remember that most plants require six or more hours of sunshine daily. Avoid sites near trees and bushes, as they will give shade, and their feeder roots rob nearby plants of needed moisture and nutrients," cautions longtime Illinois gardener Dona Popovic.

✳

If your local weed ordinance doesn't forbid it, leave weeds growing along the fence row to attract birds, suggests Illinois landscape architect Anthony Tyznik.

✳

Anyone with arthritis or knee problems can do away with weeding and save a lot of kneeling by planting everything in containers, suggests Ruth Coombs, a native of Kansas City, Missouri, who grows all her vegetables in bright yellow ceramic pots. "The herbs, broccoli, onions, lettuce, and red peppers look so pretty," she says. The pots have another advantage: You can move them to follow the sun or shade as desired.

Planting Strategies

"Don't forget the value of rotating your crops. Farmers have used rotation for centuries, but gardeners sometimes overlook it. It is an important tool for keeping disease and insects out of your garden," advises agricultural writer LeeAnne Bulman of Independence, Wisconsin. LeeAnne is a dairy farmer, freelance writer, and mother who home–schools her children in a converted hayloft, studying her own college correspondence classes along–side her kids. She juggles all this by placing a high priority on efficiency. "I consider myself the world's worst gardener," she modestly claims, "but I am quick to pick up on new and timesaving ideas." Here are more of LeeAnne's planting tips:

- Plant cabbage, cauliflower, and broccoli in the late summer after the worst of the heat and the cabbage moths are done for the year.

- If you're worried that it's still too hot, try putting the seeds in the refrigerator for twenty-four hours. This fools the seeds into believing it's cooler out than it is.

- Double-cropping helps if you have a small garden space or want to tend less footage. For example, plant peas or radishes in the spring and follow with cabbage for a fall crop.

- The use of a wetting agent helps the seeds get a good start. Some common brand names are Basic-H, L.O.C., and Wet-Sol. Use two tablespoons per gallon of water and pour it into the furrow of the rows before the rows are covered. You can also use it in the holes you dig for transplanting, suggests LeeAnne.

✳

AUTHOR'S NOTE: *Chemist Milton Palmer, product development manager of the Shaklee Corporation (manufacturer of Basic-H), explains the value of adding a wetting agent: "When a small quantity of wetting agent is added to the water, it reduces the surface tension so the water won't bead up. The water then penetrates the soil instead of puddling and running off and so also brings any fertilizer that you may have applied down to the roots."*

Here's a good time- and labor-saving tip from biologist Carl Korschgen, who gardened in Bangor, Maine, for many years and now gardens in Onalaska, Wisconsin. "After I till the garden with my Troy-Bilt Roto Tiller, I raise the tines and run the tiller again, making an impression in the earth with the tires. I run a stretched string for a good, even first row. From then on, the wheel impression helps you gauge a straight line.

"This gives a freshly compacted row to put the seeds in. I can lay out the entire garden with just a few passes—one per row. You get straight rows for planting, and you needn't hoe to make seed furrows."

✻

Which direction is best for orienting your garden rows? "Ideally they should run east to west, the way the sun travels," believes 4-H assistant Bill Hansen. That gives the plants the benefit of the sunshine, as they're not shading their neighbors. "In north-to-south-oriented rows, tall crops will cast shadows onto the neighboring rows."

On his home farm in Bangor, Wisconsin, Bill generally runs his rows east to west for a couple of years, followed by a year of north to south. "I don't think production is any different, but the garden is more inviting. It makes you feel different—if you always plant the same way, it's like wearing the same clothes every year."

Corn planted on the west end of the garden shades smaller crops; tomatoes that are shaded by corn will take longer to ripen, he cautions. Cabbages and corn, on the other hand, do well next to one another; cabbages tolerate shade and thrive when it's a little cooler.

"For more intensive cropping when space is short," advises farmer Bill Hansen, "plant early crops such as peas, onion, radish, lettuce, and spinach in rows next to spreading crops like tomatoes, melons, cucumbers, and potatoes. By the time the vines branch out and need the space, the early vegetables are already harvested."

✻

For plants that need warmth and moisture, such as tomatoes, advises Ken Johnston, a gardener in West Salem, Wisconsin, mound up the soil a little around each new plant. That gives it as much sun as possible for a good start. To avoid water runoff, though, make a small depression in the center of each mound, and then put the plant in.

"Plant beans in depressed rows to dish the water and avoid runoff," Dr. Johnston adds.

Easy-Seed, No-Weed Plotting

Here's an "easy-seed, no-weed" salad garden idea, which Chuck Comeau of Onalaska, Wisconsin, devised:

"Lettuce and carrots are very difficult to get evenly spaced. Also, carrots germinate very slowly. A solution: I marked out an area that was two arm's lengths square. Why? So I could reach the center for weeding and harvesting from the edge of the area. I mixed radish, lettuce, and carrot seeds together in equal measure. Then I stood above the area with my arm about four feet in the air and sprinkled the seeds. This gives (you hope) an even spread of seed. First radish, then lettuce, then carrots come in the same area. There is very little weeding, since radish and lettuce each shade out weeds; yet as the other crops are harvested, the germinated carrots have sun and room to grow."

Succession Planting

"I'm a firm believer in the virtues of succession planting," says Renee Shepherd of Shepherd's Garden Seeds in Felton, California. For example, it's better to plant half a row of beans for four or five weeks; you'll have a long harvest, instead of a glut of everything all at once.

✳

"Some vegetables, such as cabbage, have both early and late varieties, yet lots of gardeners simply buy them without ever considering that. Buy your plants from knowledgeable sources that can help you make informed decisions," says farmer Bill Hansen. "Be aware that at the big shopping center lots, there's more risk that the plants will lack this information and may even be labeled entirely wrong: watermelons mislabeled cucumber, broccoli with cauliflower labels. So buy from someone you trust."

Good Friends: Companion Planting

"Nine times out of ten, claims made for companion planting don't work," maintains Ruth Page, formerly editor-in-chief of *National Gardening* magazine and writer and host of Vermont Public Radio's "Earth's Gardens and the Environment."

"If you grow two things together one year (say carrots and tomatoes) and they both do just great, don't automatically assume that these are ideal companions helping each other.

"If you want to get better evidence, plant them next to each other in one part of the garden and separately in another part. Give them all identical treatment and then you'll have a little more evidence. This is not a scientific experiment, but it might be helpful to you."

AUTHOR'S NOTE: *If you want to give companion planting a try, here are some combinations that folks have planted successfully.*

* Peas and carrots go together not only on the dinner plate; while they're growing, the carrot roots benefit the peas.

* Plant onions and sage near carrots to repel carrot-infesting flies.

* Avoid planting onions (or shallots or garlic) by your peas or beans, as they'll inhibit growth.

* Although a light sprinkling of fresh dill leaves makes a marvelous marriage with cooked carrots, commingling in the garden isn't a good idea. Mature dill is believed to suppress carrot growth.

* To repel cucumber beetles, plant radish seeds in the cucumber hills.

* Sunflowers are companionable with cukes and other vines and supply a fine natural pole for climbing.

- Avoid planting sunflowers near potatoes, as they allegedly stunt the potatoes' growth.
- To repel beetles, plant nasturtiums by cantaloupe.

✳

If hot summers and strong, intense sunlight cause problems in your garden, you might consider planting tomatoes and peppers together: "The skin of peppers sometimes gets little patchy paper-like blemishes because they get burned," says Mary Gehling of Walla Walla, Washington, "so we planted our peppers and tomatoes alternately in a row. By the time the peppers are producing pods, the tomatoes are providing shelter. The peppers will be shaded from the intense sunlight, but they still receive enough sun to be nurtured."

✳

When retired schoolteacher Iona Wabaunsee of North Bend, Washington, taught on the Pine Ridge Indian Reservation in South Dakota, she learned from her Sioux neighbors that it's helpful to plant pumpkins among the corn. "They feel pumpkins do better with a little shade from the corn. The sun on those prairies is pretty hot," says Iona.

✳

Hundreds of years ago, says Mary Jane Randolph, an avocational archaeologist with the Mississippi Valley Archeology Center, Native Americans practiced this efficient method of companion planting:

Plant corn with beans and squash. The squash vines cover the ground and keep the weeds down. By the time the beans are ready to climb, the corn stalks are tall and strong enough to support them. The beans also put nitrogen (which corn depletes) back into the soil.

Bad Companions: Uneasy Relationships

"Avoid planting gardens under or near black walnut trees," advises Larry Severeid, past president of the National Walnut Council. "Keep them at least two crown distances away. Our native American black walnut trees have a growth-suppressing toxic chemical called jugalone in their roots and leaves, which can enter the soil and affect other plants. It also spreads through contact with leaves. Tomatoes, especially, will just shrivel up."

Spring Fever

"Don't fall prey to spring fever," cautions Mary Gehling of Walla Walla, Washington. "We had a really warm spring early this year. We knew better, but we put in our garden and probably are going to lose half of it due to subsequent cold weather. Be disciplined enough to hold off planting the tender vegetables, even if you have to tie yourself in the closet!"

It's not only tender plants that are at risk in spring if the weather turns cold again, Mary warns. "If you plant seed too soon, the ground is too cold for germination and the seed will rot in the ground."

Weeding and Cultivating

Looking back on nearly a century of gardening experience, Dan Young of La Crescent, Minnesota, says, "A hoe is good for cultivating as well as weeding, because you can get closer to the plants with it."

"Cultivate after every rain," advises Dan. "When it gets dry enough to monkey around with a hoe, scratch around the plants a little bit and then go through the rows with a cultivator. This brings moisture up, and helps keep it where the plants can benefit from it."

AUTHOR'S NOTE: *Lightly cultivating the top of the soil creates a protective dust mulch that keeps groundwater from evaporating as quickly. Don't overdo it, however, because garden soil, like pancake batter, is better off when left a little lumpy. If cultivated too often or too zealously, soil becomes less absorbent and more vulnerable to erosion. It also decomposes the organic matter so rapidly that it's less attractive to soil-building earthworms.*

❋

Ideally, you should work your garden soil only when it's dry enough to crumble readily in your hand. Unfortunately, Mother Nature doesn't always cooperate, and you may have to do your planting when the soil is wet.

In those instances, advises farmer Bill Hansen of Bangor, Wisconsin, try to walk around as little as possible, and rake over your footprints as you leave the garden. Otherwise, the footprints leave spots where water collects and you will have lumps in the soil that make further cultivating more difficult.

❋

If you have a garden tiller, you can cut down on hand-weeding dramatically, using the system devised by physician Tony Holt for his huge garden in Grants Pass, Oregon.

"I built a row marker with 40-inch row spacing that I drag behind my six-horsepower Troy-Bilt tiller. After working the soil in the spring, I mark the rows in two directions, north-south and east-west, to form a grid; then I plant everything in hills, including the corn," Tony reports. "This spacing allows tilling and cross-tilling, and leaves only a small area of about 1 square foot at each hill to be hand-weeded."

States of Mind

When you feel downcast, get out there with your hoe, and you'll feel better.

—JOE BORNTREGER, CASHTON, WISCONSIN, AMISH GARDENER

CHAPTER NINE

Tucking in Your Garden Bed: Mulching for Protection

You can't keep taking out of the ground; you have to put something back.

—NICK WEKSETH

hen it comes to gardening, our choice of even the most basic methods has as much to do with our temperament, philosophy, and
sense of aesthetics as it does with convenience, availability, and
affordability.

Practically speaking, mulch, or covering the soil surface with a protective layer, offers many advantages. It shields plants from temperature
extremes, keeps the soil moist, maintains better tilth, and helps prevent erosion. A summertime mulch keeps the plant roots cooler and smothers
weeds. Winter mulching shelters plants from drying winds, insulates plant

roots from the cold, and helps prevent frost heaving when soil alternately thaws and freezes. Ideally, mulch also makes the garden more attractive.

A wide variety of ground covers make good mulches. Common natural mulches are bark, wood chips, sawdust, cocoa hulls, pine needles, hay, straw, leaves, weeds, compost, and even a dust layer of scratched-up surface soil. Manufactured materials such as plastic and polyester have also become increasingly popular.

Which mulches are best? Although guidelines exist for mulches especially suited for individual growing conditions, all rules in this matter are flexible and personal preferences reign. For example, if gadgetry fascinates you, and new, labor-saving techniques add variety and interest to your gardening, you may enjoy trying some of the newly developed plastic and fabric mulches on the market.

On the other hand, if you like your methods to be as earthy as possible, the synthetics may repel you. If such is the case, tap nature's cycles by mulching with grass clippings or straw. As you'll see in some of the tips that follow, you can help both your garden and the environment by recycling trash into garden treasure, mulching with items that might otherwise wind up in a landfill.

Weighing the advantages and disadvantages of various materials involves practical considerations as well. For example, if your summers tend to be cool, black plastic will give many crops a boost by holding in heat. (In really hot weather, though, plastic can be uncomfortable for walking and kneeling on.) Synthetics offer other benefits too. While mulches made of old straw, hay, or weeds may introduce unwanted seeds, synthetic ones avoid these problems (imagine baby plastics sprouting up all over!). If you're prone to allergies, the synthetics aren't likely to make you sneeze or make your eyes water.

Synthetics, however, do nothing to replenish the soil. By contrast, most natural mulches eventually decompose into humus over time. Also, hay, bark, and sawdust offer greater flexibility: You can pile up a little more mulch when a flopping plant needs extra support or push some aside to install another plant readily. On the other hand, organic mulches temporarily deplete nitrogen from the soil, a drawback biologist Carl Korschgen will tell you how to prevent.

In this chapter you'll find tips on summer mulching, natural mulches of various sorts, mulching with leftovers ranging from carpet scraps to last week's newspaper, mulching with synthetics, and winter mulching. The innovative variety of mulching options is dazzling.

Summer Mulches: Hold in Moisture, Block out Weeds

In general, use at least 3 inches of compost above the soil as a top dressing. Mulch this with hay or pine straw for additional moisture retention. "As it rains, the nutrients flow to the plant's roots, feeding and watering, but not compacting or crusting the soil," advises Bill Bricker of Augusta, Georgia, president of Bricker's Organic Farms, Inc., a manufacturer and mail-order distributor of organic garden aids.

❋

Save your weeds. Even if they're dead, they make good mulch. "You can't keep taking out of the ground; you have to put something back," holds octogenarian garden expert Nick Wekseth of Onalaska, Wisconsin.

AUTHOR'S NOTE: *Like Nick, I too recycle weeds this way. Pluck them when they're immature, not after they go to seed.*

Winter Mulching

"One spring," says Helen Mayville of La Crosse, Wisconsin, "I raked up the leaves I had put on my perennials for winter mulch and raked up a nest of bunnies. I was just sick. I tried to shove them back under the leaves in the hope that their mother would come back to them. Just don't put a heavy covering of mulch down until the ground is really frozen and the little animals have already found places for the winter."

*

Waiting until the ground freezes will also help you avoid the risk of mildew, advises former New Jersey landscaper Ernie Hartmann. When the cold weather sets in, fungus won't flourish—it too goes dormant. "However, if we get an Indian summer and the plant hasn't yet gone dormant, it's still vulnerable," Ernie notes. Premature winter mulching will add to the mildew-prone conditions.

*

Are you one of those lackadaisical gardeners who put off cleaning their garden beds at the end of the season? Are you abashed by gardens with every dead twig banished and soil so tidy it's practically combed? Well, feel abashed no more.

"Your plants will be better off if you don't clean up the dead foliage until the spring. The best you can do is leave the old foliage over the winter," says nurseryman Randy Baier. "Normally, it flops by itself; if it stays erect, just smash it down with your hand and let it lay over the crown of the plant (where the top of the root and base of the stem meet, and where new growth will sprout).

"The old foliage mulch shades the plant from the sun, keeping it from alternately freezing and thawing. The alternating cold and warmth of temperature fluctuations are hard on plants. The old foliage also catches snow and holds it. A blanket of snow makes a wonderful insulator," he adds.

AUTHOR'S NOTE: *Snow was once regarded as a "poor man's fertilizer" for its insulating qualities and for the modest amount of atmospheric nitrogen it washes down into the soil.*

*

There's something forlorn about the sight of old Christmas trees sitting on the curb waiting for the garbage truck. You can make the holiday spirit last longer by stacking the limbs from the Christmas tree over your perennials, as Kansas City native Ruth Coombs does. The branches allow air to circulate but offer some protection from the drying winter winds.

✳

As mentioned earlier, unprotected plants are subject to alternating thawing and freezing, a situation that heaves the plants and possibly damages their root systems. Mulching in wintertime protects perennials from this stress, counsels Raymond Rice of Kutztown, Pennsylvania. He adds a new twist to the mulching alternatives.

"It's better to use straw covering than leaves. Leaves have a tendency to compact and smother plants, whereas straw remains loose," he says.

Not all perennials need winter mulch, however, says Raymond. "Heavy-rooted plants like peonies do better without mulch. Deeply planted bulbs need no covering. Iris prefer no covering, except perhaps a light soil covering, even though they may heave somewhat."

✳

"Don't forget to check your mulch periodically during winter," reminds Charlet Givens of Southfield, Michigan. Melting snow sometimes erodes it. When plants start coming up in late winter, if they're not covered, they'll freeze, she warns.

Sawdust Mulch

"I mulch my garden heavily with sawdust because, unlike straw or hay, it's free of weed seeds," says U.S. Department of the Interior biologist Carl Korschgen. First the sawdust smothers weeds and holds in moisture. Later, as it decomposes, it improves the soil's tilth.

"The problem with sawdust, though, is that as it decomposes, it depletes nitrogen from the soil, so you have to replenish it a couple of times a season. For this, I apply ammonium nitrate, which is a high-nitrogen fertilizer, or a 12-12-12 fertilizer (equal parts nitrogen, phosphorus, and potassium)."

AUTHOR'S NOTE: *Mix the fertilizer with the sawdust, or water it in. The same principle pertains to other organic mulches as well.*

Grass Clippings

It's okay to mix grass clippings into the soil to give it better tilth, but don't use it as a surface mulch; it tends to clump into a dense, soggy mass when it gets wet, advises nurseryman Randy Baier of La Crosse, Wisconsin.

Other Views on Grass

"I take grass clippings and pile them around tomato and garden rows to hold in moisture and hold down weeds," says Ed Wojahn, who gardened in Galesburg, Illinois, for sixteen years.

✳

AUTHOR'S NOTE: *Never mulch food crops with grass clippings if they've been treated with weed killers. Toxic chemicals such as the form of arsenic used in some preemergence crabgrass applications don't decompose immediately and may translocate to the vegetables you eat. Translocation occurs when substances taken up by plant roots move up through the plant. Toxic chemicals such as arsenic could migrate into the edible portion. For more on grass mulch see page 211.*

Hay

Ruth Ann Davis does double duty as a gardener. She maintains a garden six months of the year in her Tucson, Arizona, home and another up north, where she lives the other six months.

"You don't need access to a farm or stable for hay," she says. "I find out when my county crew will be mowing the side of the road and follow with a rake and pitchfork. Although the freshly mown green material does introduce weed seeds, it makes a good mulch anyhow, because it adds a little extra moisture. If water is scarce, as it is in my case, that's a valuable consideration."

The Answer Is Blowing in the Wind: Leaf Mulches

When those piles of autumn leaves are all raked up, is it wise to use them as mulch in their uncomposted state? Even garden authorities are not always of the same mind.

Illinois landscape architect Anthony Tyznik is a proponent of mulching with uncomposted leaves during the summer.

"In the fall," says Tony, "my son brings a truckload of leaves for our home garden, which I store in bags over the winter. After the garden crops come up the next spring, you can put these whole, undecomposed leaves on top for weed control. I like to use maple leaves because they decompose quickly. Soon the foliage covers them up. In the fall, you can till the leaves into the soil."

"Some moisture–loving perennials and many rock garden plants also profit from leaf mulch. But avoid it for plants that need a dry environment, like alyssum," advises Tyznik.

※

"If you mulch in winter with leaves," says horticulturist Ernie Hartmann, "timing is important. Uncomposted leaves rot due to poor circulation and drainage. So remove them early in spring before the soggy mass gets warm and develops fungus. And don't shred them first. Shredded leaves compact too much and keep out air."

AUTHOR'S NOTE: *Allow leaves to decompose before mulching with them, and you will avoid potential fungus problems caused by poor air circulation.*

✻

We don't know much about the gardening practices of the ancient Druids, but legend has it that the oak tree was sacred, probably because oaks possess the seemingly magical quality of attracting lightning. Oaks are special in another way too. "Their leaves are the one exception to the disadvantages of mulching with uncomposted leaves: Because of their structure, they won't pack tightly, and so they don't need to be composted first to be a fine winter protection," says nurseryman Randy Baier.

✻

Mary Carter of Gold Beach, Oregon, finds that partially decomposed leaves make a fine garden mulch. "I pick up bags of raked leaves that people are throwing away. This gives a greater variety of leaves than ordinarily grow in one's own yard, with a wider acid–alkaline range. This balances the pH better," says Mary.

Here's how she does it:

- Run the leaves through a lawn mower to chop them finely for quick breakdown.

- Put them in garbage bags and then before closing them, wet the leaves down with a hose to help them decompose over the winter. Lay the bags on the cleaned-up garden bed or pile them up somewhere in the sunshine for the winter.

- In the spring, the leaves will be partially broken down. Pile them around the perennials about 4 inches deep, but don't cover the plants or it will smother them. If some leaves are drier and less decomposed, pile up wetter leaves on top.

- The leaf mulch keeps a late spring frost from hurting emerging perennials. Push the leaves back from the stems a little, so they're not smothering the plants. Later, as the plants grow bigger, you can add a few more inches of leaves while the supply lasts. This keeps the soil moist, so the few weeds that come up are easy to pull.

Other Natural Mulches

To stretch your landscape dollar, buy bark mulch in bulk, advises landscape contractor Steve Taylor of Corbin, Kentucky. You'll pay $4.00 to $5.00 a bag at a nursery, versus a whole truckload from a sawmill for $10.00 to $20.00.

AUTHOR'S NOTE: *Shredded bark is best when aged a year or more so the fibers break down. To be safe, keep mulch piles at least 25 to 30 feet from your house and avoid deep mulch near the foundation. Under some conditions it has the potential to bring termites, and they may even crawl into the frame of brick homes.*

＊

AUTHOR'S NOTE: *Keep in mind that some mulches are fantastic for one crop but not really advisable for another. For instance, pine needles make a good mulch for strawberries. But never use them when planting seeds, because they inhibit seed germination.*

＊

"Avoid gravel mulches around flowers. Gravel absorbs too much heat, and translocates the heat to the soil. The plant roots will get too hot and be harmed," horticulturist Randy Baier cautions. "Unlike more deeply rooted trees and shrubs, most roots of both perennials and annuals are in the top 4 inches of soil."

"Think twice if you're tempted to mulch evergreens with white quartz. The intensity of the light reflected by the rock," says Randy Baier, "is actually so strong that it damages foliage."

There is an exception, though. "If you have evergreens on a shady northern exposure, bark mulch makes it look even darker and may mold from dampness. In such instances, gravel will give a brighter look, and because it stays drier, is less likely to mold."

What Makes a Good Garden?

People are afraid they'll make mistakes. Who's to say what's good taste and bad taste? We're overly concerned with what's proper in plant selection—gardening is supposed to be recreation.

—ERIC LAUTZENHEISER, DIRECTOR, SAN ANTONIO BOTANICAL GARDENS

Garage Sale Mulches

AUTHOR'S NOTE: *The ability of quack grass (Agropyron repens) to overpower the garden is nothing short of cursed. Even a small fragment of the root will take hold and grow a new plant. Its pale, sharply pointed roots are so invasive that they'll burrow right through many substances. I've seen its roots poking through heavy-gauge plastic sheeting and even right through potatoes while they're growing! If you have a problem with this determined weed, you'll appreciate the following tip from Hilda First.*

"I have quack grass real bad," says Hilda, a native Virginian, "and it overtakes the perennials early when they're short. So when I want to start a new bed and kill all the grass around it, I put down old carpeting. I put it upside down because the hemp backing doesn't look as ugly." To allow the plants room to come up, Hilda cuts holes in the carpet in the places where each plant is set.

To avoid having to mow close to your shrubs, Hilda adds, cut out circles of old carpeting, slit them, and place them around shrubs. "Be careful that your lawn mower doesn't catch on the edges, or the carpet ravels," she warns. "Depending upon what's in your garage, you can also cut circles from roofing paper or leftover asphalt shingles to put around small shrubs. They won't catch as easily in the mower."

＊

"When I lived in Seattle, I had a friend who hated to weed," says Kathy Deering of Sioux Falls, South Dakota. "So she bought some green indoor-outdoor carpeting for two bucks at a rummage sale. She put the carpet down in her vegetable garden. She just cut slits and planted her plants through them. When she watered, the water went through. When I saw it, she'd already had it for several years, but it still looked terrific," Kathy says.

＊

Mariel Carlisle of La Crosse, Wisconsin, has carpeted aisles in her garden with strips of brown commercial-grade carpeting recycled from an apartment-complex remodeling project. "I've rolled it up and rearranged it for four seasons now. I've used jute-backed carpet, but foam-back works, too," says Mariel. "It elicits teasing, but it's wonderful for walking on with bare feet—no muddy feet! And it looks natural."

Newspaper Mulches

"One year I tried mulching my potato field with newspaper instead of hay," recalls rancher R. J. Bootzin of Jemez, New Mexico. "It was bad news. When the top papers dried, the wind blew it all over the pasture. And then in the fall, the blobby wet papers didn't mulch into the ground as well as the hay did."

＊

Farmer LeeAnne Bulman of Independence, Wisconsin, uses grass clippings to hold down the layers of newspaper so the wind doesn't blow them away.

＊

"I always hated to weed, and I no longer have to," says Patty Emery, a cobbler in La Crosse, Wisconsin. "I scrape back about an inch of the top-soil between plants and spread newspapers in layers of about three sheets. Then I sprinkle the topsoil back over the paper. The newspaper disintegrates, and you lose no topsoil."

✻

"Where I live in southeastern Minnesota, the soil is sandy and porous, so it's a real challenge to hold in moisture," says Dick Gagne. "As well as amending it with compost and peat moss, I mulch both the vegetable and flower beds with newspaper. This prevents surface evaporation and also distributes the water more evenly along the surface; it also keeps weeds down." Dick offers this technique for newspaper mulching:

"First, remove the slick advertising inserts, which are less absorbent. Then soak the newspaper sections in the bathtub. It's better to go too many than too little. Use no less than two dozen pages, and preferably more, for the mulch layer, leaving enough space around each plant so that it won't smother, and so you'll be able to water. The paper won't blow around if you keep it moist, but a little soil on top will anchor it and is more sightly."

✻

Is it safe to mulch with colored newspapers? Many gardeners are apprehensive, fearing colored ink is toxic. Don't worry, assures nationally known garden writers and radio hosts Doc and Katy Abraham. In accordance with federal regulation, the inks used today are not toxic and are safe for use in the garden, they say.

Plastic and Other Synthetic Mulches

Says Ruth Coombs, a native of Kansas City, Missouri, "You can mulch perennial beds with breathable black plastic to keep weeds out. For an attractive, more natural look, cover this with bark chips."

AUTHOR'S NOTE: *Breathable plastics have millions of microscopic holes that allow air and water to reach the soil. Several brands are currently on the market, including trade names such as Miracle Mulch.*

✳

To protect your perennial beds in winter, cover them with Reemay, a spun polyester material that is reusable if you treat it with care, advises Ruth Coombs. To hold the layer in place, stake it into the ground with V-shaped pieces of wire cut from clothes hangers.

Because Reemay allows sunshine and water to penetrate and holds in warmth, you can leave it in place as long as you wish. "It really gives a head start to strawberries—they come in twice as fast," says the Kansas City native.

✳

AUTHOR'S NOTE: *Keep in mind that many varieties of plants need their blossoms pollinated by bees in order to produce fruits and vegetables: strawberries, melons, and cucumbers, for example. So if you're using Reemay on these crops, remove it as soon as they start blossoming so the bees can reach the blossoms.*

✳

"Years ago," says artist Dale Kendrick, "I saw onion fields near Las Cruces, New Mexico, protected by black plastic and decided to try it in my garden. I just love it. Plastic mulch has lots of advantages. It makes the garden easier to take care of—as you only need to till every four years or so, and all you have to weed is the hole by each plant. It also prevents weeds from robbing nutrients, channels fertilizer and water where they're needed, and keeps produce cleaner because dirt doesn't splash up when it rains."

Start with rolls of black plastic. Lay it over the garden plot, holding it down every 6 feet with a small 2-by-4 piece of wood. For each planting hole spray paint a circle on the plastic using a round object with about a 6-inch diameter; a two-pound coffee can is perfect for the task. Just move it along, spacing each circle as desired for each crop. Then with a razor blade or scissors, cut out the planting holes.

To make hills for vine crops such as cucumbers, space each hole in the middle of a 4-foot-square section. Use an object with a 12-inch diameter to trace the planting holes; an ice-cream bucket makes a good template.

AUTHOR'S NOTE: *It is possible, of course, to cut out the planting holes directly and omit painting circles. But spray painting allows you to lay the whole garden out in advance and see where to add or change before you cut. Also, Dale argues, "gardening design" is an art form and gives aesthetic pleasure.*

"The paint remains visible, giving each plant a halo of color," says artist Kendrick. "So instead of merely using leftover paint, consider purchasing gold, silver, or metallic car paints—they really look spectacular!"

"Plastic mulch will last about four years," says Dale, "depending upon your climate. In the fall, clean up all the vegetation from each hole. The next spring, slide the plastic lengthwise about one foot so the formerly covered ground becomes the new year's hole; the following year, slide the plastic over a foot crosswise. Each year rotate crops, planting a different vegetable in the old hole," advises the Wichita, Kansas, native.

Listening to Mother Nature

To destroy a 15,000-year-old alpine meadow to get peat moss for our garden doesn't make sense.

—KEN BALL, AUTHOR AND COLORADO LANDSCAPE ARCHITECT

CHAPTER TEN

River of Life: Watering

More plants die from kindness than from neglect.
—EVE SIMON

There's an urgency about watering that you don't find with most of the other tasks of gardening. If you get your plants in a little bit late, for instance, the worst that's likely to happen is you'll harvest a little bit later. If you put off weeding, the weeds, of course, will grow bigger. But unless you wait so long that the weeds get out of control (which takes a very long time) or go to seed, it isn't going to be a major problem. The same applies to chores such as cultivating, fertilizing, and turning the compost pile. Today might be ideal, but tomorrow or the day after tomorrow or even the day after that is unlikely to be critical.

Watering is another story. Put off watering shallow-rooted seedlings, hanging baskets, or container plants for even a few hours after the soil dries out and the plants become dehydrated—you can prepare to kiss them goodbye forever. Water supplies a plant with essential hydrogen and oxygen, dissolves minerals from the bedrock, transports nutrients to the roots, and firms the plant cells.

Like us, plants are made up primarily of water. It's hard to believe, considering how leathery the leaves are and how tough the wood is, but during the growing season a fruit tree is 80 percent water. Our instinct to pay close attention to the garden's need for water is closely related to our own dependence on water. Luckily, the rules are generally simple and the symptoms of neglect unmistakable.

The contributors to this chapter offer tips to help you water your garden easily, efficiently, and successfully. They share some observations on the relationship of water and climate, and they add hints on water and soil, water quality, and coexistence for plants with conflicting needs. You will gain from their experiences meeting the water needs of trees and shrubs and the irrigation needs of container plants and garden vegetables. The chapter concludes with some labor-saving shortcuts and innovative homemade irrigation gadgets.

These tips will also make gardening more fun and will help increase your confidence. One of the most pleasant aspects of watering is that it doesn't require great skill or experience. There's no art to watering as there is to pruning; nor is there much guesswork as there is in, say, knowing when to mulch the roses. When the ground starts looking dry, just turn on the faucet and go to it.

Water and Climate

Sometimes mild winters are harder on plants than severe winters are because of the drying effect of a cold wind without the protection of a good snow cover.

So, if the thermometer reads above freezing, it's a good idea to get out that hose and water your plants, says Ruth Coombs, a native of Kansas City, Missouri.

AUTHOR'S NOTE: *Those brief moments out in the garden are also great for chasing away the winter blues.*

✳

To give your perennials, roses, shrubs, and trees the help they need to cope with winter dehydration, provide a thorough, deep watering before they go dormant in the fall, advises University of Wisconsin–La Crosse horticulture professor emeritus Dr. Ernie Hartmann.

✳

"Water is the desert gardener's chief concern," holds Kathy Leslie of Thousand Oaks, California. "In the summertime, twice–a–day watering is often necessary. This is best done in early morning and early evening. When watering only once a day, morning is by far the better choice, since the foliage will have a chance to dry; evening watering sets up your garden for predatory snails and nasty funguses."

✳

During the California desert's hundred–plus degree days, Kathy Leslie advises, a midday spray of water can lower the temperature briefly and add some much–needed humidity to the air. This will lower the stress on gardens and lawns, says Kathy.

✳

"If the summer is very hot and dry, you may have problems with hanging baskets. Because they are open to the sun, and because the water runs right through the drainage holes, even the plastic pots tend to dry out quickly. Yet, last year, even when we had drought, my hanging baskets were so pretty that many people asked me how I do it," says gardener Jeanette Manske of Stoddard, Wisconsin.

"Before I plant my baskets, I take a plastic bread wrapper and open it up. I poke a couple of holes for drainage and line the pot with the plastic before putting the dirt in. This lining really helps the pots hold moisture longer. The plants dry out three times faster without a liner."

Coexistence for Plants with Conflicting Needs

Hand-watering isn't as enervating for you if you water at night or very early in the morning, advises Renee Shepherd of Shepherd's Garden Seeds in Felton, California. If even that is too much of a chore, put in a drip irrigation on a timer. The added feature of such a setup is that each plant gets its own emitter, and plants with different needs will get just the water they require.

If you plant drought-tolerant species next to ones that need a lot of moisture, a water-absorbent gel is really helpful, finds Jennifer Cohn of Syracuse, New York. It's also great in patio containers for reducing the need to water as frequently, and for working into lawns before planting. When you're transplanting moisture-needing plants, mix some gel directly into the soil of your planting hole. "A little goes a long way," observes Jennifer.

AUTHOR'S NOTE: *The gel that New York gardener Jennifer Cohn recommends consists of tiny polymer granules that absorb up to 500 times their weight in water and gradually release it. A relatively new product, it's marketed under several trade names, including Water Grabber and Terrasorb. These granules are non-toxic and eventually degrade into the soil.*

Water Quality

The success you achieve with your plants depends not only on the quality of your soil but upon the quality of your water, observes Lori Bauer, a grower for Bauers Market & Nursery in La Crescent, Minnesota. For instance, well water may be too acid or alkaline, and city water may have high levels of chlorine and other chemicals.

If you have a well, it may be a good idea to have the water tested. If you have city water, check with the municipal water works department, which may be able to give you an analysis.

✳

Before watering her houseplants, Mary Wrodarczyk of Linden, New Jersey, boils the water to volatilize the chlorine, which, in high concentrations, can be harmful to plants.

"When I washed my hair with regular tap water, it wouldn't shine. But when I boil the water, my hair looks really good. I figured if it was good for me, it would be good for the plants. A chemist friend said boiling for just a few minutes would be okay, but I boil it for ten minutes just to make sure."

AUTHOR'S NOTE: *Letting your water sit in a pail for a while will also eliminate the chlorine, but Mary Wrodarczyk's method is quicker. Keep in mind that if your water has other toxins, long boiling may serve only to increase their concentration as the water evaporates, so don't overdo it.*

✳

If your home water supply is heavily chlorinated, use rainwater for houseplant watering, suggests Elizabeth Pomada of San Francisco, California. If you have a dehumidifier, use the water it pulls from the air; it's good for plants because it's distilled.

"If you can avoid using water that has been through a water softener, your plants will be better off," Elizabeth adds. "The softening process takes out the calcium, magnesium, and iron from the water and substitutes sodium ions. If you do have to use softened water, fertilize to replenish the necessary elements. When you water, continue until the water flows out the drainage holes. That and occasional repotting will take care of any sodium buildup in the soil."

AUTHOR'S NOTE: *In the same way, if your outdoor plants are watered with naturally soft water, your soil is more likely to be deficient in calcium and magnesium. If your water is hard, it will carry beneficial minerals to the soil.*

Trees and Shrubs

"People fuss about grass; there's that mystique about having it green. Yet grass will bounce back after a drought—trees won't. It's a lot more expensive to replace a fifty-year-old tree in your yard than to get that grass green again," says arborist Jeff Davis of Davis Tree & Shrub Care in Onalaska, Wisconsin. Jeff shares these tips for healthier trees:

- "When trees need watering, people tend to water right at the trunk. But in time, the root zone may be 50 to 70 feet away from the trunk—make sure you water beyond the edge of the leaf canopy (drip line)."

- "The faster-growing trees like willows, cottonwoods, and soft maples can even have a root spread three times the distance of the drip line. So when watering such trees, keep in mind that if there are 10-foot branches, there can be 30-foot roots."

- "A lawn sprinkler isn't suitable for watering your trees. If you sprinkle the lawn for half an hour and then dig with a shovel, you'll see the soil is only wet 3 inches deep. Most tree roots are in the top 24 inches of soil. So let the hose run two hours, then move it to a new spot on that drip line area to puddle and force water deep into the soil."

Water and Soil

As most folks grow increasingly sensitive to the urgency of protecting our natural resources, it is harder to squander them with such impunity. If you wash dishes by hand, remember that the leftover dishwater needn't be wasted, says Mary Germann of Onalaska, Wisconsin. Once the dishes are done, consider using the water to water flowers.

✳

Keep in mind, though, that some detergents contain harmful chemicals that will alter soil chemistry. If you want to recycle washwater, be sure the cleaners you use are biodegradable, cautions arborist Jeff Davis. "Any time you alter the balance of your soil, you affect the plant life."

Water Needs
of Container Plants

"Having just replaced my pansies in the pots on the pool deck," says Phoenix resident Eve Simon, "I'll share the tip of the nurseryman who sold me the new batch: More plants die from kindness than from neglect. He suggested overwatering might be the cause."

✳

Do you have a plant that dries out so fast that every time you look, it's wilting? Put the pot within a larger pot and insert sphagnum moss between the two, suggests Pat Shedesky of La Crosse, Wisconsin, whose garden features have appeared in *Better Homes & Gardens, Flower & Garden,* and *Organic Gardening.* Keep the moss moist, and the potting medium will also stay moist longer.

Three years ago Pat Shedesky's big palm needed water only once a week; now it's dry within a day. The longer a plant is in a pot, Pat points out, the more rootbound it gets and the more quickly it dries out.

✳

Plant roots need air from the soil in order to live. If left too long in standing water, they suffocate and rot. So if you use plant saucers, be careful to empty them after each watering, advises Renee Shepherd of Shepherd's Garden Seeds in Felton, California. When gardening in containers in very hot locations, suggests the California seed authority, use the container–inside–a–container method, and pack the space between them with gravel, dry peat, or perlite to insulate the plant against the heat. Remember to establish drainage holes in both containers first.

✳

"Container gardening is a smart way to go for a desert gardener," advocates Kathy Leslie of Thousand Oaks, California. "You'll conserve water and you'll be able to have plants that you couldn't otherwise grow in the hard alkaline soil.

"Many people resist the container approach at first, wanting a 'real' (in other words, English cottage) garden. But after a few years and a few astronomical water bills, the containers start to make a lot of sense," Kathy says.

For conserving water far more efficiently, she adds, consider plastic terra–cotta–colored pots when choosing containers. "A plant in a traditional clay pot may need to be watered three times daily during the summer; plastic will give you a two– or three–day break between watering. Best of all, plastic won't show the white crust that accumulates on clay after a few months, owing to the salts that leach out of the hard water."

Watering Vegetable Gardens

Cucumbers need a lot of water in the summer, or they don't grow. When the sun is hot, however, cold water shocks the leaves. You'll also have trouble dragging the hose around the vines once they have spread.

The solution to both problems is to lay a soaker hose in each cucumber row before the vines grow and to leave it in place all season. Turn the hose so the holes face downward and the water flows directly into the ground. When you wish to water the cucumbers, merely connect the soaker hose to your main hose, advises Ed Wojahn, who gardened in Galesburg, Illinois, for many years.

✳

Spreading vines such as those on cucumber, squash, and melon plants have more surface area and so have more exposure to sunlight. As a result, vine crops consume more water than other plants, says retired agriculture instructor Jim Ness of Onalaska, Wisconsin. So unless you get ample rain, be sure to give them plenty of water.

✳

Josephine Drudick grew up on a farm in Alexandria, Louisiana. Even today, at the age of eighty-five, Josephine still mows two acres by herself in Onalaska, Wisconsin, with a riding mower and grows enough vegetables to sell the surplus.

"My pump water is so cold, I don't think it would be good for the plants, especially on such terrible, hot summer days," says Josephine. Instead, she waters the plants in her prolific vegetable garden with warmer water by catching rain in tubs, boilers, and barrels and using sprinkling cans.

Trickle Irrigation

Tatiana K. Bodine's tip for watering tomatoes is especially handy during drought conditions. The Sioux City, Iowa, gardener suggests that you make holes around the bottom of a three-pound coffee can. Bury it in the garden and plant three tomatoes around the outside of it. If there's not enough rain, fill the can with water. "It's more economical," says Tatiana, "because the water goes right to the roots without waste."

✳

For an efficient, gentle, water-saving way of irrigating tomatoes or other plants, says retired veterinarian Ken Johnston of West Salem, Wisconsin, drill a hole no more than ⅛ inch in diameter in the bottom of a gallon jug. Put the jug on the ground at the base of your tomato plant, refilling it about twice weekly. "The water slowly drips in at the root, instead of running away," he says. "Another advantage: it stays dryer between the rows, so you'll have less weeding to do."

✳

Here's a no-spill method from Elizabeth Pomada of San Francisco, California, for watering hanging baskets in awkward locations. "Simply place a few ice cubes on the surface of the soil, avoiding contact with the plant. The ice cubes gradually melt and trickle into the soil."

Recipe for a Greener Thumb

I sincerely believe there are green thumbs or blue thumbs when it comes to watering. You can't water a plant by schedule, like spraying for insects. I think maybe it's an inbred instinct.

—BENNY SIMPSON, DALLAS, TEXAS, RESEARCH SCIENTIST

CHAPTER ELEVEN

Tools, Gadgets, and Garden Aids
From Homemade to High Tech

Tap nature's own secrets and you hardly have to spend a nickel.
—ERNIE HARTMANN

Not far from where I used to garden, archaeologists have unearthed prehistoric hoes fashioned from the shoulder blades of bison. Except for the bones being rustless, they don't really differ much from the tempered-steel hoe we just bought at the farm supply store.

Ever since the first primitive gardener scratched a seed furrow with a pointed stick, people have been tinkering with ways to make gardening easier and more successful. Today, thanks to the advances of plant science and technology, we have some dazzlingly sophisticated garden devices. Even so, many folks still prefer traditional tools for their simplicity and the sense of historical continuity they impart. In this chapter contributors share their experiences with garden implements ranging from high-tech dazzlers to homemade gizmos. Especially with today's environmental emphasis on reducing waste and recycling, more and more folks are seeking ingenious applications for household items like jar lids, shower curtains, pop bottles, and newspaper.

One of the most welcome tips comes from Anne Hoskins, president of the Garden Club of Kentucky. For many of us the embarrassing price of being a gardener is having to go around with dirty fingernails from March to November. Preventive measures like Vaseline or soap under the nails never really work; gardening gloves feel cumbersome and soon get wet and muddy; and pumice, Goop—even drastic measures like bleach and scouring powder—are of little avail. Anne tells us how it's possible to be spreading compost one minute and dashing off to a meeting the next, with immaculate hands.

Now if anyone can come up with an entire body glove, they earn star billing in the next edition.

Hand Tools

Do you ever wonder what basic tools you really need for gardening? It's easy to be lured by seductive ads making fabulous claims for the wide array of gardening gadgets on the market. Indeed, some make gardening easier, but lots are just needless expense.

"Tap nature's own secrets, and you hardly have to spend a nickel. You don't need all these gimmicks," insists Ernie Hartmann of La Crosse, Wisconsin. Dr. Hartmann has been a landscape supervisor in Pennington, New Jersey; a city forester in Price, Utah; a park superintendent, a college grounds superintendent; a landscape contractor; and a university professor—and he doesn't even own a hoe. For a good "wardrobe" of basic garden equipment, he recommends the following:

- a pair of pruning shears
- a pair of big, long-handled loppers (clippers)
- a decent pruning saw (two are better—one with finer teeth)
- a spade
- a weed-cutting tool (or hoe or weed cultivator)

"Buy quality tools, especially pruning equipment. The cheap ones are made of bad steel," says Ernie. "Spend an extra $5.00 or $10.00, and they'll last a lifetime," Ernie advises.

*

One of the most essential gardening tools is a good sharpening stone, holds Richard Schnall, New York Botanical Garden's vice-president for horti-culture. To keep your tools in tip-top working order, Richard advises, "start off with sharp tools and keep an edge on them. At least once a week, clean off the dirt, sharpen, and apply a light coat of motor oil with a rag to pre-vent rusting."

*

Weed with a cultivator instead of a hoe to help prevent new weeds from sprouting, says Amish farmer Joe Borntreger. "A blade hoe just scrapes off the weeds, but a cultivator keeps the ground loose. A lot of weeds need to push up to sprout. If you keep the ground loose, they don't have anything to push against. I like to cultivate every week if it's not too wet," the Missouri native says. "Work the soil every week for a weed-free garden."

*

From a post–World War I garden almanac comes an old-fashioned tip still practical today: To clean garden tools and prevent rust, fill a box with sand and pour in old crankcase (motor) oil. Before putting your tools away after use, plunge them into the sand several times. The sand will scrub them clean, and the motor oil will coat them and prevent rust.

*

Today Dr. Michelle Metrick of Chicago, Illinois, earns her living as a healer, but she didn't start out that way.

"I grew up in Glencoe, Illinois," says the pediatric neurologist. "We had a rock garden, and the weeds would pop up between the rocks. They were so hard to pull, we absolutely hated weeding. When I was about fourteen, my father gave me and my little sister and brother blowtorches. If you blow-torch the weeds, they fry. We torched them down to zero—we loved it."

*

Freek Vrugtman's Flanborough, Ontario, garden is so steep that his wife calls it "a hill in a hole." Because of the incline he's forced to spade by hand instead of tilling. Afterward he's left with lumpy soil that resists the efforts of ordinary raking.

"The normal garden rake has fingers too close and it's too narrow. It's also too heavy," says the retired curator of collections for Hamilton's Royal Botanical Gardens.

So to smooth soil (and to rake scythed meadow vegetation for composting), he's devised a tool like the handmade nail rakes from his native Netherlands. Here's how:

- You'll need ten 4-inch common nails, a 1-by-1-by-24-inch hardwood crossbar, a long handle from an old tool such as a rake or broom, one nut and bolt with two washers (or a screw and epoxy), and about 40 inches of heavy-gauge fence wire for reinforcing.

- Drill a hole in the handle about 12 inches from one end. In the crossbar drill a hole in the center for the handle, and holes about 2 inches from either end for the reinforcing wire.

- In the crossbar drill holes for the nail tines 3 inches apart, at right angles to the handle and wire holes.

- Insert the nails, fit the handle end nearest the hole into the crossbar, and bolt (or screw and epoxy) to secure.

- Thread the wire through the handle and crossbar, and secure at both ends.

- Treat the wood with linseed oil.

Recipe for a Greener Thumb

A sharp hoe is the best tool you've got. But it won't work alone. Somebody's got to be on the end of that there handle or it won't do nothing!

—DAN YOUNG, NONAGENARIAN

Gadgets from Recyclables

"It used to be difficult to sow tiny seeds sparingly so they didn't overcrowd the flats. Then I discovered this simple technique.

"It's helpful for sowing outdoor seed beds as well," says retired nurseryman Vernon R. Carse of Central Point, Oregon. "Put a small quantity of seed inside the lid of a screw-top jar (such as a peanut butter jar). Hold the lid close to the soil, almost on edge. Rotate it until the tiny seeds find their way to the open ends of the lid's threads. Slowly move along the row, tapping lightly with a pencil.

The seeds will drop in a line where, and as thin as, you want them. A shaker-type spice jar with relatively large holes in the top also works great," adds Vernon.

✳

If you've ever experienced the frustration of accidentally hoeing up your tiny new plants, you'll appreciate this practical and economical tip from Hilda First of Edgewood, Maryland. Hilda started farming as a sixteen-year-old bride and learned to make do without the luxury of expensive garden gadgets.

"All year, save any kind of disposable plastic knives and forks you may have occasion to use. Write the names of your plants on them with a permanent marking pen, then stick them in the ground next to each plant. These weather well," says Hilda.

✳

Retired school principal Wendal Mitchell of Corbin, Kentucky, suggests how to make durable, no-cost plant markers. Cut strips from empty bleach bottles, label with permanent felt-tip pens, and staple to wooden stakes.

✳

To lay out curved flower beds, use several lengths of garden hose curved to form a design. Use flour or dots of spray paint for marking the pattern, advises Mona Stevens, master gardener for Hamilton County, Indiana.

✳

Trimming, weeding, and grooming create mounds of greenery that need to be removed from the garden area. Here's a great labor-saving idea: Spread an old plastic shower curtain and toss the debris on it. When the job is completed, cleaning up is easy—just drag the piece of plastic to the dump area or compost pile, advises Shirley Watterson of Morrow, Georgia.

✳

To keep rose cones from blowing away during windy winter storms, staple them into the ground at each corner with stakes made from wire clothes hangers, suggests Kansas City, Missouri, native Ruth Coombs. Here's how to get two elbow-shaped staples per hanger: Using a wire clipper, cut the hangers in half by clipping at the center bottom and top. Discard the hook. These staples easily pierce the styrofoam and push into the soil.

✳

To focus garden spray so that it won't blow onto nearby plants, cut the bottom off a plastic pop bottle, making a large funnel. Place the funnel bottom over the target plant, poke the sprayer nozzle through the bottle neck, and spray, advises Clarence Kelly of Bel Air, Maryland.

For a Successful Operation

Surgical gloves are more practical than regular cotton garden gloves because they're supple and don't get soggy and muddy, discovered registered nurse Anne Hoskins, president of the Garden Club of Kentucky. "Those from medical supply houses are the best because unless they tear on something sharp, they're reusable," says Anne. "When removing, peel inside out, sprinkle with bath powder, then turn rightside out again."

Stakes

May Vang, a member of the H'Mong people, is now an interpreter in western Wisconsin. May brought her native Laotian gardening methods with her to the United States when she was forced to flee the Communist invasion.

You can avoid the expense of buying garden stakes for such crops as peas, beans, and tomatoes if you have access to old tree branches, May says. "Cut to size the straightest branches you can find. At the end of the season, pile them up and save them for next year," May advises.

For cleaner produce and ease in picking, says May, let your peas crawl on string strung between stakes. But for economy don't spend a lot of money on garden twine. It's far cheaper to let the peas crawl on old yarn recycled from rummage sales or thrift shops.

✳

A cattle panel and two 5- or 6-foot T-posts from a farm supply store or ranch catalog work well for climbing plants that need staking, such as peas and pole beans, suggests farmer LeeAnne Bulman of Independence, Wisconsin. Pound the posts into the ground, then tie the panel to it with wire.

AUTHOR'S NOTE: *For city slickers who don't know what a cattle panel is, it's a piece of interwoven wire normally used for making animal holding pens, explains LeeAnne.*

Keeping Control

You don't have to buy expensive edging strips in order to confine rapidly spreading plants, holds Phil Normandy, curator of Brookside Gardens in Wheaton, Maryland.

For small perennials, cut out the bottom of joint compound buckets, industrial paint buckets, or frosting pails from doughnut shops. Sink them into the ground (wash them thoroughly first) and plant inside them.

"To confine aggressive, deeply rooted bamboo, cut the top and bottom off a fifty-five-gallon drum and bury it—or pour yourself a concrete wall," warns the Maryland curator.

✳

In Oklahoma, Bermuda grass is a terrible problem, says Robin Maxwell of Oklahoma City. "You'll dig it out and two weeks later you have a lawn in your garden. The roots are thick and really hard to pull, and they grow very deep and send out runners."

If you too are fighting a battle with grass creeping into your vegetable garden, Robin advises running 4- to 6-inch strips of carpet along the edges to create a barrier. "It's not really noticeable except at the beginning because the plants grow up and overhang most of it. If the grass starts growing through the carpet—as it will in time—just lift up the carpet to break off the shoots and tamp it back down. Repeat every couple of weeks or so to take care of new shoots."

To buy yourself a little more time in the Bermuda grass battle, it also helps to use plastic lawn edging as an additional barrier, Robin adds.

✳

If you have fond memories of elementary school art classes, you'll like this multipurpose papier-mâché mash that's fun to make and even more fun to use in the garden. Horticulturist Barbara Voight makes this practical material out of uncolored newspapers.

To make the mash, you will need one or more large pails (your choice depends upon the quantity of mash you want to make; a five-gallon pail or even a thirty-gallon garbage can will do), a plumber's plunger, one-third cup of ammonia for each five-gallon-size container to help break down the paper structure, and sheets of uncolored newspaper, unfolded.

Fill your container three-quarters full of very hot water. Add ammonia. Add opened newspaper sheets, one at a time. After about every third sheet of newspaper, give a plunge with the plunger to help the paper absorb liquid and break up.

When the paper no longer freely floats, stop adding more. The paper immediately becomes a gray, gloppy slurry, about the consistency of mashed potatoes. Use right away, or keep on hand for future use. You can use the mash in several ways:

- As a confiner for sprawling or collapsing plants. Construct a collar or cone to hold up the plants.

- For preventing squash borer penetration. Spread flat around the base, and build up onto the lower part of squash-family plants.

- To throw on dandelions and small weeds in the early spring before the ground is workable. Spade in later. ("It's very satisfying to say 'Take that!' when you plop it down," says Barbara.)

- As a garden edger. "I place mounds along the lawn and garden edge and stomp it down. The lawn mower's two inner wheels ride on this "plate," and we don't have to do hand clipping. This paper-mulched edge isn't noticeable and grass doesn't grow into it. It decomposes after two summers."

"If you stick to uncolored newspaper," Barbara says, "it's less noticeable."

✳

Do your tall perennials tend to flop over and look unsightly? You can avoid the nuisance of staking them up year after year if you keep a round tomato cage permanently over each plant. Nebraska native Sharon Imes supports yarrow, beebalm, and tansy on her naturally landscaped hillside lot this way. "The foliage prevents you from noticing the wire," says Sharon.

AUTHOR'S NOTE: *If you mulch your perennials thickly in fall for cold weather protection, these cages will also help hold the mulch in place.*

Protective Shields

One of the best garden advances in recent years is the Wall O'Water, holds Peter Tonge, a director of the National Gardening Association and previously garden editor of the *Christian Science Monitor*.

You can get a jump on the planting season with these polyethylene tubes designed to keep both plant and soil warm by soaking up heat from the sun during the day and slowly releasing it at night. When filled three-quarters full, the walls lean in like a tepee, closing the top and protecting tender plants from cold weather. After a few weeks you can keep the tops open by filling the sides so the walls stay vertical.

"I put out my tomato plants and two days later we got snow. The plants were fine," says Peter.

A homemade substitute for the Wall O'Water is to ring each plant with one-liter soda bottles filled with water, Peter adds. Place them upright and side by side so that they touch one another. The opening at the top leaves plants vulnerable to cold, however, so drape a piece of clear plastic over it. "When the sun is shining, you might want to remove the plastic, but it's not absolutely necessary—the water in the bottles absorbs the excess heat," Peter says.

For warmth-loving plants such as peppers, eggplant, and tomatoes, you can also bury one or two one-liter plastic soda bottles up to the neck just outside the Wall O'Water. Fill them with water that is nearly boiling. Every few days remove, empty, refill, and replace the bottles. "This starts the warming process at the root level and is one way of getting your plants off to a very quick start," says Peter.

✳

With a little imagination gardeners can recycle all kinds of recycled plastic products: "When we're setting out small, tender plants such as tomatoes and watermelons in early spring we put scraps of PVC or rubber tubing over them for protection from weather conditions," says Karen Ballhagen of New Hartford, Iowa. "The tubes provide shelter from frost, wind, hail, or rain, while allowing the sun to shine in.

"We use tubing with about a 6- to 8-inch diameter, and cut sections about as high as milk cartons."

✹

If you visited Mary Carter's garden in Ames, Iowa, in the spring, you'd see it full of milk jugs. She cuts the bottoms out and slips the gallon jugs down in the soil over her tender new plants. It shields them from sunburn, pounding rains, and cool nights, says Mary.

✹

To provide shade for newly planted seedlings until they take hold, cover them with round ice-cream cartons (with both ends removed, of course), recommends Eileen Langner of Albuquerque, New Mexico.

✹

Despite all the high-tech garden gadgets available, an old-fashioned cold frame made from an old storm window is still practical for giving spring plants a head start, says retired University of Wisconsin Extension agricultural agent Jim Ness.

Choose a south-facing location. Dig a hole 3 feet deep and the same length and width of the window in a sloping soil bank (a slant catches the most sun rays). Fill the bottom with 2 feet of fresh horse manure (which generates a lot of heat), then cover with 6 to 8 inches of dirt.

To support the window sash, use old 1-by-8-inch boards to make a simple rectangle with the same dimensions as the window, and lay this on the top of the hole; this allows the requisite 6-inch clearance between the top of the maturing seedlings and the pane.

As spring progresses, open the window a little each day, propping it with a stick, to gradually acclimate plants to the cooler outside air before transplanting into the garden.

✹

When you're planting flowers (or vegetables) in the garden, take empty cans, remove their bottoms and tops, and bury them in the garden with the rim 1 inch above ground. Fill with dirt and plant your seeds.

"That way you can weed all around and you know exactly where your plants are," says herb grower Terry Kemp of God's Green Acres Herbary and Gifts in Onalaska, Wisconsin. "It saves you from accidentally chopping them."

The cans also protect the plants from cutworm. Soup cans are fine for most flowers, but for large plants, use large coffee cans.

Shredders

Garden shredders grind leaves and other garden wastes so that you can make mulch and speed up the compost process. Unfortunately, they don't come cheaply.

"I bought a five-horsepower used shredder," says Stan Schabert of Roselle Park, New Jersey. "I had to keep cleaning it out, starting it, and restarting it. It can be frustrating. If the leaves are still green, moisture tends to clog it up, and you'll find that you need one with a bigger opening and more horsepower. I ended up buying an eight-horsepower Tomahawk. If you can afford it and you know you're going to use it, buy a more expensive shredder," advises Stan. "Those bigger ones are usually better and last longer."

Lighting

Commercial salmon fisher Lynne Leuthe rushes to get her Midwest garden planted each year before commuting to Alaska for the salmon run. "I rig up an inexpensive grow light from a simple shop light available in building supply stores. It's the type of setup with two fluorescent light tubes and a metal cover.

"If you don't need a portable grow light, just fasten two upright supports to a table, then suspend a dowel between them. Use two lengths of chain with hooks on each end to suspend the shop light from the dowel. With this arrangement, you can raise the light as the seedlings grow, so that their tips are 4 to 6 inches from the light.

"For a smaller, portable setup, attach the upright supports to a shallow wooden box. Attaching the supports with screws or bolts permits dismantling for easy storage."

AUTHOR'S NOTE: *I once had a garden near Oregon's Rogue River that was so glorious I felt I'd died and gone to heaven. No credit to me, though—the former owner was a childless flower grower who devoted all her energy and money to the garden. I'll probably never again have such regal roses and huge wisteria, or such a plethora of daffodils. One luxury of that garden was good, bright night lighting. A lighting system is great for gardening after dark when it is cooler outside, and it's even fun for weeding at midnight. Just keep in mind that you might never use the lights if you live in Mosquitoland, as we now do. The light attracts hordes of these vampires.*

✳

Be cautious of the increasingly popular photosensitive lights that automatically illuminate the walkway or garden all night long. Nationally syndicated garden columnist Jan Riggenbach notices that where the yardlight shines on her Glenwood, Iowa, garden the spinach goes to seed faster. "It may affect lettuce, too," Jan warns.

✳

If you use garden lights (or even if you keep your porch lights on), you are essentially extending your natural day by a couple of hours. This practice won't harm you, but it may harm your garden.

Artificial light may interfere with the normal functioning of nearby plants. Some plants need a rest period of consecutive dark nights to trigger blossoming, cautions Ernie Hartmann, formerly a landscaper in Pennington, New Jersey.

AUTHOR'S NOTE: *In California carnation growers were bewildered by a dramatic drop in flower production. It turned out that the headlights of nearby freeway traffic were to blame. The growers solved the problem by "tucking the plants into bed" each night with light-blocking covers.*

What Makes a Good Garden?

It is something to think about that the same technique that brought about dwarf rice and corn could also produce a race of men that would exert much less pressure on the physical environment. Maybe instead of more food, we need smaller people.

—ARTHUR E. PETERSON, WISCONSIN SOIL SCIENTIST

CHAPTER TWELVE

Intimate Enemies: Keeping Insect Pests at Bay

Before any spraying, ask yourself is it really necessary?
Is there another way of eliminating the bug?

—FREEK VRUGTMAN

I've always been intrigued by insects. When I was a little kid, my room was crammed with beetle-filled jam jars and shoebox grasshopper houses. In the third grade I found an insect egg case at recess and put it in the classroom's science corner. Over the weekend the case hatched, and when we came to school the next Monday, the classroom was swarming with hundreds of infant praying mantises.

As a grown-up gardener, I still haven't lost my fascination with these curious ancient residents of our planet. Garden product commercials encourage us to view insects as enemies, and yet without them many plants couldn't pollinate and we wouldn't have any gardens. In fact, without pollinating insects we probably also would not be alive.

During the middle decades of the twentieth century, we were optimistic that the "Green Revolution" of plant science and chemistry would transform agriculture. Instead of ending world hunger, as we had hoped, we wreaked havoc with the ecosystem, and the insecticides we so zealously applied poisoned our soil, water, birds, beneficial insects, and sometimes even our own crops.

Now, thankfully, we are more aware of the consequences of broad-spectrum insecticides, and home gardeners as well as large-scale commercial growers are turning toward more specific, less toxic, environmentally friendly means of insect control.

Back in the days when people worried little about child labor, and even less about "quality time and educational play," you didn't need high-tech means to keep bugs out of the garden. My friend Martha Schams recalls helping out in the garden as a four-year-old, back in 1916:

"There were ways we could get rich, such as picking one hundred potato bugs for one cent. We children had many an argument with Mother about how unfair it was to count a leaf with many hundreds of eggs on the back as only equal to one bug. Mother stood her ground, as she pretended to count the crawly orange and black bugs before crumpling the paper and putting them into the fire in our big black range."

Now this old-time method of removing bugs manually is gaining respect again, to which several contributors below attest.

As Anthony Tyznik points out in this chapter, a healthy garden cannot ignore life's natural balance—it will never be totally insect-free.

Tony and his fellow gardeners share tips for utilizing natural insect controls and suggestions for curbing pests by means of companion planting. You'll read ideas for ridding your garden of insects by mechanical methods, insect barriers, and commercial products. Home-style recipes, including insecticidal soaps and ashes, offer yet other alternatives to toxic chemicals. The chapter concludes with ideas for coping with cutworm, biting insects, slugs, and snails. (Although slugs and snails are really mollusks, you'll find them here with insects instead of in the "Critters" chapter where, technically, they belong. For despite what the zoologists say, in most folks' minds these cold-blooded creatures are more akin to bugs than to the world of fur and feathers.)

Listening to Mother Nature

A few insect holes in a garden may be the sign of a healthy environ-ment. When insects can't live, a garden is sending out its distress call.

—ANTHONY TYZNIK, ILLINOIS LANDSCAPE ARCHITECT

Nature's Allies

"I am convinced that the growing population of bluebirds and other species is responsible for the dwindling population of bugs and worms that chew on my plants," maintains Georgia garden writer Virgil Adams.

For a mutually beneficial relationship, mount bluebird nesting boxes near the garden. If you have bluebirds in your area, they will gratefully accept your hospitality. Now that the old wooden fence posts are gone and the telephone and power poles are treated with preservatives that keep them from rotting, bluebirds must be desperate for housing, Virgil says.

✳

To attract insect-eating birds to the garden, add a birdbath to the garden bed, suggests Doniphan, Missouri, native Ann Korschgen.

More Earth-Friendly Strategies

Nature tends to time a given plant's growth stages to coincide with that of its common predators, so the predators will have a food supply. When a crop grows a little earlier or later than normal, it's out of sync with the predator's destructive phase.

"If you have a cold frame, plant cabbage, cauliflower, and broccoli early to outdistance the bugs," proposes farmer LeeAnne Bulman of Independence, Wisconsin. Then they'll be ready to harvest before the infestation of destructive cabbage worms appears.

✳

AUTHOR'S NOTE: *Here's an easy, nontoxic way to capture marauding cabbage worms by "fighting fire with fire": Bait your cabbage heads by picking a leaf from the bottom of the plant (one of the big, tough, wormy outer leaves you would eventually have discarded anyway). Lay it on the top of the cabbage plant. Early the next morning it will be covered with cabbage worms.*

✳

In Transylvania sprinkling holy water keeps vampires away. Former New Jersey landscaper Ernie Hartmann's spider mite tip is less dramatic, but it's the same principle, more or less.

Spider mites hate cold water. If your flowers, vegetables, or evergreens are plagued with them, a weekly dose of cold water will deter them. Using a coarse spray and steady pressure, hose down the entire tree or plant.

✳

If your trees are plagued with bag worms, here's another water-warfare tip, from master gardener Owen Marredeth of Wauwatosa, Wisconsin. "Many folks knock these pests out of a tree with a stick and then destroy the mess on the ground; another method, especially if they're high in a tree, is to give them a shot with the hose at a high stream. Not only do they drown, but your tree gets moisture and maybe you get a bath," says Owen.

✳

Does the idea of using chemical insect repellents repel you too? Entomologist Phil Pellitteri, director of the insect diognostic lab at University of Wisconsin–Madison, suggests a nontoxic, natural way to fight off insect predators.

"When an aphid infestation is found, just crush two or three aphids by hand. The injured aphids release pheromones, chemical signals that cause the others to fall to the ground. Most aphids are not overly intelligent and will not climb back up the plant," says Phil.

✳

"Before any spraying, ask yourself, 'is it really necessary? Is there another way of eliminating the bug?'" counsels Freek Vrugtman, retired curator of collections for Royal Botanical Gardens in Hamilton, Ontario.

While he was working as a volunteer in Belize with the Canadian-based SHARE Agriculture Foundation, Guatemalan refugees taught Freek this simple, no-cost, biological control for ants: Take a shovelful of soil and ants from one ant colony and dump it on another one. Ants are fiercely territorial. They'll fight and control the population. "It's environmentally friendly instead of using poison," Freek says.

✳

For the insect war in his Georgia garden, garden writer Virgil Adams extols the virtues of two insecticides: Dipel (*Bacillus thuringiensis*) and his fingers. "The Dipel did a good job on the cabbage loopers, and my fingers worked better than Sevin ever did on the Colorado potato beetles. Picking bugs by hand is not as time-consuming as you might think. Anyway, saving the lives of beneficial insects such as ladybugs is worth a little extra effort," he says.

Harmful to Their Health

"Once I read a magazine article about a plant in a nursing home that was doing fantastically compared with all the others. It turned out that it was where two old guys would always sit chewing tobacco, and they'd spit tobacco juice into the plant," recalls farmer Jeanette Manske of Stoddard, Wisconsin.

"Well, I had some coleus that was infested with bugs, so I got some tobacco leaves from our tobacco shed and put them in a coffee can filled with water. Every once in a while I'd water the plants with this tobacco juice, and from then on I had no more problems."

✳

AUTHOR'S NOTE: *If you live where tobacco is grown, you may want to try this natural organic insecticide (or you can use Black Leaf 40, a tobacco extract similar to tobacco leaf tea). Before you rush out to find a tobacco shed, though, be forewarned that tobacco can cause health problems in the vegetable kingdom as well as in our own. Tobacco leaves sometimes carry viruses that can infect related plants such as tomatoes (both plants are in the Solanaceae family). Gladiolus may also be affected, so be careful where you use it, and wash your hands and tools thoroughly after handling.*

High-Tech, Low-Tech Antipredator Devices

James M. Szynal of Florence, Massachusetts, is an inventor, a mechanic, and a farmer who loves to tinker. In answer to the plea of nearby farmers, he has invented a vacuum cleaner that sucks insects off potatoes. With slight modification in the air flow, James's device cleans up many kinds of insects from beans, peppers, tomatoes, cucumbers, and even strawberries. "I thought strawberries were really delicate, but it didn't hurt the plants at all," he marvels.

He has modified his large farm model to create a home garden model called The Beetle Eater. (For information you can contact James at The Bugs Unlimited, P.O. Box 371, Florence, MA 01060; telephone 413–586–5040.) Can you drag your Electrolux into the garden to vacuum up the bugs? "It wouldn't hurt the plant at all!" James believes.

AUTHOR'S NOTE: *If you feel like experimenting, use the kind of vacuum with wand attachments, not the upright carpet-sweeping models.*

✳

Missouri native Joe Borntreger is proof that you don't need high technology to get rid of potato bugs. For Amish gardeners such as Joe, mechanization is taboo. Joe uses a stick to knock bugs off the plant and into a can with a little kerosene in the bottom to kill them.

Companion Planting

"In the spring, after we've prepared our garden area by spading 10 to 12 inches deep and pounding down large clumps of soil with the back of a rake, we plant marigolds. Marigolds repel tiny soil worms called nematodes that feast on the roots of many garden species," says short story writer Dona Popovic of La Crosse, Wisconsin. "We edge our whole garden plot with marigold plants and put more of them between the rows of tomatoes, green peppers, and squash."

✳

AUTHOR'S NOTE: *The suggestion to plant marigolds for their insect-repellent qualities was one of the most common tips I received, contributed by dozens of gardeners. Be aware, however, that some authorities scoff that it won't be effective unless you virtually blanket your entire garden bed in marigolds to the point where you crowd out the vegetables.*

The almost-legendary insect-control powers of marigolds are due to root secretions. The repugnant odor of the leaves also helps repel above-ground insects.

✳

If you plant beans with your cucumbers, says Mary Claire Fehring, a native or Rockford, Iowa, the beans help repel the cucumber beetles.

✳

To keep aphids away from roses, plant garlic cloves in the soil around the base of each rose bush, advises nonagenarian gardener Anne Goldbloom of Vancouver, British Columbia.

✳

"I love to plant flowers and vegetables like cabbage in the same area," says organic farmer Bill Bricker of Augusta, Georgia. "I've found by doing this most of the slugs attack the cabbage, not the flowers. (I counted sixty-seven small slugs hiding in one cabbage plant.) So now I plant cabbage or another ornamental cole [cabbage family] crop to trap slugs."

✳

"When we were putting in an irrigation system," says Bill Bricker, "we learned how to enhance the population of insect-eating toads in the garden. We used five-gallon buckets with the bottoms removed to keep soil away from the irrigation valves. Toads found these damp dark places, and they've reared many offspring there each year."

✳

"For folks reluctant to use insecticides, remember that good weed control helps prevent insects from having a habitat; they'll go to neighbors and lay their eggs there," notes retired University of Wisconsin Extension agriculture agent Jim Ness.

Mechanical Strategies

If grasshoppers are a problem in your area, till your soil in the fall. This breaks up grasshopper egg clusters (which are laid in the top several inches) and exposes them to the air, says Jan Riggenbach, author of the syndicated garden column "Midwest Gardening."

✳

If you peel a wilted zucchini plant, you can see the screwworm that caused the damage, notes Dona Popovic. "I'm kind of squeamish about worms, but if you're not, you can dig out the borer and wrap masking tape, sticky side out, over the wound. Or, you can even bandage the wound with newspaper, which will eventually decompose," Dona adds.

✻

"One of the problems with rhododendrons is root weevils. You can't hand-pick them, because as soon as the plant moves, they all drop off," says Carolyn Jones, author of *Perennials and Bedding Plants* (Whitecap Books) and horticulturist at VanDusen Botanical Garden. Here's the simple, chemical-free way Carolyn controls them in her own garden when they come out at night to feed: After you've noticed 1/4-inch, V-shaped notches along the edge of the leaves, spread newspapers under the plant in the evening. Go out after dark with a flashlight and shake the plants. The weevils will drop down onto the newspapers. Bundle them up and burn them or shake them into the toilet and flush.

Barriers

Virginia native Elsa Yeske discovered a good way to keep her broccoli from getting wormy—she ties netting over each head. "You can reuse it from year to year," she says.

✻

Kathy Deering was frustrated by cabbage worms eating the cabbages in her Seattle garden until she made collars of tar paper and laid these flat on the ground around each cabbage plant. "Cut the circles about 8 inches in diameter," she advises, "with a hole cut out of the center to accommodate the stem."

✻

To keep spinach miners off spinach plants while they're tender and susceptible, and cabbage moths from laying eggs on cabbage and broccoli throughout the summer, cover them with Reemay (a spun-bonded polyester fabric available through garden catalogs), advises Ruth Coombs of Kansas City, Missouri. Lay it over hoops cut from wire coat hangers to give the plants growing room.

"If the growing season is wet, slugs may come through the drainage holes in potted patio plants," Ruth adds. "To prevent this, put small-weave nylon tulle or Reemay on the bottom of the pot before adding the soil or other potting medium."

✳

Fiberglass screening also works. Horticulturist Barbara Voight of Madison, Wisconsin, cuts screen to size and places it in the bottom of outdoor flower pots to keep out worms and sow bugs.

Commercial Remedies

When using dormant oil sprays, temperature is a critical factor. If the temperature fluctuates below forty-five and above eighty-five degrees Fahrenheit within one month, you can't use them. "Sometimes that's hard to predict," notes Beth Weidner, assistant park manager for the Alfred B. Maclay Gardens in Tallahassee, Florida.

Newer, ultrarefined oil sprays are less temperature-specific. "If temperature fluctuations are a problem, go for those," Beth advises.

Beth is concerned, however, that folks may not follow printed guidelines for correct use. Sometimes people read pesticide directions that call for one teaspoon of pesticide per gallon of water and figure that if a little is good, a lot is better.

"They don't realize but not only are they harming the environment and their plants, but they're also breaking the law. It is illegal to use any pesticide in any way not in accordance with the label," stresses Beth Weidner.

Hindsight is 20/20 Vision

What's sitting in your garage? How do you get rid of it? If you do buy a garden chemical, buy the smallest you can, so you don't have anything left over, because the safest way to use it is to use it up according to label directions.

—ROBERTA SLADKY, MINNESOTA HORTICULTURIST

Homemade Recipes

"It is difficult to pick a favorite tip or two after sixteen years of garden writing," says Jan Riggenbach, who reaches close to a million readers through her magazine features and syndicated garden column. "The one tip, however, that has generated hundreds of letters and many reports whenever I go to speak on gardening is the fruit tree jug tip. It works so well that the tip has spread like wildfire. One of my readers shared it with me originally. I have never failed to get a huge batch of mail every spring from people who are sold on the method, but can't remember the recipe."

Here's Jan's recipe for inexpensive homemade traps to keep worms out of fruit: Put one cup of vinegar and one cup of sugar in a gallon milk jug. Fill the rest of the jug with water. Shake it well and add the peel from one banana. Hang one jug in each apple tree before the blossoms open. (These also keep bugs from lilac bushes.)

You can use the same potion in the garden in five-quart ice-cream buckets with lids. Cut V-shapes in the lids and bend the cut edges up so the bugs can get in. Set these pails between tomato plants to attract bugs.

❋

Farmer Jeanette Manske of Stoddard, Wisconsin, has reported success with these traps and suggests that you set some on the ground in the rows among raspberry and rhubarb plants as well. These will lure and trap insects all season without replenishment.

A Sudsy Solution

If you bring ornamental patio plants indoors for the cold season, be aware that they may harbor hitchhikers. "There's an effective, safe, non-toxic way to prevent such insects from ruining your other houseplants," says Beatrice Sperling of Vancouver, British Columbia. "I learned this tip from the advisory service of Vancouver's famed VanDusen Botanical Gardens.

"When your bars of soap get too small to use anymore, don't throw them away. Shave them with a vegetable peeler, put the shavings in a spray bottle, and fill the bottle with water. Spray the plants thoroughly, remembering to wet the trunk and underside of the leaves, too."

✳

At eighty years of age, artist Ruby Nicks is still experimenting with better ways to paint—and to garden. She sprays her apple trees with Fels Naptha laundry soap to keep her apples worm-free.

"Shave the soap with a knife," says the gardener in Onalaska, Wisconsin, "and soak the shavings in good hot water. Use about one fourth of a bar for every two gallons. Leave the soap mixture overnight to soften, then spray it on, drenching the whole tree and the ground to the drip line. I spray twice while the trees are blooming, starting as soon as the blossoms appear, and then once a week till little apples form. Now I have the best apples I've had in twenty years."

✳

Although commercial insecticidal soaps work well, homemade insecticidal soap is also effective. To make your own solution, mix four tablespoons of liquid dishwashing soap to each gallon of water, counsels Beth Weidner, assistant park manager at the state gardens in Tallahassee, Florida.

✳

A spray solution of soap and water kills soft-shelled insects (such as aphids, scales, thrips, spider mites, and mealybugs, which are the most troublesome pests because they're too prolific and small to pick off by hand). It kills them by softening their protective waterproof waxy coating.

"It won't kill plants, but if the solution is too strong, it may burn the leaf tips a little in bright sun," cautions chemist Milton Palmer of Castro Valley, California.

✳

Does it matter whether it's soap or detergent? Dishwashing liquid, laundry powder, or facial bar?

"No," says Phil Pellitteri, director of the Insect Diognostic Lab at University of Wisconsin–Madison. The key ingredient in household soaps, unlike insecticidal soaps specifically formulated for horticultural use, may vary not only from brand to brand but even from one batch to another within the same brand, Phil notes.

"When spraying plants with any of these products, the purer they are, the better," says Phil. "Avoid scented ones, as the perfumes may harm plants. A soap and water solution of 1 to 2 percent soap (or detergent) is best—go no stronger than 2 percent or it could burn plants."

AUTHOR'S NOTE: *I've been using Shaklee's Basic-H, a nontoxic, organic, biodegradable household cleaning product as virtually my sole plant insecticide for more than twenty years and been well satisfied. Although its manufacturer makes no insecticidal claims for Basic-H, I feel comfortable using it as it is approved by most states as a soil conditioner to make the soil more absorbent. (Ivory liquid also appears to be reliable and safe.)*

Bugs and Ashes

AUTHOR'S NOTE: *Many organic gardeners hail ashes as the answer to numerous insect woes. Now it seems they may not, after all, be quite so harmless as we believed. For more on ashes see page 63.*

✳

Sprinkle wood ashes from your fireplace in the soil around any plant that is susceptible to cutworm, advises Jeanette Baker of Onalaska, Wisconsin.

✳

To keep cutworms away from your tomato plants, Bob Neuhaus, another gardener in Jeanette's town, advises digging a ring 1 inch deep and about 3 inches in diameter around each plant. "You'll save having to bend if you make these with a broomstick. Then take a pail of ashes and fill each ring to the top. Wood ashes have lye in them. It goes into the ground, and the cut-worms will avoid it."

Wood ashes will also stop the worms from eating your onions, Bob Neuhaus finds. Give a light sprinkling of ashes after planting, and the lye will soak in.

✳

Hardwood ashes are the most effective kind for repelling insects, counsels Jim Ness, retired University of Wisconsin Extension agricultural agent.

✳

"To keep down insects," advises Ruth Ann Davis, a resident of Tucson, Arizona, "I strew ashes between the plants after the seedlings start coming up. My husband and I run a resort in the summer, and the seventeen wood stoves in the cottages provide an ample supply."

Slugs and Ashes

Use wood ashes as a slug deterrent by sprinkling them around the plants, counsels Wisconsin gardener Dona Popovic.

"To protect squash or other plants that are vulnerable to the squash borer," adds Dona, "I've also had success mixing wood ashes into the dirt when planting outdoors. Black pepper also may be used for this purpose, but it's expensive and must be reapplied after each rain."

✳

"Wood ashes will dry up potato bugs," says Amish farmer Mattie Born-treger of Cashton, Wisconsin. An alternative, says her husband, Joe, is sprinkling lime on the potato plants. "It won't hurt the plants," he says. "It just dries up the bugs."

GADD: Gardeners Against Drunk Destroyers

AUTHOR'S NOTE: *If you are bothered by slugs in your garden, put a little beer in a saucer. The next morning you're likely to find dozens of slugs trapped there. Gardeners from all over the United States and Canada recommended this potion.*

❋

If you're squeamish and loathe the idea of having to clean up a saucerful of drowned slugs, just bury a nearly empty beer can in the soil, suggests native Josephine Broadhead of Carson, North Dakota. "When it's full, just lift it out and throw the whole can away," Josephine advises.

❋

Jan Scott also used the booze bait for luring the little green inchworms that devoured the spinach, broccoli, and lettuce in her Dallas, Texas, garden so voraciously.

Just cut the bottoms off milk cartons so that you have a shallow cardboard dish 1½ inches deep. Bury them, Jan advises, and put a few drops of beer in them to lure the worms.

❋

"If you use a dish of beer or molasses dissolved in water to attract and drown slugs, be sure the rim of the dish is at least one inch above the soil surface. This will prevent shiny black ground beetles, which are beneficial insects, from accidentally falling into the dish and perishing also," cautions VanDusen Botanical Garden horticulturist Carolyn Jones.

More on Slug Warfare

Apparently, some slugs are teetotalers too. Ken Johnston of West Salem, Wisconsin, had no luck with beer. In fact, he counted more than 1,000 slugs in his garden in just four nights.

"If you sprinkle salt on the slugs, they die immediately," Ken says. "I also tried spraying them with saltwater, but that didn't work."

At night, when the slugs come out to dine, they're easy to see by flashlight, says Ken Johnston. "However, if you're not eager to go searching for slugs by torch in the dark, lay a 6- to 8-inch piece of board down in the garden near the plants that the slugs prey upon. The slugs go under the board to stay cool and are easy to pluck off, so check under the board daily."

＊

Gardening should put you in tune with nature, not at war with it, holds Terri Clark, manager of public affairs for the Vancouver Park Board, which oversees the fabulous Stanley Park, Queen Elizabeth, and VanDusen gardens. So instead of killing the predatory insects in her garden, Terri prefers humane defensive strategies such as this:

Save all your eggshells, rinsed and crushed. Scatter them under the perennials. Slugs dislike anything sharp, so this discourages them from visiting, she says.

AUTHOR'S NOTE: *Oak leaf mulch is another humane slug repellent.*

Cutworm Defense Strategies

"To protect seedlings from cutworm, I wrap the lower stem in aluminum foil," says Virginia native Hilda First. "Foil has the advantage of not deteriorating in wet conditions. If you're in a hot climate, however, the sun may scorch the tender new plant, so you'd better avoid aluminum collars."

✳

Styrofoam cups make good cutworm collars, says gardener Dona Popovic. "We use the large twelve–ounce size." For tomatoes and green peppers, cut out the bottom section of the cups and slide the root ball down through the opening. Be sure to leave 1 inch of the cup above ground as a circular shield around the young plant. The cups can also be used with zuc–chini seedlings, Dona says.

✳

To prevent cutworms from gnawing off tender new seedlings, wrap the stems with a little strip of newspaper about 2½ inches high and 5 inches long, then plant with half the paper above and half below ground level, advises master gardener Kenneth Hall of Fort Collins, Colorado. Unlike most shields, paper won't need collecting later, as it disintegrates.

Biting Insects

Many folks work in the garden late in the day to avoid the heat. To ward off the gnats that plague gardeners when the sun starts getting low, daub your-self with a few drops of vanilla as a bug repellent, advises Jeanette Manske of Stoddard, Wisconsin.

AUTHOR'S NOTE: *Most of us find that gardening is a time to relax and forget about social pressures. We tend to wear any old clothes and are grateful that we don't have to be in style or worry about what we wear. Right?*

Wrong! If biting insects plague you while you're gardening, it may be that your clothing makes you too attractive. Studies suggest that mosquitos are attracted to dark blue, burgundy, and brown, whereas white and pastel yellow have less appeal to them. Light blue clothes allegedly will keep flies away.

Turning Predators into Crops

AUTHOR'S NOTE: *The following suggestion from Danny O'Deay may be too exotic for some folk, but culinary tradition is on his side. Snails have been esteemed as food for thousands of years. Archaeological digs in the Near East have yielded the 20,000-year-old remains of snail dinners. The ancient Chinese considered roasted snails a great delicacy, and the Romans even bred and milk-fattened snails.*

Irritated by the marauding snails in his garden, Danny O'Deay of San Francisco, California, decided to utilize this predator as a crop. "These snails were originally brought over from France for gourmets who liked to eat escargot," Danny claims. "You can eat any of the garden snails that have shells. I drop the snails in boiling water, drain them, and serve them with garlic, olive oil, and onions.

"If there is any possibility the snails could have been exposed to poisonous garden chemicals in your neighborhood, keep them in a container for two weeks on a diet of cornmeal or oatmeal. Wash them daily in cold water. Discard any dead snails. If they're still alive, they'll move when touched. By the end of two weeks, any poison they might have had is gone, and you can cook them."

Listening to Mother Nature

Just live with your garden and leave the irritations to nature. There's a reason for everything: there's a reason for slugs, there's a reason for aphids, there's a reason for us. We may never know the reason, but we should be wise enough to know there is one. If you overexercise your power, you end up regretting it.

—TERRI CLARK, VANCOUVER, BRITISH COLUMBIA

CHAPTER THIRTEEN

All Creatures Great and Small: Animal Invaders

My father-in-law used to take his boots and socks off and shuffle barefoot through the sweet corn rows. If you're a good, hardworking farmer, your feet smell like the wrath of God and scare the raccoons away.

—CHERI HEMKER

Beautiful flowers and bountiful harvests are only a part of the great satisfaction gardeners enjoy. The feeling of harmony with all of nature is, for most tillers of the soil, by far the greater treasure. The rich, loamy smell of freshly turned earth, the magic of sunshine on a dewy spider web, and the hard green fruit that spring from yellow tomato blossoms tug us out of the backwash of our daily concerns and into the universal flow of seasons.

So when our gardens lure creatures from the wild, we often feel ambivalent. It's hard to be philosophical when smoothly raked beds are churned into a morass of potholes by deer, when tender pea seedlings are plucked by grackles, or when just–ripened sweet corn is stolen by raccoons. Yet if we start to view the furred and feathered intruders as adversaries to be thwarted, outwitted, and repelled, we also distance ourselves.

It is possible to protect our gardens for our own use and still maintain a sense of connectedness. As I gathered the tips for this chapter, it was reassuring to discover that the vast majority of gardeners are relying upon predator control methods that are environmentally safe and humane. These gardeners offer ingenious ideas for keeping critters at bay.

Your garden will benefit from suggestions for natural repellents, barriers, and homemade contraptions designed to cope with rabbits, gophers, moles, deer, moose, snakes, raccoons, skunks, and birds. You'll be relieved to find that the great majority of tips are inexpensive and safe for you and your garden as well as the animals and the earth.

Of all the tips I gathered, four of my favorites appear in this chapter. John Larsen and Denise Johnson's skunk and rabbit repellent is simple, natural, and, I believe, the most original I have heard. Mona Stevens and Cy Klinkner's suggestions that you protect your garden by meeting the needs of wildlife rather than by thwarting them are, I think you'll agree, the most humane.

Listening to Mother Nature

Virtually the most essential piece of garden equipment is a hammock. Instead of getting stressed out that things are not perfect, go relax in your hammock and listen to the birds.

—GARY MENENDEZ, TENNESSEE LANDSCAPE ARCHITECT

Natural Repellents

"Deer and ground hogs love peas—in fact, anything that's green," says gardener Luther Shaffer of Kutztown, Pennsylvania. "Sprinkling dried blood down the rows works to protect the plants. In the garden centers, it's very expensive, but at the slaughterhouses it's a by-product that is sold cheaply by the five-gallon can."

Dried blood has drawbacks, though. If you get heavy rains, you have to reapply, Luther says. "And it attracts cats."

✳

"Grackles were pulling my pea seed out of the ground as soon as it sprouted," complained horticulturist Barbara Voight of Madison, Wisconsin. "Then I found that if I sprinkled a small amount of red pepper over the row, they left the peas alone."

✳

If you treat your soil with water-absorbent crystals, as does Jennifer Cohn in her Syracuse, New York, herb garden, squirrels may be attracted to the moisture. To keep them away, sprinkle a little cayenne pepper on top of places where the soil is treated, advises Jennifer.

AUTHOR'S NOTE: *Some readers may be reluctant to apply cayenne pepper because of the expense. An inexpensive source of hot pepper packaged in larger quantities is the ethnic food markets. Some supermarkets or food warehouses also have institution-size containers of spices.*

✳

If you're having problems with small animals eating your flower bulbs such as tulips and lilies, don't resort to violent measures. Try planting narcissus instead. "Squirrels, gophers, and mice tend not to like them," says Deborah Paulson, formerly a catalog bulb manager for Smith & Hawken mail-order bulbs in Mill Valley, California.

✳

"Those nasty beasts that love tulips will steer clear of rhubarb. Plant the tulips among the rhubarb, and you'll have no more chewed-up tulips," says master gardener Owen Marredeth, a resident of Wauwatosa, Wisconsin. "And when it's time to divide the rhubarb, it is also time to do the same with the tulips."

✳

Chipmunks love beets. To deter them from eating yours, intersperse onions in the same row, advises Hamilton County master gardener Mona Stevens of Fishers, Indiana. "I planted onions on the outside of a 3-by-4-foot planting area and one beet, one onion, beet, onion, etc., on the inside. It worked about 95 percent of the time."

If wild animals chew the tender tops of your impatiens, it may be because they're thirsty. Set out trays of water, shallow enough for the small animals to reach, and it may save your plants, says Mona Stevens.

Rabbits

Many people have trouble with rabbits, notes retired nurseryman Cy Klinkner of La Crosse, Wisconsin. "Instead of resorting to deadly poisons which dogs and kids and birds can pick up, plant two or three rows of lettuce for the rabbits around the outside perimeter of the garden. They'll gorge on lettuce, but they won't go any further. This way, you can watch and enjoy them, too," Cy urges.

AUTHOR'S NOTE: *Do rabbits damage your trees by nibbling the bark? You can repel them by painting the tree trunks with liquefied rabbit manure. If that method is repulsive to you as well, plant onions. Rabbits allegedly will stay away from anything close to an onion.*

✳

Mary Claire Fehring, a native of Rockford, Iowa, doesn't have enough room in her garden to plant everything she wants, so she plants her beans along the outside of the garden fence. To discourage rabbits, she sprinkles the cheapest talcum powder she can buy. "Sprinkle as soon as the plants are big enough for the rabbits to eat," says Mary Claire. "Resprinkle after every rain, until the plants are grown.

But do not put mothballs in the garden to keep out rabbits, as some people advise, cautions Mary Claire. "I tried it and it worked, but my parsley tasted just terrible!"

✳

Save disposable TV-dinner trays and pot-pie pans and string them between two stakes among your garden rows, suggests farmer Jeanette Manske of Stoddard, Wisconsin. "They rattle in the wind and scare away rabbits and raccoons."

Feline Allies

"The best thing for ridding your garden of rabbits is cats," claims Pennsylvania gardener Luther Shaffer. "We have a cat and she takes care of the rabbits," Luther says.

AUTHOR'S NOTE: *Cats also do a good job of keeping snakes out of the garden—although they've been known to bring them indoors instead.*

More on Creepy Crawly Critters

Springer Hoskins of Corbin, Kentucky, has advice that allows folks gardening on urban apartment balconies to feel smug: "Never pick up a log or rock without kicking it over first. Snakes or poisonous spiders may be lurking," he cautions.

AUTHOR'S NOTE: *A few weeks ago, an acquaintance of mine was bitten on the finger by a copperhead snake that was lurking in a houseplant placed temporarily outdoors.*

Gophers and Moles

If moles are a problem in your garden, try sticking thorny twigs from raspberry canes or rose prunings in the mole holes, advises nationally syndicated garden columnist Jan Riggenbach of Glenwood, Iowa.

Pop bottles buried in the soil are another mole repellent, Jan says. Set the open mouth of each bottle just above ground. When the wind blows, the bottles whistle and the sound repels the moles.

✳

"Fritillaria imperalis is one plant that helps drive away gophers—they hate the smell," says Deborah Paulson of Mill Valley, California.

✳

"Don't plant artichokes where gophers will get them. Have you ever seen those cartoons where plants start shaking and rattling and disappear into the ground? It's amazing—and it really happens just like that!" says Coya Silverlake of Cotati, California.

If gophers are a problem, plant moleplants (Euphorbia lathyris), which they dislike, around the periphery of the artichoke patch, and they will be less likely to enter it, Coya advises.

AUTHOR'S NOTE: *Moleplant, also called Caper spurge, has roots that produce a milky latex substance that gophers and moles hate. But if you plant it, be patient: Moleplant can take a year to germinate. Because its seeds may cause skin irritation, handle them with rubber gloves and keep them out of children's reach.*

✳

If you've got the energy, advises Coya Silverlake, one way to keep gophers from tunneling into the garden is by barricading it with an underground barrier. Dig a trench about 3 feet deep and about 1 foot wide around the perimeter. Dump pottery shards into the trench and pack them densely so there aren't cracks for the gophers to squeeze through. They cannot chew through the clay, and they will not tunnel under the trench.

To get shards, ask a pottery workshop or factory to save you broken pieces. Nurseries or garden centers are also a good source. Brick, concrete block, flagstone, and rock should work too. "Scrounge in a junkyard and be creative. Just be sure the material is porous and nontoxic, so as not to disturb the ecosystem," Coya urges.

Gourmet Groundhogs

If groundhogs bother your garden, try Margaret Lindsey Markot's humane solution. The herb grower in Middletown, Connecticut, live-traps and relocates them in the woods at least 2 to 3 miles away so they won't come back. Gripes Margaret's husband, Bruce, "They were eating the herbs, the little bums—they liked the dill and couldn't get enough of parsley, and as a result, neither could I."

AUTHOR'S NOTE: *Relocation is also the humane way to relieve your garden of other pesky critters such as raccoons. You can buy live traps at farm supply stores; some humane societies and state Department of Natural Resources will lend them.*

Deer

"We have a hedge of beautiful pink roses," says Jim Nichols of West Bloomington, Minnesota. "They were being decimated by deer. They ate all the blossoms and new growth—just mowed them down. So my wife and I put a portable radio in a Zip Loc plastic bag with a hole for an electric cord so we could plug it into a timer. We put the timer in a bag also, to protect it from rain, and we just laid them on the ground near the hedge. Because the deer are active in early evening and very early morning, we timed the radio to play from just before sundown till just after sunup. One weekend we were gone and neglected the radio. Deer ate the entire petunia bed."

❋

The Nicholses kept their radio tuned to talk shows, speculating that human voices would work best. The experience of a former resident of their state, Cherie Timming of Walla Walla, Washington, found that music works well too.

"When we lived in Minnesota, we had a lot of deer and raccoon problems. They never bothered the corn until it was ripe, and then they'd clean it out in a night. To stop them, we turned on a radio at night and played loud music. It worked," says Cherie.

❋

To keep deer from browsing in the crops, string up the plastic rings that hold six-packs of aluminum cans together so that they dangle, advises Manuel Lacks of Keysville, Virginia. Space these every 15 to 20 feet apart.

❋

"A devious means of keeping deer from munching ivy is to lay Dial soap in a slit plastic bag among the plants," says Lynn Biely of Seattle, Washington. "My only other expertise," quips Lynn, "is shopping the sales at my nearest silk plant outlet."

❋

Judy Schabert of La Crosse, Wisconsin, keeps deer out of her fruit trees by hanging bars of perfumed soap in the branches.

✳

"Wrap trees with plastic tree wrap up to their first limb to repel deer and rabbits," advises twenty-two-year veteran nurseryman Hank Harris of Coulee Farm Nursery, also of La Crosse.

Commercial tree wrap is generally available at nurseries and garden supply stores. It comes in strips that one can conveniently wind around the trunk. Hank Harris prefers the plastic variety to paper wrap, because it's easier to apply and stretches as the trunk grows.

Moose

Like a lot of folks living in the Lower 48, Carolyn and Dennis Ostrander were occasionally pestered by rabbits in their Kenai, Alaska, garden. "But we had a much bigger challenge, too," says Carolyn. "We had moose. We discovered an easy and inexpensive solution to the problem by swaddling our fence with old, discarded commercial fishnet and draping the surplus along the bottom edge on the ground. The moose couldn't get through the netting."

Raccoons

"We have a lot of trouble with raccoons in the corn," says Ruth Page of Burlington, Vermont, host of Vermont Public Radio's "Earth's Gardens and the Environment" and former editor of *National Gardening* magazine.

"If I can manage to plant my vine crops like winter squashes and pumpkins with big prickly leaves early enough, they'll carpet the ground in the corn patch. The raccoons don't like to walk among the leaves.

"Plant the vines around the perimeter of your corn. As soon as the runners start growing, guide them in among the rows of corn. The problem is that when you're harvesting your corn, it's very hard not to walk on the vines, so you get on your tiptoes and kind of do a ballet dance, while sometimes teetering on one foot while you pick. But it usually keeps out the raccoons."

❋

Ask a beauty shop to save you hair clippings and strew these around crops such as sweet corn that draw raccoons and groundhogs. Leah Hochart of Keysville, Virginia, advises that she's had good success with this method.

AUTHOR'S NOTE: *Nowadays the safest, most organic way might be to find yourself an "old-fashioned" barber whose patrons don't dabble in upscale perms, tints, mousses, or sprays.*

❋

"My father-in-law used to take his boots and socks off and shuffle barefoot through the sweet corn rows. If you're a good, hardworking farmer, your feet smell like the wrath of God and scare the raccoons away," says Cheri Hemker of Onalaska, Wisconsin.

❋

If raccoons eat your corn, don't go through the trouble of putting up fencing, counsels Ruth Ann Davis, a resident of Tucson, Arizona. "An 8-foot fence around my garden didn't help at all," Ruth Ann says.

Nor should you rely on human or canine vigilance to do the trick. "My brother even tried sleeping in the garden with his dog. Neither of them even woke up when the coons got in."

❋

Judy Hansen and her husband, Walter, of Onalaska, Wisconsin, grow their sweet corn down by a creek and have to compete with the raccoons to get any. Here's how they ward off plundering. "When the corn is almost ready, we run an electric fence about 6 to 8 inches off the ground and keep it on at night. It's easy to step over and it works."

❋

Virginian Leah Hochart suggests another way to protect corn from raccoons. She saves plastic bread wrappers, and when the ears are just about ripe enough to pick—which is when the raccoons are poised to strike—she covers each ear with a plastic bag and holds it in place with a rubber band.

AUTHOR'S NOTE: *Some bread bags are printed with lead-based ink; to avoid contact with the corn, don't turn the bags inside out.*

❋

As many a rueful gardener knows, raccoons can demolish entire acreages of corn overnight. Here's a humane way to get rid of the masked little bandits and ensure they won't return. "Catch them in box traps," advises Bob Neuhaus of Onalaska, Wisconsin, "and haul them at least 7 miles away to a new home close to water."

Skunks

If you turn lawn into garden, be forewarned that you might have problems with grubs that live in the sod and develop into worms.

"One year my family planted rutabagas and potatoes in ground that was previously grass. Then skunks came. In a single day, they dug up the vegetables to get at the worms. They damaged the root crops and forced us to harvest too early," notes Jim Ness of Onalaska, Wisconsin. The grubs tend to come in seven-year cycles, Jim adds.

❋

John Larsen of St. Paul, Minnesota, suggests a novel way to discourage lawn-ravaging skunks. "When a skunk tore up our yard looking for grubs, we'd just seen the movie *Never Cry Wolf*, the account of wildlife biologist Farley Mowatt's wolf study in the wild. To keep the wolves a safe distance away, Mowatt marked his territory in the manner of many wild animals: by urinating around its boundary.

"This gave me the idea to circle the garden with my own urine. The animals never came back, so maybe it worked."

✳

We hear so much controversy about the differing innate abilities of men and women. But who would have imagined that even gardening tips could be gender-related? Male urine allegedly works to keep away some garden predators such as skunks and rabbits. "But female urine won't, because it doesn't have testosterone," says Denise Johnson from Hartford, Connecticut.

✳

Burrowing animals such as skunks may decide to dig a den under your garden tool shed. If this should happen, pour some ammonia in the hole. Then soak a rag with more ammonia and plug the hole up. The intruders will move away pronto, advises Virginia native Hilda First.

Birds

"If you plant beans too shallow, birds or cats get them," says Rosemary Muramoto of Seattle, Washington. "So I lay chicken wire on top until they start sprouting."

Open the roll of wire, crease it down the center vertically to make a shallow tent, and run it down the bean row.

✳

Here's a way to defend fragile new plants from starlings, which like to pull out plants and use them for nest building, says Bill Hansen, a farmer from Bangor, Wisconsin. It also protects tomato plants from cutworms.

"Take plastic one-liter pop bottles. Cut off the necks and the black bottom. Slit the bottles and use them to encircle plants when planting. These are easy to store in bundles of twenty to thirty. The black plastic bottoms also make ideal saucers to put under flower pots," Bill adds.

✳

To keep birds away from the garden, you need light as well as movement. String glittering, whirling aluminum pie pans about 15 to 20 feet apart, counsels Virginia gardener Manuel Lacks.

It's not only McDonald's Golden Arches that span the globe. Successful gardening tips also cross international boundaries. In Sri Lanka, where rice is the primary commodity, you'll see strings of tin cans dangling from a length of clothesline in every rice field, says Feroz Ghouse of Colombo, Sri Lanka (now living in La Crosse, Wisconsin). "Just one clothesline shaking in the wind with rattling cans is enough to chase birds from the entire paddy."

✳

Eve Simon, a gardener in Phoenix, Arizona, grouses, "Although I like birds more than vegetation, why do they have to put one hole in each of ten or twenty oranges instead of finishing off one fruit at a time? Very messy and wasteful."

If you share Eve's problem and you're willing to fly in the face of aesthetics, buy protective polypropylene netting to fling over the tree. It's available up to 28 feet square; if your tree is huge, sew several nets together.

✳

You might think that gardening on a small, high-rise balcony would be a snap after decades of tending a huge yard with pond, rose beds, and rockery. Anne Goldbloom of Vancouver, British Columbia, learned otherwise when the lush patch of nature she planted on the balcony turned out to be altogether too natural.

"The damn pigeons—I used to like them, believe it or not," Anne says. She and her husband, Tevye, returned from a winter in Hawaii to find a pigeon's nest on the balcony. Tevye, being a bird lover, thought it would be interesting to watch the eggs hatch.

"Well, the eggs hatched," says Anne. "We watched the baby birds grow—the droppings all over the carpet grew as well—and finally they were able to fly off. But the pigeons decided the patio was their home, and no matter what we did we couldn't get rid of them."

Anne phoned the university and followed its suggestions (windmills, sticky solutions on the railing, etc.), but still the pigeons stayed.

"Finally we got a dummy crow and tied streamers to it. That seemed to do the trick, and they never came back," says Anne.

Scarecrows

Have you ever seen an old-fashioned scarecrow flapping in the wind and thought you'd like to make one? Here are instructions from Leah Hochart of Keysville, Virginia.

Take a pair of old pants and fit a 6-foot post through one leg, leaving the other leg loose. Pound the post into the ground. Nail or wire a stick to the post, making a cross. Now put a shirt on the cross-piece, so that its sleeves are longer than the stick. (The arms, like the floppy empty leg, will flap in the wind.) Tie at the waist.

For the head take a plastic gallon jug such as a bleach bottle. Draw a face with nail polish or marking pens. Enlarge the opening to fit over your post, and add a hat.

The key to a good scarecrow is movement, Leah says.

✳

Sound, as well as movement, makes scarecrows more effective, so add noisemakers whenever possible, advises Bangor, Wisconsin, farmer Bill Hansen. "One of my favorites was of flexible, colored plastic tubing with metal wind-chimes," he recalls.

AUTHOR'S NOTE: *The conversation piece in our neighborhood is the department-store-mannequin scarecrow belonging to Lillian and Bob Soules. "She did the job okay until the birds wised up and even began to sit on her arms," says Lillian. She also caused further trouble for Lil, who quickly acquired a reputation for snootiness. Mistaking the mannequin for Lil, neighbors would wave as they drove by and never receive a greeting in return.*

✳

If you have faith in scarecrows, don't wait until the corn is ripe—erect one in the garden even before planting. Sometimes crows actually watch you plant and go after the seed corn immediately, Arizona resident Ruth Ann Davis observes.

When All Else Fails

You have to know how to swear, to really have some blistering words to prepare yourself for the invasion of the varmints. And it has to be loud to scare them away. It doesn't work, but it can make you feel better.

—DALE KENDRICK, ARTIST

CHAPTER FOURTEEN

Growing Great Fruits and Vegetables

If you plant too early or too deep, you're bound for trouble.
—BOB NEUHAUS

I used to dream that the life of a garden writer would be like dying and going to heaven. Caressed by summer breezes, I'd while away the mornings hoeing straight green rows, pausing now and then to pop a raspberry into my mouth or to gather sweet mild onions and tiny tender cucumbers for a fine Greek salad. Then I'd sit down and write about it and get famous and make lots of money.

Sadly, none of the above is true. Though it's fun to daydream, I never really expected the fame or money, but the garden part would sure be nice.

The reality is that, from the first chilly days when it was time to put the potatoes in until now when the corn is ripe, I've spent most of my waking hours pushing words around for this book and playing long–distance telephone tag with horticultural experts whose voice–mail codes are far more complicated than the fine points they explain about soil chemistry.

With the deadline for *Garden Smarts*'s second edition hanging over my head, I've had almost no time to devote to my garden. This was no problem with the first edition, because our vegetable plot then was only a stone's throw from our front door. No matter how pressed I was for time, I could always pluck a weed or kick a little dirt on the potatoes as I dashed by.

But recently we moved to a home enveloped in shade so inhibiting that I'd be able to grow nothing but old were it not for a gentleman down the road kindly sharing his huge sunny plot. Now, though, I have to load garden tools into a car, drive 1/2 mile, park in an empty lot, and cross a busy street—which, as LeeAnne Bulman astutely notes in this chapter's conclusion, makes all the difference.

In this chapter are suggestions for growing bumper crops of healthy, handsome fruits and vegetables, ideas ranging from the practical to the whimsical. And for all my whining about juggling competing demands, I've still managed to pick up a new piece of garden wisdom: If, while your back is turned, the finger-size baby cucumbers on your vines transmogrify into tough-skinned King Kong–size monsters, they needn't be doomed to the compost pile. With just a sprinkling of gold stars, feathers, sequins, frilly cocktail picks—and some neighborhood kids—those cucumbers can metamorphose into truly remarkable art objects.

Fruits

For the best crops of tree fruits such as apples and plums, Danny O'Deay of San Francisco, California, pinches off surplus fruit, leaving only two to each cluster. "Do this when the fruit are about the size of a pea," he advises.

❋

If you have apple scab, even on ornamental crab apple trees, be sure to dispose of all the leaves in the fall. Don't leave them on the ground (and don't add them to your compost), or eventually the disease will infect your eating apples, as well as other apple trees in the area, cautions Sheila Coombs of New Hope, Minnesota.

"This, however, will not replace a good spraying regimen using fungicides," Sheila counsels. "Contact your regional agricultural agent for pamphlets on disease controls."

Melons

When farmer David Ballhagen of New Hartford, Iowa, was a little boy, he and his grandpa used to produce especially sweet watermelon by poking a hole through the rind of the growing melon and dripping a jug of sugar water into the flesh. Nowadays David still grows incredible melons, though his grown-up technique is less exotic and less time-consuming (but not quite so much fun).

Plant the seed in soft, well-drained ground, mixing fertilizer such as cottonseed meal into the planting holes. (Avoid fertilizers high in nitrogen.) For abundant yields water daily. On unusually hot days water twice a day.

David watered his melons every day last season, and he says he had "tons" of watermelons.

AUTHOR'S NOTE: *Fertilizers high in nitrogen foster too much leafy growth and less fruit.*

✻

Cantaloupe and watermelon like a lightweight sandy loam enriched with cow manure. For a bumper crop Wisconsin melon growers Helen and Bill Halverson also add a little potash and phosphorus (but not nitrogen, which isn't helpful to profusely fruiting plants such as melons).

"Put about 1/4 of a cup of fertilizer on each side of the hill in a little trench. But be careful not to add too much, and keep the fertilizer four inches away from the tiny plant, so it won't burn. Cover up with an inch of soil, and let Mother Nature water it. As the roots spread out, they'll pick up the nutrients," the Halversons say.

Berries

For abundant strawberries it's best to be patient. The first year, advises David Ballhagen, simply pick off all their blossoms. This stimulates the plants to multiply.

❋

The secret to growing raspberries is to keep your soil in good shape with mulch, says octogenarian Nick Wekseth, a resident of Onalaska, Wisconsin, who used to sell 2,000 pints of raspberries a season.

For best results treat the raspberry plants to a good foliar feeding with one of the fertilizers suited to that purpose. Spray the leaves at night, just before it gets dark. "In the morning, it looks like a different plant!" Nick marvels.

❋

On the farm in Perthshire, Scotland, where Margaret McFarlane Gold-bloom grew up, her family raised one hundred tons of raspberries a season. Now Margaret grows luscious berries in Chevy Chase, Maryland. "The secret for growing big, juicy, beautiful raspberries is to throw on tons of farm manure," she says. "In the early spring, really feed them like crazy. They love the stuff."

Raspberries do best if you don't allow them to sprawl, advises Margaret. Put them in rows and stake them up. Tie each plant to wires strung between posts or along chicken wire. Each spring cut off the old canes that bore last year's fruit and tie up the young canes that grew during the previous season.

To ensure abundant crops of raspberries year after year, you should divide your plants almost yearly, Margaret advises. "Plants will bear fruit the second year. By the fourth year, your yield will shrink.

"At home in Scotland, raspberry plants last five years; in Maryland, after about three years you get a lousy crop. So try rotating rows for five years and see how it goes, depending on your location."

Here's how: The best time to divide raspberries is in early spring, when the buds are just beginning to show, before leaves appear. Like splitting a bulb, take new plants from the bottom of the existing plants, and make a new row parallel to existing ones. By the third year, for example, you'll have three rows of differing ages. Henceforth after three to five years (depending on your cycle), pull up the oldest, least productive row, replanting its young "babies."

If space is short, transplant new raspberry plants into a little "nursery corner" next to your compost heap, and the next year move them to the rows, Margaret adds.

Green Wisdom

"Peppers are very sensitive to cold. Wait until it's good and warm to transplant them into your garden," advises retired agriculture instructor Jim Ness of Onalaska, Wisconsin. "Many people set them out in May, and then right when they're in the blossom-setting stage, you can get cold nights. If that happens the plants won't produce any peppers."

✻

Have you ever experienced the frustration of growing beautiful, lush, abundant pepper plants that suddenly drop their blooms? That can be caused by too much nitrogen, cautions gardener Wendal Mitchell, of Corbin, Kentucky. So when you fertilize peppers, don't overdo it.

✻

If you wait until the ground warms up, it's hard to have much luck growing spinach. As soon as the weather gets hot, spinach starts to bolt and gets bitter, notes attorney Gretchen Vetzner of Madison, Wisconsin. But Gretchen has a tip for beating the heat:

"Prepare the seed bed in the fall and put down the spinach seed in September. If it's warm enough, you get a few very small pickings in October and November. It's the tenderest spinach of all. When the cold weather comes, cover the bed with a mulch and let the spinach stay in the soil all winter. I think it's tenderer than spring-planted spinach and you miss a lot of bugs. And mine is bigger than it would normally be. In the spring, as soon as there are a couple of inches of unfrozen soil, plant some more."

✻

"My mother raised a lot of endive," says Raymond Rice of Kutztown, Pennsylvania. "When the plants were 6 to 8 inches across, she tied the outer leaves up over the center leaves with strips of cloth to make the center leaves blanch. It always tasted better after the first frost was on it. We would cover it any night a frost was predicted and uncover it again in the morning."

"You'll enjoy delicious, mild broccoli late in the season if you sow broccoli seeds directly into the garden in July. Plant thickly in a short row, then transplant the strong ones. You'll be picking even after frost, and they'll be sweet and tender," says Elinor Johnston.

Cauliflower

During World War II, when the federal government launched the Women's Land Army to sustain America's family farms while the men were off to war, Marianne Williams, a city girl from Staten Island, New York, enlisted (and earned $40 a month for her work).

During her training Marianne learned this tip for growing attractive, white cauliflower heads: Wrap each cauliflower in its own outer leaves. While the leaves are still growing, lap them over one another, holding them in place with a wooden skewer.

✻

Shortage of water causes the cauliflower's curd to bolt and ruins it, cautions master gardener Kenneth Hall of Fort Collins, Colorado. "As soon as the curd is about the size of a Ping-Pong ball, cover with the plant's wrapper leaves. Check every few days and when it's ready to harvest do so immediately," he advises.

AUTHOR'S NOTE: *Slip a leg from a pair of old pantyhose over cauliflower when it starts to form a head. It holds the leaves snugly and stretches as the head grows. This prevents sunburn and keeps bugs from laying eggs on it.*

Corn

"My late husband Albert was a Potawatomi Indian, not a Sioux. But when we lived on the Sioux's Pine Ridge Reservation (where I taught school and he was a principal), he planted corn their way because it was so easy," says Iona Wabaunsee of North Bend, Washington. Here's how:

"Before you plant, prepare the soil well for the roots, tilling a good 6 inches deep. Plant the corn in hills, not rows. Make little mounds about 2 inches high, two hands' breadth wide, and about a man's stride apart. Plant three grains of corn to a hill. If all three come up, thin to two because the soil can only support two. Don't plant too deep, only an inch or so. Cover the corn up loosely so it can push up. Although my husband planted our garden, on the reservation usually an old woman made the hole with a hoe and a younger woman or a boy put the corn in the hole and covered it up."

AUTHOR'S NOTE: *When planting corn, space it 6 to 8 inches inches apart on the outer rows but farther apart on the inside rows to give the plants more sun.*

*

"For getting a head start with sweet corn, I discovered you can plant two weeks before the last frost date by covering the rows of newly planted seeds with one-and-a-half mil clear plastic," says James M. Szynal of Florence, Massachusetts. "The plastic holds heat in the ground and protects the seedlings from frost."

When he sees the corn starting to come up, James, an inventor, uses a machine he's devised to burn a small round hole in the plastic so that the plant can emerge. Home gardeners with smaller crops can simply punch holes in the plastic manually, suggests James.

Potatoes

Even garden soil that's perfectly balanced for most crops may not be acidic enough for potatoes. If the soil pH is too high, especially if the spring is cold and wet, newly planted potatoes are vulnerable to fungus before they can sprout. And if they do grow, they're apt to develop rough, warty-looking skin.

You can prevent such problems by lowering the pH with sulphur, counsels Kentucky educator Wendal Mitchell. "Just before planting, shake your cut-up seed potatoes in a paper bag with a little sulphur, the way you'd bread pieces of chicken or fish with cracker crumbs for frying," he says. "You don't need much—one pound of sulphur is enough to last the average gardener 20 years."

✳

When you cultivate potatoes, pile on dirt or straw or the like. "The more you cover potatoes, the bigger and better they grow," observes Bill Bricker of Augusta, Georgia.

✳

"When I'm ready to plant potatoes, I take plugs about the size of a melon ball from the old, sprouting potatoes in my root cellar and break off and discard the sprouts," says Hilda First of Edgewood, Maryland, who has been farming for forty-four years, ever since she was a sixteen-year-old bride.

✳

It's best to plant potatoes when the sprouts are just coming out, no more than 1/2-inch long. "If longer, discard the sprout; the eye will grow a new one," advises Bob Neuhaus of Onalaska, Wisconsin, who grew potatoes commercially for many years. "Cut your seed potatoes so that each piece has one or two eyes. Leave the cut pieces a day or so to dry before planting," he says.

"For best results, plant potatoes cut side down. This permits the plant to grow right up without curling, and you'll have straighter, healthier plants. And always put two cut potato pieces in each hill. The principle is the same as with corn: the ground can support two, and if only one comes up (which very seldom happens) you will still have even rows. Once you've planted, tamp down the soil."

✳

Biologist Carl Korschgen has good luck, however, using longer sprouts. "We always grow potatoes and store them in five–gallon buckets in a dark basement," says Carl. "But normally they don't all get eaten before they sprout. By spring, we have some with 12– to 15-inch sprouts. We take those potatoes and lay them in the garden with the sprout horizontal. After covering the whole row with ½ inch to 1 inch of dirt, we mulch with 8 inches of hay. The potatoes will grow through that, and you get early potatoes.

"Letting the sprouts grow in the winter like that really gives us a boost. We plant around the second week of April, and by the first of July they're ready. All you have to do is lift off the hay. You can actually pick and not disturb the plants. They'll continue to produce; you pick them like you would tomatoes."

✳

Rancher R. J. Bootzin tells how he grew "dirtless, digless, weedless" red potatoes in Jemez, New Mexico: "I had about a quarter–acre I put in with spuds and wanted to try an easier method to grow them, since it was such a large patch."

So Bootzin cultivated the quarter–acre with a rototiller, set the seed on top of the moistened soil, covered the seed with old, rotten hay that his stock couldn't eat, and watered it heavily.

"It's easy to check the crop—just skin back the hay off a plant now and then and put the hay back after checking. There's no need to pull out the entire bush. I never have to weed this patch either. Each time a weed came up I just put a little more hay on it. The hay kept in the moisture, which saved watering. Each time I felt under the hay to see if the plants needed water, I was frequently surprised as to how moist the soil continued to be. Obviously, there was no digging: When the crop was ready I just raked back the hay, and there were the 'taters nice and clean. That fall I mulched the hay back into the soil, which made a great light composted bed for next spring's planting."

Sweet Potatoes

To get a good start with sweet potatoes, suggests Bee Whirley of Keysville, Virginia, put some tubers in water indoors. Soon you'll get rooted sprouts. When the ground is warm enough, break off the rooted sprouts and plant them in the garden (sweet potatoes grow best in sandy soil).

✳

"You can plant just about a whole garden from one good sweet potato," promises Ruth Switzer of Nehawka, Nebraska. "Look in the grocery store for a nice one. Take a quart jar with a big top so it will fit in there. Fill it with water and put the sweet potato in the jar, root end down. When shoots grow and get about 6 inches tall, pull them off and place them in another jar with water. They'll form roots on them.

"Sometimes you can get a dozen shoots at a time. As you take the bigger ones off, new ones will grow. I guess eventually you'll get thirty or more from one sweet potato. I'll do five sweet potatoes and give some to friends."

Onions

If you purchase onion sets in bulk, you may be tempted to pick out the biggest sets in the mistaken belief that they'll yield bigger onions. But the contrary is true: For the best onions pick out the smallest sets, not over ½ inch in diameter, advises Colorado master gardener Ken Hall.

✳

If you wish to plant a fall crop of green onions, you may have trouble finding onion sets for sale late in the season. So buy twice what you need in the spring and store the extras in the refrigerator in covered coffee cans until fall, suggests Wendal Mitchell of Corbin, Kentucky.

Don't plant sets that have already sprouted, Wendal adds. "A lot of times that sprout will die and the bulb will rot."

✹

When you cultivate onions, don't cover them up, as you should potatoes, advises Georgia gardener Bill Bricker. "Remove the dirt from the top as you cultivate, and the onions will be large and nice."

Carrots

Do you have trouble growing carrots successfully? If so, you're not alone.

"If you plant too early or too deep," warns octogenarian gardener Bob Neuhaus, a retired commercial grower, "you're bound for trouble. I never plant carrots till about the time you set out tomatoes. And most people put too much dirt on top," he adds. "Just put seeds in a little furrow and sprinkle dirt over them with your hand, no more than 1/4 inch deep. Otherwise, they won't come up."

After sowing seeds, always tamp the ground to get the air out; the seeds will do better, advises Bob. "Carrots are the one exception: tamp carrot seeds very lightly, or they may be pushed too deep into the soil."

✹

Carrot seeds take so long to germinate that it's easy to "lose" the row. Many a gardener has intended to pull up weeds and has inadvertently hoed out the newly emerged carrots as well. You can avoid this error if you do what Kenneth Hall of Fort Collins, Colorado, and Elinor Johnston of West Salem, Wisconsin, do: They sprinkle some radish seeds in with the carrots. "Radishes are quick-germinating. By the time the carrots are up and growing, the radishes will be on your dinner table, so you won't have to worry about them competing, Elinor says. "In fact, they'll help loosen the soil."

Kenneth Hall adds more counsel on this slowpoke vegetable: "Carrots must be kept moist while germinating," he advises.

More Buried Treasure

"Everybody raises radishes, but lots of folks don't know how to grow mild ones," insists octogenarian Bob Neuhaus, who sometimes raises as many as seven radish crops in one year. "Here's how to grow the mild-tasting radishes like the ones they serve in restaurant salad bars," says the former restaurant owner:

"As soon as you put radish seed in the ground, water it immediately. The next morning, water again. They'll sprout right away. In three days' time, you can see the rows, about twice as soon as normally. Radishes that are quick-started this way won't taste as strong as ones that get moisture naturally from the ground and sprout more slowly," Bob counsels.

✳

The hardest vegetable to grow, believes Nebraska gardener Ruth Switzer, is parsnips. "They're so temperamental in sprouting. They take even longer than carrots to sprout. And from a whole seed package, you're lucky if you get a half dozen plants. The rule for parsnips is: space far enough apart—not too thick. Don't plant too deep, and keep them moist."

✳

"Peanuts need sandy soil. If your soil is too heavy, as ours is, it may not be worth your time to try. We had a bad experience attempting to grow them," confide Lil and Bob Soules of Onalaska, Wisconsin. "The tops of the plants grew beautifully, but the peanuts underground came out the size of lima beans."

Vine Crops

"Every bean has a little spot on its hollow side," notes Rosemary Muramoto of Seattle, Washington. "That's where the roots come out. If you plant the bean upside down, it sprouts upside down and smothers and rots. So be sure that spot is turned down."

Here's how Rosemary recommends planting pole beans:

"Make little bean hills of mounded dirt about 2 inches high and as big as a large hand span; put a 5-to-6-foot pole in the center. "Plant about ten beans in a circle and expect about six to germinate. If one looks weak, pull it out; otherwise there's no need to thin."

✳

"If you're growing pumpkins and want them to be especially big for jack-o'-lanterns, leave only one or two pumpkins on each plant and snap off all the other blossoms when they start to form," advises Mary Gehling of Walla Walla, Washington.

✳

"When I plant my cukes and squash, I put a lot of compost in the ground. Then instead of laying the seeds flat, I lay them on end, point up," says Ed Wojahn of Onalaska, Wisconsin. "When the shell breaks open, they can pop straight up. The plant doesn't have to fight the dirt and comes faster."

✳

Do not allow soil to dry out while cucumbers are fruiting, warns Colorado gardener Kenneth Hall. "This will cause stunted growth on the end of fruit. And pick the cukes frequently; if allowed to mature, plants stop producing and your yield will be reduced."

(Other crops requiring lots of water and moist soil, Kenneth adds, include squash and peppers.)

A Matter of Gravity

Cucumbers twining along the garden fence are a beautiful sight, holds Louis Ferris of La Crosse, Wisconsin. The fence puts them out of reach of rabbits and makes them easier to pick. "Gravity must affect their development," Louis says, "because when cukes grow hanging down, they grow long and straight with none of their typical curl."

Gravity was also a consideration for the enterprising gardener in Laramie, Wyoming, who supported his cantaloupes by stapling his amply endowed wife's bras to the fence.

Designer Pumpkins

You don't have to be a yuppie to have designer vegetables. Personalized pumpkins make truly special gifts for friends. Children will be thrilled with these, says Jeanette Manske, a gardener in Stoddard, Wisconsin.

When the pumpkins have ripened to a light yellow (but before they've hardened), "monogram" them by scratching a name into the skin with a nail. "Don't scratch too deeply or the pumpkins will rot," Jeanette says.

"Magic" Pickles

Most of us have seen ships in bottles, but have you ever seen a cucumber in a bottle? For two generations Jeanette Manske has been astonishing kids, grandkids, and friends with her "pickle in the bottle" gardening trick. You can try it too.

When your cucumbers are just starting to develop, take a small bottle with an opening about the size of a dime (a small Coca-Cola bottle will do). Gently poke a tiny cucumber (still attached to its vine) into the bottle. Lay the bottle on its side and tuck it under some cucumber leaves so it won't cook from too much heat.

"Don't expect them all to grow," warns Jeanette. "You'll know within a day or two if it's going to make it, and then you can try again. The cuke will grow to fill the bottle, and you'll have everybody wondering."

What Makes a Good Garden?

The closer your garden is to your house and a window that you look out of often, the more likely you are to weed and nurture it.

—LEEANNE BULMAN, WRITER

CHAPTER FIFTEEN

The Taste of Summer: Mouthwatering Tomatoes

When green, [tiny yellow pear tomatoes] . . . make good weapons for kids. They'll leave nice pea-sized welts on siblings' foreheads.

—SHIRLEY SAULS

I s a tomato a fruit or a vegetable? Common sense tells us it's a vegetable—after all, we'd never toss tomatoes with grapes and peaches or slice them over chocolate fudge sundaes. But whenever we refer to them as vegetables, some smarty-pants is bound to argue because, botanically, tomatoes are berries.

In everyday language we say *vegetable* when we are talking about non-sweet edible plants and use the word *fruit* for sweet ones, irrespective of botany. Technically, though, the seed-containing fleshy portions of any plant are considered fruit, even eggplants and hot chili peppers. But ever since Spanish explorers brought the tiny, tart Indian *tomatl* from the New World and no one was sure what to do with it, the controversy has lingered.

Tomato sauce soon became a hit in the Spanish court, but it was 300 years before tomatoes gained wide acceptance throughout Europe and Colonial North America. Although the French believed that tomatoes were aphrodisiacs and called them "Love Apples," most gardeners grew them only for ornament, and belief that this scarlet fruit was deadly earned it the nickname "Wolf Peach."

Finally, in 1830 Robert Gibbon Johnson, an ardent tomato fan with a flair for showmanship, debunked this myth by eating an entire basket of tomatoes before a crowd of 2,000 onlookers in Salem, New Jersey. All the while the firemen's band played dirges and his physician stood by, predicting he would foam at the mouth, be stricken with appendicitis, and risk brain fever.

Once rid of their dread reputation, tomatoes quickly became the most popular crop in the home vegetable garden. They're versatile, delicious, extremely nutritious (an excellent source of vitamins A and C), and easy to raise. They grow so rapidly, in fact, that sometimes it seems as if they're burgeoning forth before our very eyes.

If you yearn for the perfect tomato, this chapter offers suggestions for delicious varieties. Whether or not you've grown tomatoes before, you'll welcome the advice for climate protection. Most folks—even experienced gardeners who know better—get impatient and put tomatoes in too early, but it's best to resist gambling with the weather. Although tomatoes tend to be vigorous and prolific once they get a good start, they need warmth to thrive, and they freeze easily.

This chapter's practical and whimsical planting tips, recommendations for plant care, and innovative alternatives to tomato staking will be sure to interest you.

Since the first edition of *Garden Smarts* came out, I've been delighted to hear from readers reporting excellent results from its various tips. If I hadn't seen them with my own eyes, I would have been hard-pressed to believe the near-miraculous results that one reader achieved by combining three tips from the original tomato chapter with three more of his own which you'll find herein. While other tomato plants for miles around were still knee-high and scarcely flowering, his, laden with tiny green tomatoes, towered overhead like trees. I hope you'll agree that success stories like this do more than help us to grow bigger, better tomatoes. They also serve to remind us that we're privileged to be part of an awesome network of knowledge and experience that links gardener to gardener across distance and time.

Finding the Top Tomato

Many of today's tomato hybrids are genetically manipulated for uniform color, thick skins, and uniform shape. Intended for market, they ship and store well. If you long for the joys of fresh vine-picked tomatoes, choose varieties that are bred for flavor, says Renee Shepherd of Shepherd's Garden Seeds in Felton, California.

"Three French tomatoes bred especially for flavor as well as disease resistance are Carmello, Dona, and the very early, yellow tomato, Chello. These are meant for the home or local market," adds Renee. "They taste best when picked fully ripe, and they aren't shippable."

❋

AUTHOR'S NOTE: *Don't bother to save seeds from hybrid varieties. The offspring of hybrids often inherit less desirable traits from prehybrid ancestors. Hybrid seeds may even be sterile.*

Tomatoes need a lot of sunshine to thrive and develop peak flavor. If your climate isn't sunny enough and you've been disappointed with your tomatoes, try Fog tomatoes, suggests California gardener Elizabeth Pomada. "Here in San Francisco, this is a really popular variety because it does well despite our foggy weather," Elizabeth says.

❋

Many gardeners like the tiny yellow pear tomatoes because they're easy to grow and look pretty in pots. But moms and dads should be forewarned that they also possess other characteristics. As Atlanta, Georgia, native Shirley Sauls notes, "When green, these make good weapons for kids. They'll leave nice pea-sized welts on siblings' foreheads."

Last summer Shirley nearly lost her whole crop to a violent hailstorm. "I would have stood over them with an umbrella, only there was lightning, so I couldn't. Within three or four minutes, hailstones and yellow tomatoes were all over my deck. They were mostly still green. I was trying to eat the ripe ones, while the kids were zinging each other on the heads. It was all over in a few minutes, like an earthquake."

✳

"Sweet 100 cherry tomatoes are unbelievably prolific growers," says Mary Gehling of Walla Walla, Washington. "They produce hundreds and hundreds per plant. If you like a really sweet cherry tomato, they're just like candy."

Climate Protection

Master gardener Kenneth Hall of Fort Collins, Colorado, faces formidable short season challenges. "When that sun goes down in the evening it's as if somebody opened the refrigerator door. In a single day 50 degree temperature swings are not uncommon," he says. Here's his strategy for harnessing and holding heat, which should be effective for other warmth-loving crops as well:

Lay wide black plastic down the row to absorb the heat during the day and warm the soil. Cut holes for the plant by making 4-inch-long X's in the plastic. Dig planting holes, add fertilizer, plant, and protect against cutworm.

"Because of our weather, tomatoes can be sporadic as far as successful growth and harvest," says southern Oregon gardener Tony Holt.

"I buy starts from a local nursery and transplant them to 6- to 8-inch pots in mid-April. I pinch the lower leaves off and bury as much of the stem as possible to stimulate vigorous root growth. I keep these in the cold frame, generally transplanting to the open garden in late May."

✳

The common way to plant tomatoes is to bury the roots and leave the stem aboveground. But Amish farmer Joe Borntreger has a better way.

"When we plant tomatoes, we lay the plant in a shallow trench in the soil, with the buried leaves trimmed and just the top 3 or 4 inches of the plant exposed," says the Missouri native. "With the bigger root system that develops through trenching the tomatoes, the plant won't fall over as easily."

✱

If the spring weather in your area tends to be cool, another benefit of planting tomatoes in a relatively horizontal trench instead of planting them upright is to stay above the deeper, cooler soil, notes nurseryman John Zoerb, president of La Crosse Floral in La Crosse, Wisconsin. Tomatoes need warm soil as well as warm air to get a good start. If the temperature of the soil is below fifty–five degrees Fahrenheit, the leaves yellow.

If your summers get very hot, however, your tomatoes will do better if the roots are deep enough to stay relatively cool. To cope with the challenge of a cool spring and hot summers, plant shallow for early soil warmth and, as the temperatures rise, create shade with mulches.

✱

A late spring frost won't kill tomato plants if you rig up temporary mini–hothouses from 6–inch mesh concrete construction wire. New Jersey native Stan Schabert offers these instructions:

For each plant make a wire cylinder about 3 feet in diameter and 5 feet tall. Wrap with translucent four–mil plastic (which lets sunlight pass through but is cheaper than clear plastic) and seal with duct tape.

If you expect a severe frost, cover the top of each cylinder with garbage can lids or leftover plastic; otherwise, leave open. The plants are less likely to freeze if they don't come in direct contact with the plastic, so you might have to prop the plastic with stakes to leave an air pocket.

Remove the plastic after a few weeks when the tomato plants are larger; if the temperature warms quickly, remove the plastic sooner. Crowding, humidity, heat, and poor air circulation will attract white flies, so watch the plants carefully. Leave the cages in place after the plastic comes off; the branches grow through the mesh and you don't need to tie them up.

Planting

Don't go overboard when planting tomatoes. While it is useful and important to keep a few extra plants in reserve "for insurance," three or four tomato plants will supply more than enough fruit for four to six people, counsels Renee Shepherd of Felton, California.

✳

"For lack of garden space when we lived in the city, we planted Big Boy tomatoes in bushel baskets along the driveway," recall Lil and Bob Soules of Onalaska, Wisconsin. "We kept them well watered, and they yielded a very good crop, producing until frost came."

✳

"Mary Claire's Folly" isn't only a creative space saver; it's a good conversation piece. Mary Claire Fehring punches a hole in the bottom of a pail, then plants a cherry tomato plant upside down so that the plant's stem dangles through the hole. This makes an attractive hanging basket for the porch, and is also handy for reaching a quick handful of tomatoes without going out to the garden, says the Rockford, Iowa, native.

Care

When his tomato plants are about 12 inches high, drywall contractor Cornelius McFarland, Jr., of Corbin, Kentucky, mulches them with Sheetrock scraps (available free from drywall contractors). This reflects sunlight onto the fruit, yet protects the roots from intense heat. It also gives you a clean surface to walk on after a rain. "While others mire up knee deep, we can get right out there and work," says Cornelius.

Push tomato cage prongs right through the Sheetrock, leaving 3 to 4 inches of exposed earth around the stem for watering. After the growing season, plough the scraps under, and they'll add lime to your soil.

✳

With many plants, such as chrysanthemums, it's best to keep pinching off the center growth to encourage the plant to branch out and become bushier. "With tomatoes, do the opposite," advises Rosemary Muramoto of Seattle, Washington.

"Keep only three or so lateral shoots off the main branch. Pinch off all the others as soon as they start to develop, so that the main stem grows tall," says Rosemary. "If you leave the plant with fewer branches, you'll have larger fruit."

✳

"Never water your tomatoes on a hot day in full sunlight," warns longtime Illinois gardener Dona Popovic. "Tomatoes will crack and the blossoms will fall off if you do. Always see that your garden has a chance to dry before the sun goes down. I usually hold my hose down close to the base of each plant when watering by hand," Dona says.

✳

If you have the space, protect tomatoes by encircling each tomato plant with an old tire. The black rubber holds heat and radiates it back to the plant, advises Oregon State University's Extension Service master gardener Joseph Moos of Grants Pass, Oregon.

AUTHOR'S NOTE: *Be sure to mound enough dirt inside so that water can't collect in the tire and attract breeding mosquitoes.*

✳

Extremes of wet and dry can cause the soft dark spots on fruit known as "blossom end rot," cautions Renee Shepherd of Shepherd's Garden Seeds in Felton, California. She recommends that you keep your soil evenly moist. Mulching when the plants are 8 to 10 inches tall is also a good strategy.

✳

Mulching with grass clippings around tomatoes to a depth of 3 inches will prevent or retard tomato blight fungus, advises fish pathologist Fred Meyer, retired director of the National Fisheries Research Laboratory and a gardener in La Crescent, Minnesota.

*

This technique from orthodontist Herm Silver of White Plains, New York, discourages slugs, grubs, and other insects from devouring your tomato plants. It also confines water and other nutrients to each individual plant.

"Cut the bottom from the pots so the roots can grow, but leave the sides intact so that you have a bottomless cylinder. Plant the pots in weed-free, well-turned fertile soil. Water each plant at this step.

"Then surround each plant with a cylindrical cage made from wire fencing approximately 5 feet tall. This keeps the plants upright as they grow, resulting in cleaner fruit and helping protect them from animals and insects."

Stake, Cage, or Sprawl?

"I always cage my tomatoes to keep the fruit off the ground. They don't rot or get dirt spots, and they stay nice and firm and red," says Wisconsin gardener Ed Wojahn. "I used to use wooden stakes and tie them. Then I switched to cages, and like them much better."

*

Tomato cages can be much cheaper, stronger, taller, and more convenient than the store-bought kind if you make them the way retired veterinarian Ken Johnston does. He suggests that you buy rolls of 5-foot cement reinforcing wire. Cut the wire to make cages 2- to 2½-feet in diameter. So that they'll nest inside one another for storage, make three sizes: ten, twelve, and fourteen spaces wide (the mesh is about 4 by 6 inches).

Cut off the bottom horizontal wire, leaving vertical strands exposed; poke them into the ground to anchor the cage. Slightly overlap one lengthwise edge around the other, and twist a few loose strands to secure the cylinder.

When erecting these in the garden, stick a 1-by-2 stake into the ground alongside each cage to hold it against the wind. As the plant grows, you can easily reach through the mesh openings to tend it.

*

When he read the first edition of *Garden Smarts*, Wendal Mitchell, a retired school principal in Corbin, Kentucky, was inspired by Ken Johnston's prior homemade cylinder tip, Stan Shabert's protective blankets idea (page 209), and Peter Tonge's Wall O'Water suggestion page 152) So he combined all three, plus a few strategies of his own. The result? Incredibly early, giant, profuse tomatoes! Here's how:

- For each planting hole dig the earth knee-deep to loosen, and mix it with aged manure.

- Plant your tomatoes about six weeks earlier than usual, and surround them by tomato cages. Because the wire's protruding prongs are stiff to bend and painful if they poke you, Wendal secures the cylinders with twine, instead. "Then in the fall, you can cut the string and open the cages flat for convenient storage," he says.

- Until the weather warms up, keep your plants twice as warm with both the water-filled tepee and a plastic covering over the cylinder.

- To encourage the plants to grow straight, cut sticks (such as bamboo cane) a few inches longer than the cage diameter. Crisscross a couple of these horizontally through the mesh wherever the stem needs support. As the plant grows, move the sticks or add more as needed.

✳

If storage is a problem for you, you may prefer master gardener Kenneth Hall's method of growing tomato plants supported by wire rather than tomato cages. Here's how the Fort Collins, Colorado, resident does it:

When your plants are 1 foot high, drive a 6-foot 2-by-4 sharpened at the bottom end, into the ground every 7 to 8 feet.

Staple smooth wire (such as electric fence wire) down the row and up the other side 9 inches above ground, so that it supports the main stem within the 4-inch space. Add wires about every 9 inches as your plants grow, going up four to five strands, as needed.

At the end of your growing season, take off the wire. Roll it back on the spool, and stack the 2-by-4's until next year. "You can reuse them almost forever," says Kenneth.

✳

If you'd like your tomatoes to be especially abundant and beautiful, try this tip from longtime Wisconsin market gardener Nick Wekseth. He raised 735 tomato plants from seed and averaged seventy-five tomatoes per plant with his method.

Plant the tomato plants about 3 feet apart, or a little farther than you normally do. When they are about 1 foot high, pile straw almost level with the plant, so you can barely see the tops. Don't worry about smothering the plants—the straw soon settles. There's no need to stake up the plants or use trellises or cages; the limbs lay on the straw as they grow, and the tomatoes are clean when you want to pick them.

"I got big money for my tomatoes because they looked so nice. Also, there are no weeds, and the straw holds the moisture," Nick says.

AUTHOR'S NOTE: *You may have the best luck with Nick's tip in a dry climate. I tried it during an exceptionally rainy summer, and to my dismay, the straw rotted.*

❋

If staking tomato plants seems like a lot of fuss to you, don't bother. "They'll be stronger if left unfettered," counsels Judith McCaslin, former Cornell University Extension specialist for agriculture education.

"Simply lay an old wooden extension ladder horizontally in the garden and use blocks to prop it about a foot above the ground. Plant the tomatoes between the rungs. They'll grow through them and sprawl along the ladder. This elevates the plants just enough to protect developing fruit from contact with the ground, which could cause tomatoes to rot," says Judith.

Gardens Grow Gardeners Too

You never tell a gardener something can't be done. For every rule of gardening there are 25 exceptions.

—FRED WICHE, FARM DIRECTOR, WHAS-TV (LOUISVILLE, KENTUCKY)

CHAPTER SIXTEEN

Herbs and Everlastings

If you give herbs too much love and kindness . . . they don't do well!
—DEBORAH WHITEHOUSE

erbs have a certain mystique that makes many gardeners leery of growing them. Most of us have grown up in a meat–and–potatoes culture where salt, pepper, and ketchup were the basic seasonings. For some of us the most exotic seasoning in our kitchen was soy sauce or paprika. Yet early in the New World's history, every kitchen garden had an herb plot, whose fragrant plants were used to flavor soups, cure headaches, and rid the house of ants. For the most part we have lost touch with the herbal arts, reaching instead for the supermarket shelf to supply our culinary, medicinal, and household needs.

The recent influx of immigrants from Latin and Asian countries, however, has reminded us how delicious herb–seasoned food can be, and the growth of the environmental movement has made us far more interested in turning back to natural, homegrown products. We are discovering that our own gardens can supply a wonderful cornucopia of plants that meet more of our needs than most people realize.

At last we're discovering that herb culture isn't really more complicated than growing petunias or potatoes; indeed, with just a little knowledge, it can be simple, successful, and immensely satisfying. As more home gardeners venture into herbs, local nurseries and mail-order seed houses are taking notice, so that now, even in small towns, you can find a wide variety of culinary, medicinal, and decorative herbs.

This chapter offers advice from experienced home growers as well as from some of the leading Canadian and American herb experts on smart shopping, best picks, successful growing, and propagating, harvesting, preparing, and enjoying your herbs and everlastings.

Recipe for a Greener Thumb

A plant without a scent is like a beautiful person who has no personality—nice to meet at first but not someone you'd want to spend a lot of time with.

—TERRI CLARK, VANCOUVER, BRITISH COLUMBIA

What to Plant: The Right Stuff

"When buying garden herbs, don't rely on the label," cautions Conrad Richter, vice-president of the renowned Goodwood, Ontario, herb mail-order house Richters. Many herb plants and seeds on the market are inferior varieties, Conrad cautions. For example, suppliers often sell oregano seeds and plants of a wild type that has no flavor, instead of a variety such as Greek oregano, which has a wonderful flavor. By the same token, Russian tarragon is common because it's cheap and easy to grow commercially, though unlike the superior French tarragon, it has no flavor or scent. "So take a sprig and squeeze it and smell it and taste it," he advises.

✳

Herb plants grown from quality seed will be more vigorous than those transplanted from mass-produced six-packs or pots, and you'll have the advantage of growing choice strains, advises Renee Shepherd of Shepherd's Garden Seeds in Felton, California.

Best Bets

Which herbs are especially easy to grow and practical? Better Homes & Gardens Special Interest Publications garden editor Kate Carter Frederick recommends these thirteen for a good basic repertoire:

Basil	Rosemary
Cilantro	Sage
Dill	Savory
Fennel	Tarragon
Garlic	Thyme
Greek oregano	
Parsley, curly leaf or Italian flat leaf	

✳

For an herb that does double duty, plant coriander (*Coriandrum sativum*), suggests Renee Shepherd of Shepherd's Garden Seeds mail-order house.

Coriander seed is a popular, traditional spice in curries and cookies, but many people don't realize that the bright green cilantro essential to many Mexican and Asian dishes is coriander leaf. All cilantro grows quickly from leaf to seed, so succession-sow every few weeks for a continuous supply. It will be most abundant in cool conditions, notes Renee.

✳

For a fun plant to grow, try licorice mint (*Anise hyssop*), suggests Terry Kemp of God's Green Acres Herbary & Gifts in Onalaska, Wisconsin. "It makes a really nice tea; you can add it to fruit salad and even use it as a breath freshener. It's good in anything that calls for a licorice/anise type of flavor."

This hardy perennial is easy to grow, but Terry cautions it's best to confine it somewhat because it propagates by dropping seeds, and one plant will produce hundreds.

✳

Purslane (*Portulaca oleracea*) is a spongy low–growing succulent that is notorious as a weed. "I bet there isn't a garden that doesn't have it," notes Syracuse, New York, native Lee Rodman. "If it comes up where I want it to be, I just weed around it, and I let some go to seed for the next year." Raw purslane leaves have a pleasant, slightly tart flavor and add an interesting texture to salad. In Greek cuisine purslane is also used in vegetable soups, notes Lee.

> **AUTHOR'S NOTE:** *Ironically, the much–scorned purslane has turned out to be somewhat of a miracle food. Lipid biochemist Norman Salem, Jr., of the National Institute on Alcohol Abuse and Alcoholism has found that purslane, of all the leafy greens, is the richest known source of the cholesterol–reducing omega–3 fatty acid.*

In a letter appearing in the *New England Journal of Medicine* (November 16, 1989), Salem and collaborator Artemis P. Simopoulos of the American Association for World Health reported that purslane–eating hens produce eggs with ten times the omega–3 fatty acid found in typical supermarket eggs.

The Right Environment

Most of our popular culinary herbs have Mediterranean ancestry and thrive when you replicate the conditions of their origins, notes Kate Carter Frederick, a master gardener and herb specialist in Des Moines, Iowa. Though ocean–sprayed, rocky, windswept land may be impossible to reproduce, at least aim for a sunny location with good drainage.

"Allow the soil to dry out between waterings," Kate advises. "Herbs don't like to sit with their feet wet." Kate scoffs at the myth that herbs thrive best in poor soil, however. "I think that's a fallacy. The more compost you put, the better they do."

✺

"If the summers are wet where you live, don't bother to grow statice," counsels commercial everlasting grower Ralph Cramer of Columbia, Pennsylvania. If you get rain the last two weeks before harvest, as Ralph sometimes does in his part of Pennsylvania, the statice turns brown. "Desert dwellers who have problems getting many varieties of everlastings to grow should have good luck with statice," Ralph Cramer says.

✺

"Even if you live in a colder climate, don't be afraid to grow some of the tender or semi-hardy herbs, such as basil, rosemary and some of the sages," counsels Deborah Whitehouse, director of Niagara Parks Botanical Gardens & School of Horticulture in Niagara Falls, Ontario. In the fall, bring the plant indoors. If it's too large, you can separate a section that is already rooted to enjoy on your windowsill over the winter.

✺

Raising herbs successfully in a hot, dry climate can be frustrating, however, says Kathy Leslie of Thousand Oaks, California. The answer is to select xerophilous (drought-tolerant) plants. The following varieties will restore your confidence.

For culinary use try chives. They do well in a dry climate, as does gray sage. Rosemary, especially the upright Santa Barbara variety, never needs water after the cuttings are well established, and it can go months without rain.

For fragrance, plant scented geraniums, English lavender, and lavender cotton (*Santolina chamaecyparissus*).

✻

"Most people have a hard time growing rosemary in the house during the winter," says herb grower Terry Kemp of Onalaska, Wisconsin. "I put mine right by my heater and it's just thriving. The heater dries out the plant quickly, though, so I water twice a week."

✻

If you raise dill, you'll sometimes find it's reseeded itself. Then simply transplant it where you wish, advises Mary Jane Randolph of La Crosse, Wisconsin.

Too Much of a Good Thing

"Some mints can be invasive," warns Ontario horticulturist Deborah Whitehouse. To prevent them from spreading out of control, plant in an upright cylinder such as a tile sewer pipe or a coffee can with the bottom cut out of it.

Starting Everlasting Flowers Successfully

Crested celosia is easy to start from seed, counsels Ralph Cramer, a well-known authority on everlastings and the proprietor of Cramer's Posie Patch in Columbia, Pennsylvania.

Sprinkle the seed on a prepared bed. The seeds are very fine, so be careful not to spread them too thickly. Drag an upside-down lawn rake gently over the bed to cover it lightly. "I cover the beds with garden matting such as Reemay, but you could use old, sheer muslin curtains; this lets rain and light pass through, but gives wind protection," says Ralph.

After about a month remove the cover. Thin if needed. When the plants are 3 to 4 inches tall, they're ready to transplant (if they are not already in their permanent bed). Wet the soil to soften it, and gently pull the plants with your fingers.

✻

"For the beginner, globe amaranth is one of the hardest things to germinate. It can drive people nuts," says Ralph. He grows six acres of this beautiful everlasting, selling it nationwide. If your soil is too cold to get good germination outdoors early, try this:

Spread the seeds on top of moist soil or planting medium in flats. Very gently tamp the seeds with your hand, being careful not to bury them. Mist with water. To hold in moisture, lay a piece of black plastic over each flat, tucking it under the bottom for a snug fit. Stack the flats on shelves with air space between each flat. For example, if the flats are 12 inches wide, you can space two about 11 inches apart and set a third flat over the space.

Use a small electric space heater with the thermostat set to hold the temperature between ninety and a hundred degrees Fahrenheit. You can also use a heat lamp or even a hundred-watt light bulb; if the heat source has no thermostat, check frequently with a thermometer to be sure it doesn't get too hot. Wrap flats, heater, and all in black plastic, tucking the edges under to make what Ralph calls "a little sweat chamber." Be careful to keep the plastic far enough from the heat to avoid melting.

Between eighteen and thirty-six hours later, the plants will pop up, so start checking after eighteen hours. As soon as most of them have germinated, take the flats out of the dark to prevent the plants from getting long and stringy.

Once they're growing, take appropriate steps to prevent damping off, and water them as needed. But don't get them too wet; people commonly make the mistake of overwatering seedlings. When the first two true leaves develop, transplant the strongest plants into individual cells or pots until they're ready to go in the field.

Propagating Herbs

"To root thyme, never, never attempt to lift a fat wad and pull it into sections to replant. This rarely works," says one of America's leading herb authorities, Bertha Reppert, owner of Rosemary House herb and spice shop in Mechanicsburg, Pennsylvania.

"Small pieces, however, will almost always root readily in receptive soil, especially with the aid of rooting powder, sandy soil, and—most important— a rock. Press one end of the thyme cutting into the soil and anchor it with the rock. It marks the spot and serves as a firm mulch, retaining just enough of the soil moisture to sustain life. This will produce a lively, vigorous plant, one that will quickly produce another fat wad of thyme."

✳

For full, bushy basil plants, start pinching off the center growth of stems to stimulate new branches as soon as the seedling starts to form a strong plant, three to four weeks after planting. To keep the plant leafy and prevent it from going to seed (which basil easily does), continue pinching all summer. "Then, at the end of the season, let it go to seed, and next year you may not have to plant any," says floral designer and herb grower Terry Kemp, proprietor of God's Green Acres Herbary & Gifts in Onalaska, Wisconsin. "You can also save the pinchings of basil, mint, hyssop, and rosemary and root them in water or sand for new plants," Terry adds.

The Frugal Gourmet

People put too much fuss and work into preserving leftover seeds, insists Iowa garden editor Kate Carter Frederick. Kate saves her surplus seeds in a cool basement, all jumbled together in one jar.

"If I get 25 percent germination, that's still plenty," she holds. "I've used five-year-old basil seed, and it's just taken off like crazy!"

Nurturing Your Herbs

If you have time for only one task in the herb garden and you need to make a choice between weeding or clipping, Clip! Clip! Clip! "The more you clip, the more you get," says Bertha Reppert, author of *The Bride's Herbal*. "It makes me sad when people ask in September 'When can I harvest the plants I bought in the spring?' They have already missed several harvests, alas. For some reason, cutting herbs is intimidating to the new gardener.

"Woody plants should be clipped more judiciously than non-woody herbs such as mint, chives, and lemon balm, which can be cut sometimes every week. One quickly learns as one clips away. But don't deny yourself the bountiful harvest available all season long from these productive, useful plants," urges the herb expert in Mechanicsburg, Pennsylvania.

✳

Just as pinching off the tips of flowers makes the plants fuller, pinching off the growing tip of herbs stimulates branching too. "You're removing the place on the plant with highest concentration of growth hormone. The highest concentration remaining is at the leaf nodes, so you'll get new growth there," explains Goodwood, Ontario herb grower Conrad Richter.

That's also why the best place to cut a branch for propagating is right underneath a leaf node. "This is the same hormone, Auxin, that's sold as rooting powder," Conrad says.

✳

"If you give herbs too much love and kindness—overfertilizing, pinching, fussing, constant cultivation—they don't do well," insists Niagara Falls horticulturist Deborah Whitehouse. Just prepare the soil well with organic matter before planting, mulch, and keep plants watered, she advises. "I put mine in half a dozen years ago; I used rich loamy soil, and fertilized with manure, but haven't fertilized since."

✳

"For greater vigor, fragrance, and flavor for your herbs," counsels Bertha Reppert, "treat your plants indoors and out to an occasional dose of Epsom salts (magnesium sulfate). Mix two tablespoons of Epsom salts per gallon of water and treat your herbs to sturdier stems, increased growth, insect control, and intensified aroma."

AUTHOR'S NOTE: *Some sandy soils that are otherwise ideal for herb growing tend to be deficient in magnesium. In Chapter 4, soil scientist Professor Emmett Schulte explains how plant metabolism is affected by magnesium, an essential element for plants.*

Preserving Herbs and Everlastings: Drying, Freezing, and Storing

Drying herbs allows you to enjoy homegrown flavor long after the growing season is past. Rinse off sand from the harvested stems, and shake off excess water. Tie five or six stems together in bunches with old yarn or string, and hang upside down in a dry, dark place.

You can also dry herbs by hanging the tied bundles from a clothesline in the attic, says Mary Jane Randolph of La Crosse, Wisconsin. Depending upon the humidity, they take a month or two to dry. "The herbs feel crinkly when they're dry enough to store," Mary Jane says. "Drying sage makes the whole house smell clean—and it sure clears your sinuses."

If you want ground herbs, try this method from Mary Jane. Put two or three dried bundles at a time in a paper grocery sack. With a rolling pin or your hands, rub very hard. This will knock the leaves off the stems. Remove the stems from the bag and discard them.

Pour the leaves into a colander. You'll see many small stems still mixed with the leaves; remove as many as you can. If you have an electric coffee grinder, blender, or food processor, put in a small amount at a time. Give a whiz, and in a few seconds the dried herb is ground up. If you don't have a blender, push the dry leaves through the colander with your fingers or a wooden spoon, and catch them on a plate or paper towel placed underneath.

To store dried ground herbs, says Mary Jane, save interesting jam and mustard jars. They make nice gifts. "For Thanksgiving, I put sage in plastic sandwich bags and send them to relatives for seasoning their holiday fowl. This also makes a nice gift at Christmastime, or any holiday when your family or friends cook a turkey," Mary Jane says.

✴

AUTHOR'S NOTE: *Maybe Mary Jane's house smelled clean from drying herbs but that's not always the case: Be forewarned that basil gives off an unpleasantly pungent odor while it's drying. I kept trying to figure out where one of our tomcats had misbehaved until we discovered that the stench emanated from some basil left on top of the refrigerator to dry.*

✴

AUTHOR'S NOTE: *You can also dry herbs quickly in a microwave oven. Rinse, blot dry, and put between two microwave-safe paper towels. Microwave two to four minutes per cup of herbs on full power, turning every half-minute. Don't overcook or the herbs may scorch and the paper catch fire.*

✴

Dried mint is a welcome gift from the home garden, suggests gardener Richard Bunker of Salt Lake City, Utah. "You can get a good crop from just a few plants," he notes. "One year we dried it in the electric oven. It takes about a day or a day and a half. Don't turn the oven on—just leave the door ajar and the heat from the oven light bulb is enough to dry it."

✴

"I discovered a great way to dry thick-stemmed and succulent herbs, such as basil and parsley, that tend to dry slowly and turn brown when air dried," says Chris Weingand, an herb grower in Kalaheo, Hawaii, on the island of Kauai. Here's how:

Put one to three cups of herbs, minus the stems, in a paper bag (for a small amount use a lunch bag; for a larger quantity use a grocery sack). Fold closed, and put in the refrigerator. (Cover or wrap other foods in the refrigerator so their odors and flavors won't mix with the herbs'.) Turn the bag over at least once a day to change the position of the leaf surfaces. Depending upon the amount, the herbs will take one to three weeks to dry.

"I've had no problems with mildew. The best part is, the herbs stay a pretty olive green and keep their flavor better than when air dried," says Chris.

✹

"My favorite way to dry herbs is a dehydrator," says herb fancier Terry Kemp. "It's faster than air drying and they stay green."

✹

"If you are drying and storing a large crop of decorative herbs (such as artemisias and statice) or everlasting flowers (such as celosia, strawflower, or globe amaranth) for later use in arrangements and wreaths, store them with spices to deter insect damage," advises Phyllis V. Shaudys, publisher of the herbal networking newsletter *Potpourri from Herbal Acres.*

Phyllis advises layering your dried materials in boxes with tissue paper, sprinkling mace and cloves on the tissue covering each layer. Many authorities suggest using moth balls (which can be toxic when inhaled) for this purpose. "I find that the spices work just as well, and add fragrance to the botanicals too," Phyllis says. (For information about the newsletter, write to *Potpourri from Herbal Acres,* Washington Crossing, PA 89771.)

Freezing

Another simple way to preserve herbs quickly is to rinse them thoroughly under cold water, pat them dry with a paper towel, put them in freezer bags, and pop the bags in the freezer, suggests Wisconsin herb expert Terry Kemp. "I usually stick them in whole and pull out pieces as needed. They're too limp to use in salads, but they are fine for cooked dishes," Terry says.

AUTHOR'S NOTE: *You can prevent herbs from clumping together when you freeze them by spreading them in a single layer on a cookie sheet to freeze. Then bag them. Each piece freezes individually in short order.*

Love-Hate Relationships: Attracting and Repelling Insects

Flowering herbs will draw beneficial insects to your garden, so interplant herbs in your vegetable and flower beds and let some of the plants bloom freely, counsels Renee Shepherd of Shepherd's Garden Seeds.

✳

One of the most respected names among herb fanciers is Phyllis V. Shaudys of Washington Crossing, Pennsylvania. Her book *The Pleasure of Herbs: A Month-By-Month Guide to Growing, Enjoying, and Using Herbs* (Garden Way) is considered a classic in its field. Phyllis suggests the following ways to use herbs as companion plants in your flower and vegetable beds.

• Plant basil, parsley, chives, and/or thyme (which attracts bees for pollination) in and around your tomato plants for healthier production. Then harvest the herbs with the tomatoes to season any and all tomato dishes, especially spaghetti sauce. The chives and thyme are hardy, so place them near the tomatoes on a border where you won't be rototilling. Annual basil and biennial parsley should be replanted around the tomatoes each year, advises Phyllis.

• "Border any patch with annual catnip (which self-sows) for flea and beetle control. The catnip will provide a paradise for your kitty and a lovely herb tea for you," Phyllis says.

- Dill, to season any fish dish or to use for pickling, is a good friend to any plant in the cabbage family.

- Annual summer savory complements all bean plants and, either fresh or dried, all bean recipes.

- "Garlic and rue, bitter enemies of Japanese beetles, are beneficial in the rose and raspberry beds to deter these pests," Phyllis says. "Dry the garlic bulbs each year for year-round culinary enjoyment, and dry the attractive, but inedible, rue for a moth and insect repellent. If you are allergy-prone, avoid skin contact with rue foliage," Phyllis cautions.

✳

The hardy perennial rue (*Ruta bluemound*) is a terrific insect controller that also enhances the beauty of your garden. Its striking mounds of blue-green foliage are suitable for edging walkways and other borders and make it a lovely highlight plant all by itself. "Any flower would look pretty next to it," herb grower Terry Kemp believes. "It's real care-free, and one of my favorites."

Terry plants tansy around the foundation of her house to keep ants away. "You can also lay tansy leaves where ants are a bother, and they'll stay out," she says.

Though tansy is a fine ant repellent and has pretty yellow button flowers that are nice dried in arrangements, it is very aggressive, advises Terry.

In colonial times tansy was a common bug repellent for ants and other pests. Even today, in spite of its aggressiveness, savvy gardeners like Jack Laws of Buffalo Mills, Pennsylvania, plant it between the rows of cucumbers, peas, and cabbage to keep insects out.

✳

"In the 1700s," says Jack's wife, Vi Laws, a tour guide at Old Bedford Village in Bedford, Pennsylvania, "colonists sprinkled fresh wormwood leaves on floors and under mattresses as a bug repellent."

✳

The Herbe Sainte Marie of colonial times was the name for what we call costmary (*Chrysanthemum balsamita*). "People used this fragrant mint to make crowns to wear around their head," says Pennsylvania herb grower Vi Laws. "Later, with the invention of books, costmary leaves became popular bookmarks."

The costmary protected books from being devoured by silverfish and was used especially in Bibles, adds herbalist Terry Kemp.

Cosmetic Uses

Cooled basil tea is a fine rinse to bring luster to summer-dulled hair, advises California seed merchant, grower, and garden writer Renee Shepherd.

Recipe for a Greener Thumb

Plants are like people; they're all different and a little bit strange. The more gardening you do, the better you get at it—you learn the tricks over a period of time. You have to have faith in yourself; even if you go to the books, common sense is the answer 90 percent of the time. You have to be persistent, have a little self-confidence, and keep plugging at it.
—JOHN KEHOE, PARK SERVICES SUPERVISOR, COLT PARK, HARTFORD, CONNECTICUT

CHAPTER SEVENTEEN

Foliage Fitness: Trees and Shrubs

*The flowers are like advertising. But most of them only bloom
for one or two weeks. You have to live with the tree
the other fifty weeks, too. Like in any romance, the date
may be wonderful but the marriage might be awful!*

—GARY KOLLER

If you plant a petunia or a tomato without having any experience or
knowledge, the worst that happens if the plant fails is that you're out a
few pennies and a couple of moments. You might even have time to try
again the same growing season. But when you plant a shrub or tree, you're
forced to dig deeper into both ground and pocket. You expend more energy,
more money, and also more time.

Be aware too that if a tomato poops out on you, it most likely happens
right at the start of the growing season, but trouble with a tree or shrub may
take years to develop, with far more costly results.

I, for instance, felt so clever when I found $1.99 poplar whips at a
nursery close-out sale that I bought dozens to flank our driveway. Neigh-

bors warned me that this tree is short-lived and should be avoided, but I ignored them.

Lombardy poplars are quick growers, and in no time at all our new trees transformed our humble gravel drive into a lush green archway. By the seventh summer, however, we were left with a towering leafless tunnel, looking like the entrance to Village of the Damned. Taking into account the fee from the tree service we needed to remove them (few homeowners have the equipment to remove huge, hazardous trees and their deeply embedded stumps), those bargain trees ended up costing hundreds of dollars.

This chapter will help you avoid such problems. Smart shopping tips introduce the importance of considering site location, budget, and future growth when choosing trees and shrubs. You'll read tips on transplanting and keeping trees healthy, and you'll learn more about flowering shrubs. Folks who are confident with other kinds of gardening often feel on shakier ground with plants such as azalea, camellia, and lilac. If you feel this way too, these tips will put you on a more solid foundation by explaining their few special requirements.

By and large, gardening is a salad of common sense tossed with a bunch of experience. One aspect that tends to be a little more technical, though, is the theory and technique of pruning. The pruning tips in this chapter offer counsel for trimming flowering shrubs, evergreens, and deciduous trees.

If, as you read, you become aware of the mistakes you've made in your own garden, don't be dismayed—take comfort in knowing you're not alone. Much of the advice in these pages originally came not from books but from the School of Experience. "And experience," my daughter Ingrid reminds me, "is what you get when you don't get what you want."

States of Mind

Spring is Hell.

—RICHARD SCHNALL, VICE-PRESIDENT FOR HORTICULTURE,
NEW YORK BOTANICAL GARDEN

Smart Shopping

"When you buy a plant," cautions Gary Koller, senior horticulturist for Harvard University's Arnold Arboretum in Jamaica Plain, Massachusetts, "don't rely on what the salesperson says. They want to sell, and they'll tell you what you want to hear. Take a good garden book with you when you shop to help you be an informed consumer, or go over and look at their books containing information about the plant you intend to purchase. All good garden centers have a reference library."

✱

"Don't make your decisions in the nursery—that's impulse buying. Buying trees is like buying a computer or a car. The last thing you want to do is go to the showroom, or you'll get seduced," believes Phil Normandy, curator of Brookside Gardens in Wheaton, Maryland.

"When you are choosing new trees, shrubs, or perennials, choose smart. You want to do your homework first. Consult with the staff at your local botanical garden or read a garden encyclopedia," urges Phil.

✱

Deciding What to Plant

If you are choosing a flowering shrub or tree, don't let the flowers sway you, warns Gary Koller.

"The flowers are like advertising. But most of them only bloom for two weeks. You have to live with the tree the other fifty weeks, too. Like in any romance, the date may be wonderful but the marriage might be awful!

"It's better to buy a shrub or tree or herbaceous perennial when it's not in bloom. That way you'll make a better choice based on growth potential, environmental needs, and year-round suitability," Gary says.

✱

States of Mind

When in doubt about the right time to move or prune a plant, I always keep in mind garden writer Christopher Lloyd's advice: "The right time is when you have the time."

—SARAH PRICE, CURATOR, NEW YORK'S CENTRAL PARK CONSERVATORY GARDEN

"Today's average length of residence in any one home is somewhere in the neighborhood of seven years," Brookside Gardens curator Phil Normandy notes. "Part of the throwaway society we live in is the attitude that 'I'm gonna be out of here in a few years.'"

"Don't put in plants that will grow too large and cause problems for the next owner," urges Phil. "I suggest people look at smaller shrubs. People's time is getting more compressed, and control measures tend to be drastic and lethal, so match the plant to the site."

❋

"When we buy a shrub or tree," says Michigan native Pat Ostrander, "we don't buy a perfect one. We look for the one with a crook, because it looks more natural and has more character."

❋

"Beware of 'cute little things' in the garden center—they have the potential to turn into monsters," warns Arnold Arboretum's Gary Koller. "Most people put in trees and shrubs and spend the rest of their lives trying to control them by pruning. Know in advance their mature height; don't select solely on the basis of flowers, fruit, or autumn colors, but consider rate of growth, height, width, shape, and volume of the plant. Will it still please you five years from now?"

Practical Choices

"Trees are like people. They have their own individual personalities. When we come to understand them, we come to know them and love them," says Cy Klinkner of La Crosse, Wisconsin.

A longtime nurseryman, Cy confesses that he's so passionate in his zeal for good landscaping principles that he sometimes has trouble restraining himself. He has driven by homes with landscape plans so inappropriate that he's stopped the car to proffer unsolicited advice.

"A couple of times, I got my head taken off," he admits. Cy shares some of his best tips:

- Barberry (*Berberis thunbergii*) was once popular because of its pretty red foliage. Often touted as the "traffic stopper," it has long, sharp thorns that would certainly deter trespassers. "I don't recommend barberry," says Cy. "It's dangerous, and can cause injuries."

- Many homeowners plant silver maple for fast shade, but this beautiful tree is far from problem-free. "To begin with, they aren't structurally strong, and they split easily in wind," says Cy. "Because they're shallow-rooted, they eventually bulge into sidewalks and driveways. Be aware that their roots go out looking for moisture, seeking out water and sewer lines."

  Furthermore, adds Cy, female silver maple trees are loaded with seeds that sail down like little helicopters and make a big mess in your yard.

AUTHOR'S NOTE: *If you're a kid, though, that's great. The little winged seeds are fun to split open and stick on your nose.*

- Because they're inexpensive and grow quickly, Chinese elms also used to enjoy great popularity, especially for hedges. But this is another tree to avoid because eventually the hedges revert back to being trees; like the silver maple, this elm is prone to splitting and also generates messy seeds.

- When planting birch trees, don't run out to a nursery lot and choose the first pretty birch you see. Look for the new varieties that are more resistant to birch borer and birch leaf miner.

- If you're grappling with basement dampness, "plant red twig, yellow twig, or variegated dogwood," advises Cy Klinkner. "The roots of this moisture-loving plant will absorb a lot of the water and help relieve the dampness problem."

✳

Many people looking for a quick-growing privacy screen make the mistake of planting bamboo, which spreads aggressively and gives lots of problems, observes Phil Normandy, curator of Brookside Gardens in Wheaton, Maryland.

A good alternative (for up to Zone Six) is the tall, narrow, dark green Leyland cypress that is so popular in England for hedges, Phil says. Shaped like a fat exclamation point, it's quick growing and stays green in winter. If you want a privacy screen, you can plant them 2 to 7 feet apart (depending on your budget), and in five years or less you'll have a good, dense hedge. You can even plant them as close as 2 feet apart, but only if you plan to keep the hedge clipped. (If left unclipped, the mature plant can reach at least 40 feet in height under optimum growing conditions.) Plant only in full sun.

Deciding Where to Plant

Planting any tree too close to your home can wreck your foundation. Old homes had 2-foot-thick stone foundations; today they're just 10-inch concrete block. To protect them from root damage, it's safest to go at least 30 feet for major trees, cautions retired agricultural agent Jim Ness.

✳

Pointers on Planting

The old saying "Big is best" is not necessarily so, says arborist John Kehoe, park services supervisor for Colt Park in Hartford, Connecticut.

When it comes to choosing trees, the bigger ones are seductive. "But the larger the tree, the more shock its root system will experience when you transplant it," John says. "Whereas an annual may take several weeks—or sometimes just days—to recover, a tree may not recover for six to fifteen years."

For large, transplanted trees, advises John, proper care is critical. To help the tree to recover from transplant shock, you need to irrigate in drought, fertilize every year or two, and monitor for bugs and diseases. "That's where people make a mistake. They pay all that money for a big tree and then abandon it, leaving it for God to take care of. That's throwing money away."

✳

"The number-one problem in gardening is putting a five-dollar plant in a fifty-cent hole," holds Ralph Snodsmith, garden editor for ABC-TV's "Good Morning, America."

"Put it in a fifty-cent hole and in three weeks, it goes to its last rites. Instead, if a fifty-cent plant goes in a five-dollar hole, we'll have a five-dollar plant shortly.

"A 'five-dollar hole' means the total planting environment," Ralph elaborates. "Any time you plant with the right temperature, the right light, and the right wind, soil, and fertilizer, it will grow for you.

"It's the same as human beings—if you put someone in the wrong environment, they won't be happy. But people can move, and—other than the walking fern—plants don't have that ability." (Walking ferns put out roots that enable them to gradually creep across an entire woodlot in time, Ralph explains. "But it still can't get across the interstate.")

✳

"When you're doing any transplanting, put the majority of your effort below the ground," recommends Ernie Hartmann, who landscaped Henry Ford's Long Island estate when he was landscape supervisor for Howe Nurseries in Pennington, New Jersey. "If the roots are happy, the rest is happy." Ernie shares these tree planting tips as well:

- When digging a hole for a tree, avoid making the V-shaped holes most people dig. A tree hole should have a wide bottom and narrow top so the roots can spread out.

- The shape of your shovel will influence the kind of hole you'll dig. For planting trees and shrubs, use a square-edged spade with a flat, level shape. (It's also great for the clean cut you need to edge the lawn and create flower beds.) If you have only a scooped shovel, cut the sides of the hole with the shovel inverted.

- Container-grown plants probably already have a feeder root system, but bare-root or burlap-wrapped trees have probably lost 75 to 90 percent of their feeder roots. "Those tiny, hairlike feeder roots are the only ones capable of absorbing nutrients," says Ernie Hartmann. "You have to create a comfortable environment so those tender roots won't be stressed and can get established as quickly as possible."

- Compensate for root loss by trimming back top growth. "People hate to do that," says Ernie. "You have a heck of a time convincing people that the better you balance, the quicker the plant will respond and bounce back. You've got to have the same square footage of root as there is top growth in order to supply water and nutrients."

- When planting bare-root shrubs and trees, don't apply nitrogen fertilizer for several weeks. Nitrogen stimulates the foliage, but right after transplanting the tree or shrub's roots won't yet be able to absorb sufficient moisture and nutrients to support lush foliage. Instead, add a slow-release, long-feeding phosphorous fertilizer to stimulate root growth. "One of the easiest and safest to use is bonemeal. This organic source of phosphorous is mild and won't burn," says Ernie.

✹

Don't expect dramatic growth on newly transplanted ornamental trees. McKay Nursery landscaper Pat Haugen of Holmen, Wisconsin, likes to quote this saying to her customers: "The first year it weeps / The second year it creeps / The third year it leaps."

✹

Says Connecticut arborist John Kehoe: "If you have a cavity, you go to the dentist—you don't go to the butcher. A transplanted tree is like a patient; it has a shocked root system; it's sickly, and it needs to be nurtured to recover health. Have a trained, knowledgeable plant professional, an arborist, or a state–certified landscape contractor come in once a year to examine your trees and advise you."

Baby Boomers

Have you ever considered starting with infant trees instead of purchasing larger ones? Having a hand in growing your own trees is economical, and it also adds to the fun of gardening, says retired nurseryman Cy Klinkner. He suggests that you buy trees when they're small (and inexpensive). Plant them in rows, in open ground safe from lawn mowers, ball players, and the like.

After about two years move the trees to another spot. This serves as a root pruning, stimulating fine feeder roots in a small area, so when you eventually transplant the trees to their permanent places, they have a sturdy, denser root system. After the fourth year transplant again. After the sixth year transplant to your desired permanent location.

Keeping Trees Healthy and Happy

Did you ever wonder why evergreen foundation plants often turn a dreary brown? It's not the result of summer scorching, as many people assume. Instead, says Hank Harris, another veteran nurseryman of La Crosse,

Wisconsin, the reflection of bright sunlight bounces off windows, house siding, and even snow, burning them. Ideally, evergreens such as yews shouldn't be planted where they'll be exposed to a lot of sun. But if they're there already and tend to discolor, try staking tents of burlap over them for protection during the winter, Hank advises.

✹

In spring you can bring back a bright green color to evergreens that have browned over the winter by mixing a solution of Sterns Miracid in a sprinkling can according to package directions; water directly onto the foliage, advises Texas native Esther Pertzsch.

✹

Sometimes you see maple trees disfigured by long splits the entire length of the tree trunk, usually on the west side of the tree. Why? On sunny winter days the sun raises the sap, and then at night the sap freezes. As the ice expands, the trunk splits, observes Kay Risberg, whose family-owned Onalaska Tree Service in Onalaska, Wisconsin, specializes in shade trees.

If you live in a cool climate and like maple trees, she advises you to wrap the trunks until they've grown thicker than 4 to 5 inches in diameter. The wrap lasts several years, and it won't hurt to leave it in place, as it stretches as the tree grows. "The wrap not only prevents the trunk from splitting; it also keeps away mice," Kay adds.

Fruit Trees

"If you're short on space, put three fruit trees that cross-pollinate one another in the same hole," suggests chemist Milton Palmer of Castro Valley, California. "Select varieties with different ripening times so you spread out your bearing season. (You'll also have a better yield because of the cross-pollination.) The trees crowd one another, and this stunts the growth a little, but it hasn't been a problem in my yard. I did it fifteen years ago with plum trees, and they're doing great."

AUTHOR'S NOTE: *Choose dwarf varieties. Large trees will become unbalanced as they're forced to lean outward. Another option is to plant a tree with several varieties grafted onto one root stock. You can purchase these or do your own grafting.*

Azaleas and Camellias

"Azaleas and camellias make good companion plants because they have fairly similar cultural requirements," says Beth Weidner, assistant park manager for one of the South's most exquisite and extensive camellia and azalea collections, the Alfred B. Maclay Gardens in Tallahassee, Florida.

Here are some tips from Beth for cultivating these two beautiful flowering shrubs:

- Both azaleas and camellias like a slightly acid soil. Because they're shallow-rooted, they do best in well-drained soil that is rich in organic matter. Avoid planting them in dense shade, or they'll be leggy and fail to flower. A partially shaded location is preferred, and a high, shifting shade, like the kind you get under pine trees, is ideal.

- One of the most common mistakes gardeners make with azaleas is to plant them too deeply. Even if you're careful not to do that, the soil settles in the planting hole, lowering the plants. "We're still perfecting our technique, and even here at Maclay Gardens, ours sometimes die," says Beth Weidner, who suggests that "only if you plant in light, sandy soil should you have the top of the root ball level with the ground. Otherwise, I recommend planting with part of the root ball sticking up on top of the ground. If you have heavy, clay soil, raise the bed for drainage, but leave most of the root ball above ground.

    "So that the roots aren't exposed, cover them with loamy, organic matter such as leaf mold, rotted sawdust, or compost. Then add a good mulch like pine bark or pine needles," Beth advises.

- Lace bug damage is common in azaleas. Usually occurring in midsummer, it causes a bronzy, stippled look, similar to mite damage. For an organic control, soap spray is recommended.

- Camellias are plagued by few pests, but tea scale is particularly troublesome and spider mites can also be a problem.

  "In the past, we used Cygon for scale, but it's extremely toxic, so we're going to soaps (we use Safer's; there are also other brands) as much as we can," says Beth. "The insecticidal soaps have another advantage: they are good for treating mites as well as scale."

- "We have gone back to using dormant oil spray on camellias; it's a good preventive measure for scale insects," says Beth. Dormant oil spray is also good for other kinds of piercing and sucking insects on broadleaf evergreen shrubs, such as white flies on gardenias.

- Die back is common in camellias, so watch for it. A branch will wilt and die. If not removed, the fungus progresses farther back in the plant. "Prune out the affected parts and destroy them," Beth Weidner advises.

Lilacs: Chronic Malingerers

Lilacs (and phlox) often get powdery mildew. If you have this problem, you may wish to use a fungicide every two to three weeks for prevention, counsels former New Jersey landscaper Ernie Hartmann.

Do not remove the mildewed leaves during the growing season, as they are still supplying the plant with needed vigor. But in autumn clean up the fallen lilac leaves and clip off the phlox stalks so the mildew won't overwinter. Dispose of this foliage; do not compost it.

✳

Freek Vrugtman, retired curator of collections for the Royal Botanical Gardens in Hamilton, Ontario, advocates a let-live philosophy: "Powdery mildew is not a disease that will harm the plant—it doesn't really matter. Although you can spray if it really bothers you, spraying is expensive, and there's already too much lawn spraying," Freek maintains. "As powdery mildew usually occurs later in the season, it won't interfere with your enjoyment of the blooms."

And even the most meticulous gardener needn't feel apologetic about the affliction: The Royal Botanical Garden's fabulous lilac collection, reputed to be the world's largest, flourishes despite the mildew and remains unsprayed.

✳

Gary Koller, senior horticulturist at Harvard's Arnold Arboretum, which includes a famed lilac collection of 550 lilac types, shares Freek Vrugtman's tolerant attitude.

"It will not hurt them—it just makes them look unattractive. If they were mine, I wouldn't bother to use fungicide. If I were planting a new lilac, I would attempt to choose one that is not only beautiful and fragrant in flower but selected for disease resistance. The best way to avoid powdery mildew problems in lilacs is to buy disease-resistant varieties," advises Gary.

The Arnold Arboretum puts out a list of recommended mildew-resistant lilacs. (For the free list send a self-addressed stamped envelope to Arnold Arboretum, Harvard University, 125 Arborway, Jamaica Plain, MA 02130.) You can also check with your local botanical garden or Agricultural Extension Service for varieties suitable for your area.

Girth Control: Pruning Deciduous Trees and Shrubs

Spring-flowering shrubs such as lilac, rhododendron, and laurel should be pruned right after flowering, before growth begins, so they have time to develop the growth buds for the next year, counsels Raymond Rice of Kutztown, Pennsylvania. "Lilacs are vigorous growers. It's okay to prune them to contain their size—make them as small as you want," advises the Pennsylvania gardener.

"If they're old and woody, pruning out the old growth will stimulate new growth from the roots. Don't be afraid to prune aggressively. Within a year or two, they'll be blooming again," Raymond says.

AUTHOR'S NOTE: *Another important consideration is that pruning (or fertilizing) late in the season stimulates tender new growth that will lack time to harden off and will be more vulnerable to winter cold.*

✻

Caution: Your lilac may actually be a combination of two plants, with an improved cultivar grafted onto a sturdy rootstock. If you prune near ground level and go below the graft, the rootstock will grow branches, but you'll lose your cultivar.

✻

Says Beth Weidner of Maclay Gardens, "Camellias are kind of touchy to prune. A common mistake people make is to shear the outside, making them thick and bushy. Don't prune them into ball shapes—that fosters disease and insect problems."

The proper way to prune camellias, says Beth, is to keep the center open so air moves freely through the plant. Never leave a stub sticking out, because that fosters dieback; instead, prune to the juncture of another branch or an outward-facing bud, so the limb can continue to grow.

✻

"Whenever you prune deciduous trees and shrubs, consider it a rejuvenation. In the majority of cases, it stimulates new growth," says landscaper Ernie Hartmann.

If they are growing well, Ernie advises removing the occasional limb you may find that is dead, diseased, or infested with insects. "Otherwise, a light pruning for shaping and air and light penetration is all they need," he says.

"If they show signs of neglect, are in generally run-down condition, and are full of a dead wood, I give them 'a crewcut,' removing 60 to 70 percent of the top growth," Ernie says.

Evergreens

If you want to shape your evergreens, don't prune in the winter when their new growth is starting to develop; wait until June, July, or August, advises Kay Risberg. Cutting in summer will stimulate the tree to push out a new branch. Don't trim this new growth until after it has emerged and lost its softness. When it gets hard and prickly, then cut.

✳

"To maintain the shape of blue spruce, I just pinch off the little tips of new growth that appear in the spring. The tree will get fuller and denser, but it will stay the same size," says Raymond Rice of Kutztown, Pennsylvania. If blue spruce gets too crowded, however, it dies off inside, he cautions. Some pruning will prevent that problem.

✳

It's a good idea to trim evergreen trees every couple of summers to control their growth. Even if you have never trimmed your trees and they are very large, you can still trim them to contain their size, says arborist Jeff Davis.

To ensure thick growth on evergreen shrubs such as arborvitae, Japanese yew, and Mugo pine, trim them twice a season (early July and late August), or at least annually. Without pruning, the inside dies from lack of sunlight; when you cut back inside, beyond the green growth, the plant will not regenerate.

Remove fallen needles from beneath spruce trees, and trim off the lower branches at least 6 inches so they don't lay on the ground. Spruce need wind and air in their branches so that they don't trap moisture. Humidity and heat will lead to fungus, not only in spruce but in any shrubs that lay flat on the ground. For fungus protection trim them during the cold months, advises Jeff.

✳

Retired nurseryman Cy Klinkner urges self-restraint when it comes to pruning: "If I had my way in this world, I'd outlaw electric trimmers. People get carried away. We have no glue to cement those limbs back on after they've erroneously taken them off. To preserve a natural look, you should avoid severe pruning."

States of Mind

I like gardening because it knows no social barriers. Everyone can do it. You listen to the experts and you read all the books and you end up doing what you want in your own garden. That's what it's all about.

—DAVID TARRANT, HOST, CBC-TV'S "CANADIAN GARDENER"

CHAPTER EIGHTEEN

Beauty Secrets:
Tips for Flower Growing

*Virtually everything in my garden has been moved
at least once or twice. If you mounded up the dirt that I've dug,
it's probably bigger than the garage.*

—SALLY NETTLETON

There's something special about a circle that makes it seem more harmonious, more magical, than any other shape. When Rosemary Muramoto of Seattle recounted to me how she plants her mums in circles, and when Lee Rodman described sowing circles of wildflower seeds on her hillside, long-ago memories came flooding back to me.

When I was a little girl, we used to make fairy rings, poking aside the leaf litter with sticks and scratching circles in the earth. We outlined our circles with acorns and strewed wildflowers within, half-believing we could entice elves and fairy queens to appear.

As a grown-up, I've planted my garden beds with a far more rational agenda, and they've never recaptured the sense of wonder that my magic rings in the woods used to hold. Though colorful and beautiful, my grown-up gardens march across our yard like soldiers on parade, and the only Little Folk they lure are aphids, spider mites, and a miniature schnauzer from down the block.

Now, after receiving the ideas on garden design that open this chapter, I'm beginning to believe I can recapture that old magic after all. This chapter includes wonderful tips for planning annual gardens and perennial gardens. You'll learn easy propagating techniques—methods for dividing old plants, coddling new ones, promoting abundant, large blooms, and starting wildflower gardens.

Powerful though these ideas may be, I can't promise they'll lure sprites to your garden. But you will find suggestions for attracting hummingbirds and for capturing moonlight, and many for luring *you*!

Recipe for a Green Thumb

A garden is a very personal creation. Try not to be swayed by other people's opinions or current gardening fashions, but use your own creativity and imagination. Your garden is your refuge from the world and should be a personal source of pleasure.

—CAROLYN JONES, HORTICULTURIST, VANDUSEN BOTANICAL GARDENS

Planning Glorious Gardens

Did you ever buy a plant that grew into something you never expected? Or looked identical to another variety with a different name? "Many cultivars aren't reliably labelled," cautions Freek Vrugtman, vice-chair of the International Society for Horticultural Science's Commission for Nomenclature and Registration and retired curator of collections for the Royal Botanical Gardens in Hamilton, Ontario.

Sometimes one plant is known by many names; at other times different plants are referred to by the same name. "The name 'Princess Royal' dianthus has been used for at least 40 different varieties of pinks," Freek notes. "For more trustworthy information, check with the individual plant societies and/or plant registration authorities."

✳

When planning your flower garden, be aware that sometimes even when plants are genetically identical, weather and soil conditions can change their appearance, advises gardener Anne Hoskins of Corbin, Kentucky. "For example, if you have a blue hydrangea and the soil's acid content is too low, the flowers will bloom pink," Anne says.

✳

To get ideas for flowers that will make attractive beds in your yard, check out the commercial sites and industrial park entrances to see what flowers they are using. Professional gardeners want plants that look good and stand up well without a lot of fuss, counsels master gardener Mona Stevens of Fishers, Indiana.

✳

You'll never see flowers in the wild growing in the timid, narrow borders of people-planted gardens, so why must yours grow that way? Minneapolis-based registered architect and garden designer Sally Nettleton's own garden bed juts out into a 12-foot swag of lush layers and dense foliage in the style of a nineteenth-century English garden.

"It's a planned ebullience," she says. Below are more of Sally suggestions for exquisite gardens:

- A garden is alive with patterns of sun and shadow that change constantly by the season, by the time of day, by a cloud's passing. In designing your garden, consider the arc of the sun and what in its path is blocking out light to parts of a garden. Colors need to be bolder in a sunnier garden, as they will tend to wash out in the brightness. Pastels, on the other hand, show well in dappled shade.

- Take black-and-white photos when designing gardens, as Sally does for clients, in order to focus upon such qualities as balance, texture, scale, massing, and shadow.

- When rearranging plants, pick blooms and leaves and test them against plantings in other parts of the garden. See what one green looks like next to another. In her own garden, for example, "there probably are fifty shades of green out there," Sally speculates.

- Don't be afraid to move plants around to achieve the balance you desire, Sally says. "Virtually everything in my garden has been moved at least once or twice. If you mounded up the dirt that I've dug, it's probably bigger than the garage."

- You can't always count on blooms to create a striking garden, cautions Sally. "The day your favorite lily is going to bloom there could be a hailstorm, and then you're out of luck for another year." So consider other elements too in planning your perennial garden, such as layering, contrasting textures, and the shape and color of the foliage, concludes the Minnesota garden designer.

✳

"I really like the 'cottage style' garden where you let the plants go their own way," says floral designer Terry Kemp of Onalaska, Wisconsin. "When they go to seed, I clear the old dead plants out. I take the seed-heads off and shake 'em right into the dirt all over the garden. In spring, little baby plants come up all over, randomly. This is not for people who like perfect, formal rows—it looks like a field of wildflowers."

Terry's cottage garden includes phlox, zinnias, love-in-a-mist (*Nigella damascena*), globe amaranth (*Gomphrena globosa*), marigolds, delphinium, and moss roses. "It's like getting free plants," Terry says.

✳

An all-white flower bed can be dramatic in the daylight and absolutely dazzling by moonlight, notes West Coast gardener Anne Goldbloom. Consider planting such a garden by your entranceway or edging a patio where you'll enjoy sitting out after dark.

You might prefer to plant this garden with annuals, so if you get tired of the monochromatic look, you're not stuck with it for years.

✳

Planting red tubular blossoms, such as salvia, bee balm (*Monarda didyma*), and trumpet-vine, attracts hummingbirds, notes Anthony Tyznik, Illinois landscape architect.

AUTHOR'S NOTE: *For a priceless thrill, plant them near a window so you can glimpse the tiny, jewel-like creatures as they hover to sip flower nectar.*

Annual Gardens

"If annuals are already in flower when you transplant to the open garden, they don't have time to adapt to the environment," says John Kehoe, park services supervisor for Colt Park in Hartford, Connecticut.

"For example, if celosia begins to flower while it's still indoors, that's it. The red plume flowers will be small, inconspicuous, and not very vibrant," John says.

When you buy annuals, avoid those that are in flower, because the root system in the little pots didn't have a chance to develop sufficiently. "If you get them just when the buds are coming, however, you know it's a vigorous plant," counsels John.

✸

To give your flower garden a full, luxuriant look without crowding, space your annuals so they'll start to touch three to four weeks later, advises Wisconsin nurseryman John Zoerb. "If you plant the third week in May, for example, they'll look perfect from the third week in June."

✸

Impatiens, with its dazzling colors and continuous blooms from summer to fall, is a good flower to plant where overhanging trees have shaded the flower beds, suggests retired Wisconsin nurseryman Cy Klinkner. This cheery flowering plant tolerates morning sun, but total shade is best, he advises.

✹

"In Birmingham, Alabama, where we used to live," says Lisbeth Reynertson, "it was hot and humid, with lots of bugs and poor soil. We tried a lot of plants that were supposed to repel bugs, but they didn't work. The slugs would literally kill seedlings overnight. The only plants that survived were the impatiens. They were wonderful—and they reseeded."

Perennial Gardens

"Contain rapidly spreading plants at the time of planting," advises Phil Normandy, curator of Brookside Gardens, a fifty-acre conservatory 15 miles north of downtown Washington, D.C.

In his home garden Phil admits he's guilty of failing to practice what he preaches. "I put in a plume poppy, one of those vigorously running, invasive things—I liked it! I just got lazy and didn't contain it," he says ruefully.

To avoid problems, Phil advises, "dig a trench to where you hit the hard, original soil, and then go a couple of inches deeper. Insert a strip of rigid plastic, or metal for a physical barrier. It's a lot of work, but take the long view—it's worth it."

✹

Three decades ago perennial specialist Randy Baier founded Baier Nursery in La Crosse, Wisconsin, on the land his family farmed for more than a century. Randy shares these tips for flower gardening:

• "Probably 90 percent of people just go to a nursery, pick out what's blooming, take it home, and plant it. For three weeks, it looks great, but then there's nothing going on. My suggestion," says Randy, "is to take it slow. Go back to the nursery throughout the growing season to see what else appeals to you.

• "To have a perennial garden, you need enough space for a progression of blooms going on all summer. By and large, most perennials only bloom for a three-week period, though it varies from two to four weeks."

Varieties of known hardiness should be the backbone of your perennial garden. Leave a few areas open for more exotic, unique plants.

- For your hardy core, yarrow, columbines, both tall and creeping phlox, and most varieties of the cheerful bluebell campanula will do well. Gloxinia, with its showy clusters of trumpet-shaped blooms, might be used to add interest as far north as Zone Four, though it's more subject to winter damage. Of course, what is hardy for one locale may be shakier in another, so ask your local nursery.

- In a narrow, confined area such as a walkway, there isn't room for enough perennial varieties to give a progression of blooms. In those areas you're better off planting annuals, which will give blooms from spring till fall. If your perennial garden has too much open space, fill it with annuals. "A few annuals are nice in perennial gardens," Randy believes, "because they give such long-term, concentrated color."

- Pick perennial plants that have good-looking, healthy foliage all summer, even when they're not in bloom. The glossy, dark green foliage of doronicum is pretty when its yellow, daisylike blossoms aren't in flower; the same is true of penstamon, whose glossy, narrow green leaves are always attractive.

- Generally, plants that have hard, glossy leaves have fewer foliar diseases, because the waxy coating makes it difficult for disease organisms to penetrate. Plants with dull or hairy leaves have more places for fungal spores to lodge.

- If the leaves of any perennial plant start to look scraggly, dry, brown, or droopy, cut them back to 2 to 3 inches from the ground and they'll leaf again. You can cut back late in the season if you are fairly far south, but in more northerly regions cut back before mid-July, so the plant will have time to build a root reserve.

- Drainage is very important for perennials. "With few exceptions, they won't do well with their feet wet. Pick a drier, sunnier location for any plants that are susceptible to foliar disease," Randy Baier concludes.

✳

Here are some border ideas from Helen Mayville of La Crosse, Wisconsin, who has learned to pack a lot of color, variety, and beauty into a small urban lot:

- Plant perennials that will show large masses of color visible from a distance.

- Spot in a few annuals such as zinnias, Victoria blue salvia, and marigolds for late color when most of the perennials are finished blooming.

- Orchestrate the garden by moving plants until the color balance and sequence of bloom are right. Except in extremely hot weather, plants can be moved almost anytime by taking a large chunk of soil with the root ball. Move the plant in the early evening so that it has all night to adjust before the heat of the day. Water it well.

- You may want a central focal point that has something interesting blooming all the time. If the border is fairly long, however, repeat the same species at least three times so that your eye is drawn along the border.

It's hard to find plants that thrive in shady gardens. One top choice of retired nurseryman Cy Klinkner is funkia (*Hosta*), also known as plantain-lily, a perennial that used to be popular in old–time gardens. Its stalks of lilac, white, or blue bell–shaped blossoms are not spectacular, but its lush foliage makes it a good accent plant, especially when planted in the foreground, Cy believes.

Gardens Grow Gardeners Too

Rather than destroying plants that must be thinned out of a garden by throwing them in the compost or landfill, put them back into production in somebody else's garden. Organize a swap meet to share surplus plants.

—KEN BALL, COLORADO LANDSCAPE ARCHITECT

Easy to Propagate

If you envy a magnificent plant that belongs to someone else, ask for a cutting to root. Mary Shriner has a 6-foot gardenia bush in her Santee, South Carolina, yard that's yielded many offspring. She sticks a 12-inch piece in water for a couple of weeks until it roots, then plants it in full sun. With a branch broken from a fig tree, Mary has also produced a 20-foot fig tree loaded with figs in just five years.

✱

For many of us, the winter blahs are over and spring fever starts when we see the first pussy willows. It's easy to start pussy willow bushes, discovered Mary Wrodarczyk of Linden, New Jersey. "I was so aggravated—one of the girls at work would bring in pussy willows and everybody else snatched up the good ones, so I decided to grow my own.

"In the spring, after the buds turn furry, cut several branches and put them in a jar of water. Check water level daily and refill, as willows use up the water quickly. The twigs will grow roots in about four to five weeks. When the roots are about 2 inches long, plant outdoors. You'll have large, beautiful shrubs in two years," says Mary.

✱

It's easy to grow new azaleas by rooting 8- to 10-inch branches in damp sand or rooting medium, says Shirley Watterson of Morrow, Georgia. "I take evergreen azalea cuttings in midsummer, right after they bloom, and deciduous azalea cuttings in the spring, right after the leaves come out. Use a rooting hormone as directed."

(In the North the common azaleas are deciduous. In the South it's mild enough for evergreen varieties to survive as well. "Native deciduous azalea are also known as wild honeysuckle," Shirley notes.)

You can also propagate evergreen azalea by ground layering, Shirley adds. Just take a branch and scrape the bark where you want the roots to grow, but don't sever it. Bend the branch over and cover it with soil, weighing it down with a rock, if necessary.

"After a year or so, when the root system is well established, you can cut the new plant from the parent plant," she says.

✳

For abundant snapdragon plants snip off the top half when the plants are 4 to 5 inches tall, and stick the cut end of the tops back into the ground. These will soon root, giving you twice as many plants. Cutting back also makes the original plant grow fuller, instead of tall and lanky, advises Mary Froegel of La Crosse, Wisconsin.

Mary likes to plant white and assorted colors of snapdragons. "They make such a sunshine bouquet on the kitchen table. But even when you don't use them for bouquets, cut them back every ten days to two weeks so they keep producing," she says.

✳

Though it's common practice to pinch off pansies when they start to fade, you can let them go to seed and still enjoy ample blooms, assures landscape designer Yvonne Rickard of Shreveport, Louisiana.

For huge, lush, blossoms sprinkle one-half cup of blood meal around each plant every two weeks. Unless it's going to rain soon, water it in, but don't cultivate, or it will disturb the seedlings.

"If you plant something a little taller like impatiens around pansies to shade them during the hot mid-summer heat, they'll bloom longer. As they reseed, the taller plants protect the little seedlings, which bloom in fall," Yvonne says. And the new generations are always a bit of a surprise because instead of resembling their hybrid parents, they revert and flower in different colors.

✳

Ringed by skyscrapers in Manhattan's Central Park is an oasis of exquis-ite beauty—a six-acre jewel called The Conservatory Garden. In its formal French, English, and Italian garden sections, thousands of plants, both rare and common, flourish.

"We don't have greenhouses or cold frames," says curator Sarah Price.

"After the biennial foxgloves have finished blooming in early summer, we allow them to go to seed, then scatter the seed where we want next year's plants to be. The plants grow rosettes that fall and bloom the following spring, so we always have foxgloves in the garden."

*

When you grow any nonhybrid flowers from seed, pay careful attention, as one out of a hundred may be a better plant. Then you can save the seed, recommends Eric Lautzenheiser, director of the San Antonio Botanical Gardens.

Coaxing Blooms

Plant peony roots in a shallow hole, just enough to cover the growth buds with a scant inch of soil. "If you plant them too deep, they won't bloom," Pat Froegel of Onalaska, Wisconsin, cautions.

*

Here's a nineteenth-century British trick for growing fabulous lilies that Terri Clark, manager of public affairs for the Vancouver Park Board, administrator of the Stanley Park, Queen Elizabeth and VanDusen gardens in Vancouver, British Columbia, discovered in an old plant history book: Plant them in tall, narrow, cylindrical terra cotta pots called Long Toms.

"I experimented, planting lilies in the garden bed, in regular pots, and in the Long Tom. The Long Tom produced the best lilies and bloomed three to four weeks earlier than the others, because their shape lets the roots grow deeper and stay warmer," says Terri.

Be forewarned, however, that in winter the potted, dormant plants need protection from moisture, or the clay pots will freeze and break. If you don't have a greenhouse (as Terri does), wrap them with burlap and keep them in a sheltered spot such as under a porch.

Note: Long Toms are available through catalogs, specialty shops, and elite garden centers but cost much more than standard pots.

*

For stockier New England asters, advises New York City's Conservatory Garden curator Sarah Price, cut the foliage halfway back in mid-June.

✺

To prolong the blooming period for perennials that bloom in spikes, like penstamon and delphinium, says nurseryman Randy Baier, it's important to cut them back early. If you wait till they start to set seed, the plants think their job is done and won't flower again. If you cut back the stems as soon as the blooms start to fade, they'll bloom again, though usually each successive bloom is smaller and shorter.

✺

Be a pincher. Not a penny pincher or a fanny pincher, but a plant pincher. Your annuals will burgeon into a solid mass of flower instead of getting spindly if you get into the habit of pinching all summer long, advises nurseryman John Zoerb.

Pinch about halfway down at least twice during the summer; the plant will come back fuller and start to flower again in three weeks. To avoid a bald look, don't pinch the whole bed down at once. Pinch selectively, a few at a time.

AUTHOR'S NOTE: *Ontario herb authority Conrad Richter explains the rationale for pinching in Chapter 16.*

R$_x$ for Plant Health

"To prevent wilting if you have to transplant flowers on a hot day, cover the new transplants with a branch for filtered shade," advises Anne Hoskins of Corbin, Kentucky. "If a branch isn't available, placing a page of newspaper over them loosely will do."

✳

To control powdery mildew that plagues your flowering plants, it's a good idea to spray the ground with a fungicide in late fall after your fall cleanup, adds horticulturist Randy Baier of Baier Nursery in La Crosse, Wisconsin. This will reduce the disease–producing organisms (which are hard to completely eliminate because they survive freezing temperatures). Use the same dilution as directed for spraying foliage.

✳

"If you have a barren plot where you've had trouble raising other plants, or if you've had problems with a patch of lawn, cut out the crummy looking grass and put in moss roses," advises nurseryman Cy Klinkner.

"It can be the most godforsaken soil where other plants have failed, but as long as there's sun, you'll have mounds of 3– to 5–inch clusters, a constant source of flowers. Although the moss rose is an annual, if you stay away with the hoe from July onward, they will self–seed and come up every year."

Flowering Bulbs

Flower bulbs will store better if you put them in a mesh fruit bag or snagged pantyhose and hang them up so that air can circulate around them, advises Mark Rogers of La Crosse, Wisconsin.

Daffodils

To save money, plant smaller bulbs when naturalizing, suggests Deborah Paulson, formerly the catalog bulb manager for Smith & Hawken mail-order bulbs in Mill Valley, California. When you're digging hundreds of holes, the smaller and shallower ones required by the smaller bulbs add up to considerably less labor. "You'll get smaller, less showy flowers than with larger bulbs, but given proper care, in the correct zone, they will continue to grow," she notes.

✳

After four or five years, when the blooms get smaller, it's time to dig up daffodil bulbs and divide them so they'll be less crowded, observes Pennsylvania gardener Raymond Rice.

Tulips

At Stan Hywet Hall and Gardens, a National Historic Landmark in Akron, Ohio, thousands of visitors flock each spring to admire the 20,000 tulips on display. "The reason that tulips look so big and beautiful at an institution such as ours is because each year we use fresh bulbs of top quality, ones that are a minimum of thirteen centimeters," says retired superintendent of grounds Bill Snyder.

Though the bulbs are still good, after the first season they produce blooms only half as large. And the bulbs that develop in coming years will probably be two-thirds the size of the first year's bulbs, says Bill.

✳

Some guilty neglect of her tulips led Anne Hoskins, president of the Garden Club of Kentucky, to the discovery that deep planting fosters better blooming and longer survival.

"When I gardened in Pennsylvania, I planted tulips 4 to 6 inches deep and they lived for years, but here in Kentucky, the tulips were very sparse after the first year," says Anne. "Then one year, while enlarging the bed, I piled dirt on top of the tulips. I kept scolding myself, but never got back to move it."

To Anne's relief, the tulips came up as pretty as ever. "So I decided to leave them, and they were just as pretty the next year. After that, I started planting tulips 8 to 10 inches deep. I think it's the summer heat that gets to the bulbs, and the greater depth insulates them."

✳

Tulips thrive in good, loose soil. Because the bulbs multiply and need to be divided about every three years anyway, take the opportunity to repair the soil if it's compacted. To keep it soft, advises Watertown, New York, native Keitha Cooper, dig it up to the depth of your fork or shovel, and mix in some vermiculite and a sprinkling of bulb food.

In years when the bulbs don't need dividing, just scratch a little bone-meal or bulb food into the top inch of soil after the plants finish blooming.

What do you do when your tulips finish blooming? Once the blossoms have faded, the leaves turn yellow and unsightly, yet if you remove the leaves before they have died off, the bulbs won't set for the next year.

If you have just a few tulips nestled in a rock garden or tucked between a wide variety of plants, other foliage usually hides the yellowing tulip leaves. The postbloom stage can be unsightly, however, if you have big, showy tulip beds. Keitha Cooper suggests digging them up and trenching them temporarily in a holding bed in a less visible spot.

Then once the leaves have died, dig up the bulbs, sort by colors and variety, and store them to replant in the fall.

❋

Here's another way to free up a straggly looking tulip bed with less labor. After your tulips have bloomed, dig up the bulbs, roots and all, with the soil on the roots, advises Bill Snyder, garden writer for the *Akron Beacon Journal* in Akron, Ohio.

Stand them up in boxes, trying not to disturb the root system. Put the boxes in the shade until the leaves turn yellow and dry, then clean off all roots and dirt and "foof on" a dry fungicide such as Bordeaux or captan. Put the bulbs in onion bags and store them until the fall in a cool, dark place with good air circulation.

"If you plant them 8 inches deep, or deeper, they'll do fine," assures Bill.

❋

To protect tulips from winter cold, Alec Berg, a native of Onalaska, Wisconsin, recommends covering them with 6 to 8 inches of peat moss. "It works itself into the soil, and by the end of the next summer, all of a sudden it disappears. You wonder where in the dickens it went to!" he marvels.

❋

For splendid flowering, tulip bulbs need a winter chill. So if your winters are mild, store the bulbs in your refrigerator for ten to twelve weeks before planting. Just keep them away from ripening fruit, which gives off ethylene gas that can interfere with flowering, advises Elizabeth Pomada of San Francisco, California.

Iris

The exquisite and prolific iris adds beauty to the garden and serves as a readily available gift shop as well, thanks to its growing habits. The lovely purple, white, and yellow varieties in Mary Shriner's garden in Santee, South Carolina, are a source for her to share. Mary too originally received hers from friends.

Like other bulbs, iris multiply and get too crowded. Every three to four years, they need to be dug up, divided, and replanted, Mary counsels. "When you divide and replant the tubers, leave them right at the surface, partially exposed. They need to be at a shallow depth in order to bloom."

✻

Iris don't like moist soil, but if you plant them on little mounds with good, well-drained soil, they'll coexist happily with moisture-loving flowers, says Watertown, New York, native Keitha Cooper.

✻

"I plant 500 to 600 iris in my garden and grow about 110 different varieties," says Luther Shaffer of Kutztown, Pennsylvania. "Depending on the colors, the fragrance of iris blossoms is sweet, tart, and spicy, almost like cinnamon. So don't forget to smell the flowers."

Here are more of Luther's tips on iris culture:

• It's important to keep the rhizome dry. Unlike spring bulbs, iris bulbs should be left on top of the ground so the sun can shine on them and dry them out after rain. If they're put in the soil, they rot. Only the roots dangling down from the rhizome go into the soil.

- When iris are finished blooming, cut the flowering stalk as close to the rhizome as possible to prevent it from rotting and to keep the garden looking cleaner.

- If your iris leaves have streaks of brown going down through the leaf vein, it's a sign of a borer. "If you see these symptoms, try to find the borer where the rhizome is a little mushy and you see the hole. You can take a knife and gouge it out," Luther suggests.

- If you don't thin iris, the flowers will get smaller and smaller. The best time to divide them is two to four weeks after they've finished blooming. This gives the plant plenty of time to get a good start again. Dig out the roots, thinning the surplus rhizomes. To replant, dig a hole, dangling the long, stringy roots into it. Pack dirt firmly over the roots, leaving the rhizome sitting on top of the soil. If necessary, mound the soil a little so the rhizome isn't buried.

- "There's nothing wrong with brown tips on the iris leaves, but it doesn't hurt to cut the tips with shears. A lot of people trim iris leaves into a fan shape—don't," advises Luther Shaffer. "The plant needs the green leaves to put nourishment into the rhizome to prepare for next year."

Begonias

The vast majority of the tuberous begonias in the United States are forced into bloom with the help of artificial light, says Eugene Bauer, who grows 15,000 begonias a year from seed. These begonias, however, have only a 25 percent likelihood of ever developing tuberous bulbs for next year. "So if you want to grow tuberous begonias, buy them from a reputable grower who gives you the bulb type, not the seed-hybrid type," he cautions.

Dahlias

After dahlias have been stored over the winter, when they start sprouting, put them in a flat of soil or peat to grow till they're 8 to 10 inches tall. By the time they're ready to plant, they're too high for the slugs, notes gardener Terri Clark of Vancouver, British Columbia.

✻

Before the killing frost, cut the stalks off dahlia plants and dig up the tubers to store for the winter. You can store them in slightly moistened peat moss in the cellar. In the spring separate the tubers with a sharp knife. It's important that each tuber show a growth bud near the narrow end, so take care that the growth buds aren't injured or eliminated, advises Raymond Rice of Kutztown, Pennsylvania.

Gladiolus

Twenty-five varieties of gladiolus—around 600 plants in all—bloom in the shale-chip soil of Raymond Rice's southeastern Pennsylvania garden. "My main interest is to supply flowers for our church and for a sister congregation in Bethlehem. I also give a lot to people who don't have gardens, and I take them to sick people.

"Gladiolus are pretty tricky to raise, however, because they are prone to diseases. They take a lot of care," he notes. Raymond offers these tips to make gladiolus gardening more successful:

- Just before planting gladiolus in the spring, peel off the husk. Mix a captan and water solution according to directions, and soak the corms for about a half-hour.

- Plant about 6 inches deep. Corms like cool earth; at this depth they'll stay cooler when the summer turns hot. The 6-inch depth also gives more support for the stalk.

- Plant gladiolus as early as possible, starting a week or two before the last frost for vigorous bulb growth and early blooming. Stagger your planting if you want staggered blooming. "I have put gladiolus in as late as mid-June," says Raymond, "but keep in mind that some varieties require ninety days to bloom." If you have enough space, plant gladiolus in a different location every year to reduce the likelihood of disease.

- Gladiolus like moisture. If it doesn't rain, give them a good soaking every third day.

- Leave the gladiolus in the ground as long as possible. But in the fall before the ground freezes, dig them up and let them dry on the ground for a few days with their stalks still on. It won't hurt if it rains on them, but pay attention to the weather; if rain is expected within three or four days, it's best to wait. After they've been on the ground a few days, bring the corms indoors and spread them out to finish drying.

- For fall cleaning and storing, cut off the stem, but leave on the husk. Save the new corm that has developed over the summer, but discard the old, shriveled corm from last spring. To prevent disease, shake a few corms at a time in a plastic bag with captan dust. Place the corms in open trays to provide air circulation, and store in a cool place, such as a cellar, preferably in darkness. "If you turn lights on occasionally, though, don't worry—the glads won't sprout," assures Pennsylvania gardener Raymond Rice.

Chrysanthemums

"If my chrysanthemums are not winter-killed, in April I dig up the old stump, separate the plants, and replant in circles of four or five plants," says Rosemary Muramoto of Seattle, Washington. "Some will have the roots broken off, but plant these anyway; if they do take, they're nice and strong.

"When you first plant, the mums wilt down almost as if they're dying. But within a week they perk up. After a couple of weeks, start pinching off the top inch or so to encourage them to grow."

✳

"Seven years ago we purchased one plant of small, 1-inch white button mums," says Michigan native Pat Ostrander. "Now I have them all over the yard, and probably twenty people in our area have made plants from them.

"In the spring, the plant comes up, and by late June, it's 6 to 8 inches high. If you let them grow, they'd be spindly and ugly, so chop them off 3 inches above the ground.

"Strip about 3 inches of the leaves from the bottom of these cuttings and stick the bare section of stems in a bucket of water until they sprout roots. Maybe only one in ten will sprout, but you'll still have a ton of them. Plant in a sunny spot."

✳

When chrysanthemum plants grow large, they can be divided. In Pat Ostrander's garden, the white button mums grow huge by fall, so she divides them every year in the spring. Here's how:

Take a spade and dig straight down at least 10 inches, slicing straight in through the roots. Lift out half the plant, covering the remaining half with soil again immediately. Gently cut through the portion you've lifted out, so you have three plants about 3 inches in diameter. Don't pull them apart, or you'll damage the roots. Slice cleanly and leave the root ball as undisturbed as possible. Plant these without delay, advises Pat.

✳

For beautiful, large chrysanthemums, Shirley Watterson of Morrow, Georgia, advises dividing the crowns when new growth is still small, adding fertilizer to worked soil, and planting about 2 feet apart, setting them very shallow.

If your mums are the early blooming variety, after the early summer blooms fade, cut back to the ground (by early July) for fall blooms. "Fertilize again in late June and mid–August," says Shirley.

✳

Chrysanthemums depend on shorter light periods to come into bloom. In some regions it is necessary to protect the plants from frost until they bloom, in early November.

You can stimulate the plants to bloom earlier, however, by covering them with a lightweight black cloth to shorten their natural daylight (and also protect them if you get killing frosts), advises Raymond Rice of Kutztown, Pennsylvania. Here's how:

Build a frame so the covers won't rest on the flowers and damage them. Starting from about mid-September, cover them around 3:00 P.M. each day. Remove the cover by 8:00 A.M. Even after they bloom, you can continue to cover them on freezing nights and days. The daytime darkness won't hurt, as they'll soon go dormant anyway.

Wildflower Gardens

Lee Rodman, a native of Syracuse, New York, disliked having to mow her lawn, so she collected seeds from roadsides and converted her lawn into a field of wildflowers. If you'd like a wildflower garden, try this method:

Dig up the grass deeply enough to remove the roots. Plant one variety of wildflower seeds at a time. Sprinkle the seeds in circles approximately 6 inches in diameter, 1 to 2 feet apart from one another, so that nice, visible clusters will be apparent when they grow. The smaller the seed, the shallower you plant. It's not necessary to label varieties, but it's helpful to plant a little stick near each cluster.

Repeat the same procedure with the other varieties, interspersing them to vary color and blooming time. "I put shorter species in front and taller ones in back," says Lee, "but as they seed themselves, they intermingle. Be patient. The garden takes about three years to become completely full. Once your garden is established, the only work you'll have to do is pull out tree seedlings. If you find bare areas, you can reseed in the fall."

Before planting a wildflower meadow, check zoning regulations to be sure local ordinances won't give you problems (some, for instance, require the mowing of "noxious weeds"). It might also save misunderstandings to explain your plan to your neighbors. "They're still called weeds by some, instead of precious wildflowers," says Lee Rodman.

✳

AUTHOR'S NOTE: *When starting a wildflower garden, water well after you clear the grass but before you sow. This will cause many of the weed seeds in the soil to germinate. Once they appear, hoe them down and then plant the wildflowers. This gets rid of many of the weeds that otherwise would spring up and compete with your flowers.*

The National Wildflower Research Center has a wealth of information, including lists of recommended native species and commercial sources for your region. You can contact the center at 2600 FM 973 North, Austin, TX 78725–4201; telephone (512) 929–3600.

Gardens Grow Gardeners Too

Plants are living things. They'll smile at you, they'll tell you when they're happy—you have to learn their language. Leave fear in the dictionary. Plants are hardier than some humans are. Don't be timid: if it doesn't work the first time, just find out why and correct it.

—GEORGE ALLEN, OCTOGENARIAN, BROOKLYN, NEW YORK

CHAPTER NINETEEN

Beauty among the Thorns: Growing Healthy Roses

I have 700 rose plants. People ask me which one is my favorite.
That depends on the day, the time of day, and the mood I'm in.

—ROGER HAYNES

Recently I browsed through *Bartlett's Familiar Quotations* to see what famous folk through the ages had to say about flowers. There I found one lone quotation about carnations, no mention whatsoever of delphiniums or petunias, but 143 references to the rose.

The rose has captured our imagination as no other flower has. With its exquisite loveliness, haunting fragrance, and sharp thorns, it has filled the language of lovers, poets, and kings throughout history.

In 326 B.C., for instance, the Sanskrit writer Pilpay philosophized, "There is no gathering the rose without being pricked by the thorns." In

England's War of the Roses, the House of York, bearing a standard with a white rose, battled for thirty years against the House of Lancaster, represented by a red rose.

In the United States the rose has such favor that it is the official flower of Georgia, Iowa, North Dakota, and the District of Columbia. Georgia's state blossom, the Cherokee rose, originally was native to China, illustrating this flower's far-flung popularity.

In fact, the rose's family tree is as many-branched and crisscrossed as the genealogies of the aforementioned Yorkists and Lancastrians. If you're confused by the multitude of hybrids, shrub roses, miniatures, ramblers, climbers, and cabbage roses, don't be dismayed—you're in good company.

Cultivated roses fall into three main classes. Those known as old roses bloom only once a year, generally in early summer. Many of the climbers, the yellow briers, moss roses, and damask roses fall into this category. Another group, the perpetual roses, bloom in early summer and again in fall. The most commonly cultivated roses are the ever-blooming hybrids. This category includes floribundas, grandifloras, hybrid teas, and polyanthas; they produce flowers through the entire growing season.

Many gardeners are hesitant to grow roses because they fear their requirements are demanding. While roses thrive most beautifully with a bit of extra effort, their needs are easily met with some simple precautions.

When planting roses, work the top 2 feet of soil well to loosen. For a light, fertile soil, mix in well-rotted manure (fresh manure can burn the roots) in the proportions of one part manure to two parts soil.

Be sure the planting holes are deep enough so that the roots have room to spread out pointing downward. Plant the rosebushes far enough apart so that their branches don't touch and you have room to give them care without getting scratched (sometimes in our eagerness to consider the plants' needs, we forget about our own).

The older gardening books commonly recommended the use of rotted manure for mulch as well as for fertilizer, and today some organic gardeners are rediscovering this practice. In the fall, manure protects the roots from winter cold, and in the summer it retains moisture. (The rich nutrients of a summer manure mulch, however, will promote lots of surface roots, making the plant more vulnerable to drought and temperature extremes.)

If you provide your roses with lots of sunshine, fertile soil, generous watering to the roots (but no more than nature provides on leaves or blooms), decent drainage and air circulation, and protection from strong winds and extreme temperatures, they should bring you years of pleasure.

This chapter offers general guidelines for growing beautiful, healthy roses and provides information on getting free, individualized, expert advice for your own roses. You will learn how to fertilize, propagate, and prune your roses, as well as how to protect them from insects, disease, and weather. In addition, you will read suggestions for selecting outstanding varieties with more of the advantages and fewer of the disadvantages we commonly find in the rose garden.

Since life always seems to prick us with some thorns, I guess the writer Pilpay is still correct philosophically. But, at last, his words are no longer always true botanically—2,300 years after he wrote his Sanskrit proverb, plant scientists have bred thornless roses. May your rose garden be as painless as this new wonder.

Recipe for a Greener Thumb

Does your state have a horticulture publication? Often these are more helpful and to the point than national horticulture magazines. The University of Minnesota Arboretum has not only an interesting botanical garden, but an extensive library and a call-in service that's extremely helpful. See if your state has a similar service.

—DICK GAGNE, LA CRESCENT, MINNESOTA

Understanding Your Roses

Few services are free these days, but rose gardeners have an entire network at their disposal. "You can contact your local Rose Society, or the American Rose Society in Shreveport, Louisiana, and they'll put you in touch with a consulting rosarian, who will come to your garden and advise you at no charge," says Donna Fuss, consulting rosarian for the American Rose Society and rose garden consultant for Friends of Elizabeth Park in Hartford, Connecticut.

"Consulting rosarians are selected by the district society for their knowledge of roses and their willingness and ability to teach others who want to grow roses. They keep up with the newest techniques and chemicals, and their knowledge is very up to date and sophisticated," notes Donna.

The American Rose Society can be reached at P.O. Box 3000, Shreveport, LA 71130–0030; telephone (318) 938–5402.

✻

"If you know what your roses need, they will do well," assures Roger Haynes, rosarian for Brookside Gardens, 15 miles north of Washington, D.C., in Wheaton, Maryland.

They need six hours of direct sun daily, 1 inch of water weekly, and a good pruning yearly, Roger advises. Good fertilizer and spray programs are also necessary to healthy growth.

"For insecticide and fungicide control, consult your local Extension service. And for proper soil pH, it's also important to have a soil test. Roses do best with a pH of 6.5 to 7," he adds.

✻

When you're shopping for new roses, keep in mind that some nursery stock may lead to problems, cautions oral surgeon Odell Anderson of La Crosse, Wisconsin. "A lot of nursery plants are grown in sand and light materials, so when the whole pot is planted in the ground, it's going to dry out quickly. A top quality nursery is unlikely to put roses in inferior materials," he says.

"Buying plants with bare roots gives you a chance to look at the root and know what you're getting. Bare-root plants do as well. If the roots look long and scraggly or have broken ends, prune them back a little."

Odell also suggests that you mulch the soil to help minimize fungus and provide a cooler base in summer. "Shredded bark is a good mulch because it lets air circulate. It keeps the soil softer, so it won't pack," he says. This protects the leaves from water splashing up from hard ground. "Prune dead blossoms to stimulate new growth," Odell concludes.

Fertilizing

How often should you feed your roses? "Roses benefit from fertilizing once a month from the time you prune in spring," says Roger Haynes, rosarian for Brookside Gardens in Wheaton, Maryland.

"A good natural sign that it's time to prune and start fertilizing is when the forsythia start blooming," he adds. "Here in Maryland, we fertilize from May to early September, but this varies with your region. If your winters are cold enough to have a dormant season you want to avoid too much succulent growth into winter; in the South, where roses bloom all year, this doesn't apply," says Roger.

✹

Don't ever fertilize bare-root roses at the time of planting, advises Wisconsin gardener Nick Wekseth. Wait about four weeks, until they start to grow and have rooted.

✹

Many rose gardeners have favorite fertilizers they depend on to grow beautiful roses year after year. Says Mary Wrodarczyk of Linden, New Jersey, "Ross Root Feeder Cartridges give beautiful trees and shrubs, so I tried them on my roses. The results on the rose bushes were unbelievable! They just shot into the air and had to be trimmed. I used it during the summer, and the roses grew huge and had a richer color."

A special tool, Root Feeder, administers the cartridges (and works for the manufacturer's other plant cartridges too) by connecting to the garden hose and pushing into the ground. As water is released, the cartridge dissolves. "Never use it right at the trunk; the directions state how far out from the plant you should go," cautions Mary.

✳

Debbie Haldorson, proprietor of Five Oaks Nursery in La Crosse, Wisconsin, is also a fan of the root feeder method. "It's an excellent way to feed roses as well as other shrubs and trees. You're getting fertilizer and water under the soil surface where you want them to be," she says. "Also, because the fertilizer is all subsurface, it's not toxic for pets.

"If you talk to the staff at a reputable garden center, I think they would suggest you avoid rose stakes—I think they are garbage! Unless you've got the perfect soil conditions, they tend not to break down like they should to be taken up by the soil, and very few gardens have perfect soil.

"I've seen rose stakes a year later, still sitting there undissolved, whereas granular fertilizer or the root feeder cartridges dissolve readily."

✳

Keitha Cooper, a native of Watertown, New York, thinks otherwise. "The easiest way to fertilize the roses is with spikes," Keitha holds. "You just hammer in two or three spikes, depending on the plant's size. The slow-release fertilizer dissolves gradually throughout the summer. They're especially convenient if you use bark mulch, because you don't have to remove it all."

✳

If your soil is poor, dig it out and replace it with peat and black dirt, and keep up with a good fertilizer, advises Wisconsin rose grower Odell Anderson.

✳

Hartford, Connecticut's Elizabeth Park, the oldest municipal garden in the nation, has a rare and priceless collection of rambler roses. Some of its species exist nowhere in else the country. Rose garden consultant Donna Fuss advises that you encourage new growth from the bud union of your rosebushes (the base at the graft) by giving give each plant one tablespoon of Epsom salts once a month in May and June with their regular monthly feeding.

AUTHOR'S NOTE: *Epsom salts supplies magnesium, essential for plant metabolism.*

"Alfalfa is wonderful for roses," continues Donna Fuss. "It has some kind of growth hormone. Just throw a handful around the base of each rose bush. There's no need to scratch it in—just let the rain do it. We have a bunny, so we just use pelleted alfalfa rabbit food. We don't worry about wild rabbits. They're not attracted; they'd rather eat clover."

AUTHOR'S NOTE: *Inspired by Donna, I watered our roses with a cocktail of fresh alfalfa blendered with water (straight up, no ice). The fabulous results, I learned later, were due not to my bartending skills but to the growth stimulant triaconatol.*

❋

Here's a tip for tea drinkers: Toss leftover tea bags or tea leaves on the soil under rosebushes. Your roses will get a lift, not from a caffeine rush but from the tannic acid in the tea. "Roses like slightly acid soil," notes Roger Haynes, rosarian for Brookside Gardens in Wheaton, Maryland.

Battling Bugs

Japanese beetles are a big problem with roses, notes Roger Haynes. "If you only have a few beetles, the easiest method is to pick them off by hand. If it's a bad infestation, the worst-case scenario is to kill them by applying Sevin," he says.

"Another control for Japanese beetles is to set pheromone traps," adds the Maryland rosarian. "Set them as far away from your roses as you can get, because they will lure beetles from miles around, and if they see the roses, they'll dive on them. "Actually, the best approach is to buy a trap and give it to your neighbor," Roger quips.

For a biological control of the Japanese beetle, put milky spore around the beds. "It's also good to treat the turf around your whole property," advises Roger.

> AUTHOR'S NOTE: *Milky spore is a bacteria that can be safely applied to the soil, where it gradually multiplies and attacks destructive white sod-eating grubs, including Japanese beetle larvae. It's available in granular and powder forms through garden supply centers and mail-order catalogs. Use according to directions.*

*

Don't be upset if you don't get instant results trying to eradicate Japanese beetles with milky spore.

"It takes about five years to spread enough to be effective," says Connecticut rosarian Donna Fuss. "Once you eradicate the beetle grubs, the spore slowly dies, but the effect should last fifteen to twenty years."

Many rose gardeners use separate fungicides for treating black spot, mildew, and rust. Ortho, however, manufactures a chemical called Funginex that takes care of all three problems, notes Donna. "It has a very low toxicity and is a good spray."

"Insecticidal soap works just fine for aphids," counsels Donna Fuss, "but you have to apply it three times a week for it to be effective."

Gardener Anne Goldbloom of Vancouver, British Columbia, advocates a more labor-saving companion planting approach: Planting garlic at the base of the rosebush repels aphids.

*

Tobacco sweepings are a good natural insecticide for roses. The roots take up the nicotine, which is toxic to insects. "Tobacco doesn't hurt the plant—in fact, the roses like it," maintains eighty-eight-year-old Nick Wekseth of Onalaska, Wisconsin. "You can get sweepings free from tobacco warehouses if you call up in advance.

"Dig a trench as deep as your shovel about a foot in diameter around each rose bush. Add fertilizer such as rose food and bonemeal, then fill the whole ditch with tobacco sweepings and pile the dirt back on top. As the tobacco leaves decompose, the soil mound levels down again.

"With established plants, do this in early spring, as soon as you can work your ground. With new plants, wait about four weeks after planting until the roots are established. This eliminates the need to spray all summer, and you'll have no aphids or beetles," Nick says.

AUTHOR'S NOTE: *My mother-in-law used to spray her roses with water in which she soaked the cigar butts from my father-in-law's gin rummy games. Tobacco is the original native American organic insecticide. It keeps roses healthier by killing disease-transmitting insects. Nonetheless, it can spread a virus to gladiolus and to plants in the potato-tomatoes-eggplant-pepper family, so don't use it recklessly.*

Disease Control

The best ways to reduce fungus are to avoid splashing water on the leaves and to provide good air circulation, counsels Odell Anderson. "Water rose bushes close to the soil so the plants don't get wet; if possible, don't sprinkle. And water early in the morning so they won't go to bed wet," Odell says.

❋

"Just before you winterize and cover your roses in the fall, pull all the leaves off the canes and clean up all the leaves around the plant," advises Olga

French, former horticulturist at Olbrich Botanical Gardens in Madison, Wisconsin. "Otherwise, the leaves can be a source of infestation for black spot fungus on next year's roses."

✳

If you've had problems with black spot fungus, you might want to try a mulch of bark chips, as New York native Keitha Cooper did. "This kept the leaves from contact with the soil, and black spot didn't return," she recalls. "If the plant becomes infected with black spot, the fungus gets into the soil. You can dig it all out and replace the soil, but there's no way to simply sterilize it," says Keitha. "Sometimes you're forced to surrender and move your roses to a new location."

✳

If you are forced to move your infected roses to escape contaminated soil, the ideal time to do so is as early as possible in the spring when the plants are still dormant, says Ernie Hartmann, formerly a landscaper in Pennington, New Jersey. "By transplanting before the buds swell, instead of when they are in leaf, you can minimize root shock," he says.

"Concentrate on the roots when transferring rose bushes," adds Ernie. "You may want to cut back the canes to 6 inches to help the plant survive the transplant shock."

✳

Cornell University has developed an organic method of controlling black spot using baking soda, notes Fred Wiche, farm and garden director for WHAS-TV and Radio in Louisville, Kentucky, and garden columnist for *Kentucky Living* magazine. Add one tablespoon each of baking soda and regular vegetable oil to one gallon of water. Add a drop of liquid dishwashing soap and shake well before and during application.

If the weather is humid or the threat of disease is high, spray every five to seven days. Spray both sides of the leaves thoroughly at the first sign of disease. Remember, Fred adds, always test any homemade spray on a small area before spraying your entire plant.

Pruning

"Each leaf is a little food-manufacturing factory; the more you remove, the less the plant has to manufacture food and flowers," cautions horticulturist Ernie Hartmann.

"You want to encourage the canes to grow outward, though—not into the center of the rose bush. If it's congested, the junglelike growth reduces air circulation and sunlight and makes an ideal habitat for disease and insects."

So when picking blooms for bouquets, cut back to just above the first outward-growing five-leaf junction; these have a bud in their axil (junction of cane and stem) that produces the new cane.

✳

When cutting roses for flower arranging, keep in mind that you're pruning the bush as well. To protect the bush, never use an anvil pruner (the kind with a stationary bottom blade), as this crushes the stem.

Always use a scissors or a scissors pruner (the kind with crossing blades), advises consulting rosarian Donna Fuss of Connecticut.

Cold Climate Protection

Curiosity and a hankering to experiment can yield fantastic results, but folks who have these traits better have a bit of the gambler in them.

"After dutifully unhooking my climbing rose every fall, laying the canes down flat, and covering them with straw," recalls Alec Berg of Onalaska, Wisconsin, "I began to wonder: What's the difference if they're standing up or on the ground? So one year I left them upright. By the spring they were deader than a dodo."

"So if you have any climbing roses," Alec advises, "lay them down. In the spring, pick them up again, and away they go."

✳

"When covering roses for the winter, mound each rose with 8 inches of peat moss. Don't put rose cones on till the weather has been down to twenty degrees for at least a week. This protects the roses from becoming moldy, which might happen if you cover them too soon," says Kansas City, Missouri, native Ruth Coombs.

✳

Roses can flourish even in cold climates if you give them a little extra care. Unfortunately, advice about mounding and trenching, mulching and covering, pruning and not pruning is sometimes contradictory and often confusing.

Two highly respected horticulturists, nurseryman Randy Baier and Dr. Ernie Hartmann, offer a few simple guidelines for cold-weather roses. Randy Baier owns Baier Nursery in La Crosse, Wisconsin. Over the years he's often been my plant psychiatrist. Horticulturist Ernie Hartmann has been a landscape contractor, forester, park superintendent, and landscaper and is a professor emeritus at the University of Wisconsin–La Crosse.

- In heavy winds long canes will rock and gouge each other, so it's best to do some prewinter cutting early in November. When pruning, look at each individual plant's health before coming to a decision. If the plant is spindly, cut back more. If the canes are big, heavy, and healthy, don't cut as severely.

- The beautiful roses in today's gardens generally are exotic hybrid roses grafted to the sturdy stock of wild rose root systems. If the bud union at the crown dies back in cold weather, the plant reverts to the wild rose with puny, leggy suckers. To protect that bud union, wait until the frost is 2 to 4 inches deep in the soil, and then mound 8 to 10 inches of soil over the crown.

- Air can seep in between clods of frozen earth and freeze the bud graft. So while the weather is still warm, get a pile of dirt and cover it with a tarp to protect it from rain, frost, and snow. Then when you're ready to mound your roses, you'll have loose soil on hand.

- Wait until you've had a few good frosts before mulching. By then field mice have found a home elsewhere and won't nest in the mulch. Also, the air temperature is colder, so mold won't develop. (Light frosts are actually good for roses, because they toughen the twigs and make them hardier.)

- Cover the dirt mounds with hay or straw mulch, or with Styrofoam cones to protect the mounds from the freezing and thawing action of temperature fluctuation. This also protects the canes from the cold and from the drying action of the wind.

- To keep the cones from blowing away, anchor them by piling dirt snugly around the bottom 6 inches of the base, and place bricks on the corners that face the prevailing winds.

- Poke a few holes in the cones to let in air; otherwise, the warm, protected environment will become an ideal breeding ground for fungus.

- Do you get spring fever? If you use winter mulch, don't rush out at the sight of the first robin and expose your roses—the risk of more hard frost isn't yet over.

- When is it safe to remove mulch from roses? "It's always a bit of a gamble," admits Randy Baier. "You develop a feel after a few years. The safest thing to do is to remove it gradually. First, fluff up the mulch so air flows. Later, remove the mulch. Finally, remove the soil mound just when the buds start to swell."

- If you opt for cones, in the spring when the ground is still frozen but the sun starts warming the cones, start checking inside each cone twice a week, suggests Ernie Hartmann. "If the canes are starting to show life with any new green growth, they'll need sunlight to live, and it's time to remove the cones before mildew and fungus build up."

Propagating

For multiplying climbing roses try this simple method from an old family garden almanac belonging to Cheri Hemker of Onalaska, Wisconsin: Bend down the cane that you wish to propagate. Make a deep cut in the branch on the underside to stimulate root growth. Press the cut section into the ground, cover it with soil, and place a rock on either side of the wound to hold it down.

✳

AUTHOR'S NOTE: *Virtually all roses sold today are fancy tops grafted onto the roots of sturdier but less showy varieties. The time-tested technique of rooting canes is fine for multiplying wild roses or any nongrafted ones, but don't try this with grafted ones. If you do, the new canes will inherit the traits of the grafted canes, and will very likely lack the hardiness of the root stock.*

Some Lasting Favorites

Are you are looking for roses that are disease resistant and winter-hardy, with a long flowering season?

"A new series of landscape roses are now being developed by the nursery industry," says Gary Koller, senior horticulturist for Harvard University's Arnold Arboretum in Jamaica Plain, Massachusetts. Cultivars that Gary likes are Bonica, Carefree Beauty, Sea Foam, Chuckles, Europeana, and Iceberg.

"Though some of these new roses may be less fragrant and less showy, they are tougher, more adaptable, and more trouble-free than the hybrid tea roses," Gary says.

✳

If you love the beauty and fragrance of roses but hate the fuss that the fancy new hybrid tea roses require, try the old-fashioned varieties that every farm family once had, advocates Anthony Tyznik, retired landscape architect for the Morton Arboretum in the Chicago suburb of Lisle, Illinois.

"These heritage roses are hardy. You don't have to mound them in winter, and they have very minor, if any, disease problems. Their disadvantage, though, is a briefer flowering period." These robust, old-fashioned rose varieties are Tony's favorites:

- The Frau Dagmar Haastrup rugosa is a lovely, fragrant, single-petal pink rose. It blooms profusely in June, then intermittently thereafter. It grows to a height of 3 feet, with good foliage.

- Another rugosa beauty is Blanc Double De Coubert, which grows to a height of about 6 feet in a tall, rather symmetrical mound. Its pure white, double blossoms have a clean, almost penetrating fragrance.

- The "hundred-leaved" Centifolia cabbage rose and the pink or striped Gallica shrub roses are other fine varieties that once graced farm homes long ago and are well worth a place in our gardens today.

※

Muses Roger Haynes, rosarian for the beautiful Brookside Gardens, "I have 700 plants. People ask me which one is my favorite. That depends on the day, the time of day, and the mood I'm in. But a favorite with anyone who knows it, a rose that gardeners across the nation would like, is Double Delight. This hybrid tea rose was named, not for the two colors of its red-tipped, white petals, but for the double delight of its color and fragrance. It's very fragrant—the fragrance will knock your socks off!"

Hindsight is 20/20 Vision

When a plant that you love doesn't survive, view it as an opportunity to change your plan and enjoy something new. Gardens aren't static. If they don't change, there's something not right, they're not natural.

—GARY MENENDEZ, KNOXVILLE, TENNESSEE, LANDSCAPE ARCHITECT

CHAPTER TWENTY

Making Cut Flowers Last Longer

*If it costs less than $3.00, it is a "vayse";
if more, then it is a "vahze."*

—SHELLEY GOLDBLOOM

T here's an elderly woman in our town whose flower garden is so spectacular that people drive by week after week just to view its
ever-changing beauty. One day she noticed me leaning over her fence
to admire a particularly glorious display of poppies and beckoned me in.

After oohing and aahing over the lavish profusion of ferns, flowering
shrubs, and rare perennials, I eagerly accepted her invitation to come inside
and visit, expecting to see a home filled with flowers.

To my astonishment, it held only plastic ones. "Flowers deserve to be
growing naturally, not cut off and stuck in vases," she declared.

Although flowers are indeed at their most beautiful when growing, I
think most of us would argue that a very legitimate motive for growing them

is to furnish material for bouquets. They fade, of course, and we feel a twinge of regret, but it is their short-lived beauty that makes them so precious to us.

This chapter offers tips for creating more beautiful bouquets, as well as techniques for making them stay fresh longer. Because the secret to success starts in the garden, the chapter opens with tips on planting, caring for the plants, and harvesting the blossoms.

Next, florist Kathy Guenther offers basic principles for extending the life of cut flowers; you'll find that nearly every variety of flower responds to her guidelines.

Tips on spring flowers start with a method for encouraging blooms (the technical term is forcing, but I hate to use it because it sounds so violent) and continue with tips for tulips, roses, and evergreen boughs. You'll also find a wide assortment of treatments that reputedly prolong the life of various flowers. These potions range from vodka to photo-developing chemicals. As you read these tips, you may wonder how—and why—the assorted conditioning agents and techniques work. Seemingly, they promote water uptake and reduce bacteria; to my frustration, however, despite queries to numerous floral authorities, I failed to discover any substantiated scientific explanation for many of them.

Folks have been arranging flowers for centuries, though, without an understanding of principles of science, and even the unexplained tips allegedly work wonderfully. You can be the judge of their magic.

Pretty Posies Start in the Garden

"For beautiful flower arrangements, grow some cinnamon ferns (*Osmunda cinnamomea*) in your garden," suggests Luther Shaffer of Kutztown, Pennsylvania. "They are attractive while growing, they do well in partial or even deep shade, and they spread in the garden."

✻

When buds form on dahlias, peonies, chrysanthemums, and tea roses, leave the largest bud and pinch off the smaller ones in each cluster, advises another Kutztown gardener, Raymond Rice. "With this practice of disbudding, you'll have larger blooms."

✳

"Woody stems such as daisies, mums, and, especially, lilac and forsythia have a hard time absorbing water. They open up more to absorb water if you break the ends off by hand instead of using a knife," advises floral designer Scott Bjorge of Minneapolis, Minnesota. "Your second choice is to pinch them off with wire snips, which pulverizes the ends."

✳

When you make a bouquet of flowers such as snapdragons, whose own leaves are small and unremarkable, add a few leaves from a showier plant in your garden, suggests Mary Froegel of La Crosse, Wisconsin. "But watch them," she cautions. "The leaves often die before the flowers and get mushy in the water."

✳

"People let strawflowers grow too long before they harvest them," notes one of the nation's leading growers of everlastings, Ralph Cramer of Cramer's Posie Patch in Columbia, Pennsylvania. "Strawflowers continue to open after they're picked," says Ralph, "so if you're not quick enough, you end up with open flowers. Watch until one or two layers of the petals are open and then pick them."

Making Cut Flowers Last

If your homegrown flowers don't last as long as ones from the florist, don't feel like a failure. "Flower shops deal in special hybrids grown to last longer than common garden varieties," points out florist Kathy Guenther of Flowers by Guenthers in Onalaska, Wisconsin. For the freshest, longest-lasting garden flower bouquets, Kathy offers these tips:

• Cut your flowers in the cool of the day. Early morning is best; even if you wait until evening, the day's heat may have drained the flowers.

- Cut stems at an angle with a sharp knife. Avoid scissors, which can pinch the end.

- Remove any leaves from parts of the stem that will be under water—they invite bacteria.

- Plunge the stems into water immediately.

- Avoid using icy cold water, and if possible, avoid water that's been treated by a water softener.

- Hard, woody stems absorb better if you break up their tissue by laying the cut end of the stem on a table and giving it a tap with a hammer.

- Perk up wilted flowers by giving them a bath. Lay the flower—stem, leaves, blossoms, and all—in water for a half-hour or so before arranging them.

- Every day, change the water and give the stem a fresh cut, angling the bottom of the stem (a $1/4$- to $1/2$-inch cut is sufficient).

- Avoid putting cut flowers in direct sun. The cooler they're kept, the longer they'll stay fresh. If it's a hot day and you want them to look pretty for the evening, pick them in the morning and store them in the coolest room of your home.

Welcome Spring

You can coax blooms from cut branches of forsythia, pussy willow, lilac, apple, peach, or pear as early as January. Cheri Hemker of Onalaska, Wisconsin, shares this method from her old family almanac: Simply place the branches in water and dampen them with frequent spraying.

✳

For longer lasting hyacinths, squeeze the jellylike substance from the end of their stems as soon as they're picked. Plunge them immediately into very cold water mixed with five drops of peppermint oil.

Always leave on the green leaf near the flower head of a lilac. It conducts water to the bloom.

AUTHOR'S NOTE: *It's a common mistake to arrange narcissus in a tall, deep vase filled to the brim. All members of the narcissus family do best in small quantities of water, so use no more than an inch.*

Tulips

Pat Shedesky, who writes for *Flower & Garden*, *Organic Gardening*, and *Better Homes & Gardens*, raises hundreds of tulips in her La Crosse, Wisconsin, garden. She has a technique to make cut tulips last at least a week:

"The main thing is, don't wait till they're in their prime; cut them just as they're starting to open, and do it before sunup or after sundown. Then stand them up to their heads in lukewarm water (big, 46-ounce juice cans are a convenient container for this). Leave them in a cool place for twelve hours. An open porch is ideal, but keep them out of the wind, which saps moisture out of the blooms," Pat says. This method also will help peonies to last five days longer, Pat adds.

Roses

"The best time to cut roses is before 10:00 A.M.," counsels Roger Haynes, rosarian for Brookside Gardens in Wheaton, Maryland. "If air travels up the stem, the keeping quality goes down really quick. If this happens, make a new cut about halfway up the stem and hope for the best," says Roger.

✻

When picking roses, bring a container of tepid water with you to the garden, suggests Donna Fuss, rose garden consultant for Friends of Elizabeth Park in Hartford, Connecticut.

"The minute you cut, plunge the stem into the warm water. The warmth helps draw water up the stem. Otherwise, an air bubble is sucked in and bacteria grow, causing the bloom to droop," says Donna. "Then bring the roses into the house and recut under warm water, because no matter how fast you are, they'll still suck air. Keep the roses in the warm water for an hour, then put them into ice water for an hour to condition them. Change the water in your vase every second or third day, so it won't get stagnant."

✻

"Roses should have a very long, angular cut, longer than you would give most flowers (at least 1 to 1½ inches). Then split the length of the entire cut, and within ten seconds put the stem in water that is almost hot to the touch," says Minneapolis floral designer Scott Bjorge.

If your roses wilt because of improperly cut stems or lack of water, Scott suggests that you "make a new cut and lay the stems horizontally in a pan of warm (not hot) water for two to four hours, or until the roses firm."

✻

People often advise that you put roses in a cool place until you need to display them. Brookside Gardens rosarian Roger Haynes disagrees. "Put them out where you can enjoy them," he maintains. "Just keep them out of direct sunlight."

You see so many still-life paintings of flowers drooping over lush bowls of fruit that we tend to think of fruit and flowers as natural companions, but that's not so, cautions Roger.

"Don't stick roses in the refrigerator! Ethylene gas from ripening fruit such as apples do nasty things to roses—it causes them to age. Also," adds the Maryland rosarian, "the refrigerator is too cold for roses."

✻

To make roses last longer, you can also condition them first for a couple of hours in a solution of two tablespoons of powdered alum to a quart of water. But if you don't have any alum handy, table salt will do instead.

Camellias and Gardenias

"Camellias and gardenias never absorb water through the stem after they're cut," says Maria Daily of El Paso, Texas. "To help retain moisture in their petals, wrap each separate bloom in wet tissue and leave them in a cool place overnight."

＊

"Always handle gardenias very gently, as they have extremely fragile petals that bruise easily," cautions floral designer Scott Bjorge. Because of their short stems, they are best displayed by floating them in water, Scott adds.

Evergreen Boughs

Nothing is more fragrant than the spruce and pine boughs many folks cut for indoor winter holiday decorations. Unfortunately, they start to dry out and shed needles within a couple of days.

To keep boughs fresh longer, garden writer Pat Shedesky soaks their cut ends in a solution of one-half cup of brown sugar to each gallon of water for not less than twenty-four hours. (Dissolve the sugar in a small amount of water, then pour the solution into a pail of water.)

"If the boughs aren't put in the sugar water soon after they're cut, make a fresh cut, as the sap seals over pretty quickly, preventing water uptake. After conditioning the boughs, remove them from the water to use in decorations. If you plan to display the evergreens in containers, just add fresh water to the sugar solution as it evaporates," says Pat.

Multiple Solutions

"I've heard that a little vodka in the vase is supposed to extend the life of the flowers," says floral designer Scott Bjorge, "but I've never tried it." He recommends a less extravagant preservative—bleach. Add about one capful per gallon of water to stop bacterial growth in cut flowers.

AUTHOR'S NOTE: *I tried vodka on a magnificent bouquet Scott brought me, and the flowers stayed fresh for nearly two weeks.*

Have you ever wondered what magic ingredient is in the little packets that florists sometimes send along with flower arrangements? "They're basically just detergent and sugar," says Scott. "The detergent stops bacterial growth."

✹

Sodium thiosulphate, a chemical used in photography, has almost miraculous power to prolong the life of cut flowers. "A carnation, which might last four to five days normally, can last up to five weeks with its influence," says John Zoerb, president of La Crosse Floral in La Crosse, Wisconsin.

This expensive salt is only sold in bulk at present, John notes, but you may be able to cajole your local florist into selling you a smaller, affordable amount.

✹

Missouri native Betty Holey opened her garden file to share a fabulous assortment of common household solutions that prolong the life of cut flowers. By coincidence, Anne Goldbloom of Vancouver, Canada, sent a newspaper clipping dated 1954 that included many identical recipes.

For best results, first cut stems on a slant and strip the foliage from at least the lower 4 inches of the stem. Immediately plunge the stems into the conditioning solution you have chosen, and keep them away from direct sun and drafts. Cut the flowers in early morning and allow the stems to absorb the solution for several hours. Or cut in late afternoon and soak them overnight. Here are the "recipes" for specific flowers:

• For longer-lasting carnations and dianthus, soak them in cool water up to their flower heads; don't submerge the blossoms.

- Violas and violets stay vibrant if you bunch them together, submerge them for two hours, and then arrange them in a container holding ice water.

- Submerge ferns under water for twelve hours. When you're ready to use them, shake them well before adding them to your arrangement.

- The secret of a longer life for dahlias is to burn the stem ends, and then condition them in two quarts of ice water with five tablespoons of alcohol added.

- Burn the stem ends of hollyhocks, poinsettias, poppies, and milkweed, then condition them in a solution of one handful of rock salt to two quarts of water.

- "Fresh as a daisy" conjures up the image of a natural radiance. Who would guess that even daisies benefit from beauty potions? A conditioning bath of one quart of water with eight drops of peppermint oil helps daisies live longer.

- Snapdragons look snappier if conditioned in a solution of two tablespoons of salt to two quarts of water.

- Marigolds stay perkier after a cocktail of two tablespoons of sugar, one tablespoon of salt, and a quart of water.

- Your gladioli will keep longer if they're preconditioned in a quart of water mixed with five tablespoons of vinegar.

Recipe for a Greener Thumb

Nature is my library. It is living material waiting to be understood.

—ANTHONY TYZNIK, ILLINOIS LANDSCAPE ARCHITECT

Containers

What do you call your flower containers? My college roommate used to insist that if it costs less than $3.00 it is a "vayse"; if more, then it is a "vahze." Regardless of what you call it, just be sure that it's absolutely clean.

When your flower arrangements endure especially long, remember which container you used; some materials seem to have a beneficial influence on the life of cut flowers. For example, when I put flowers in the silver pitcher that my husband gave me on our twenty-fifth anniversary, they stay fresh three times longer than they last in other containers. A plant physiologist would no doubt explain that it's a chemical reaction, but I think it's magic.

Recipe for a Greener Thumb

I don't believe that anybody can learn gardening from a book. The way you learn is with dirt under your fingernails.

—BENNY SIMPSON, RESEARCH SCIENTIST, TEXAS A&M UNIVERSITY

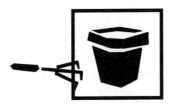

CHAPTER TWENTY-ONE

Container Gardening and Houseplant Horticulture

Schubert's Unfinished Symphony *really helped my droopy plants perk up. On the other hand, they didn't like Wagner.*

—RUTH SIMONS

While writing *Garden Smarts*, I spoke with one gardener who owned an entire square mile of fertile land, others who tended a few pots on an apartment balcony. But regardless of their garden's scope, the force creating green, growing life from sunshine and water is the very same magic.

As you'll read in the tips that follow, container gardening is a way to go not only if you have limited space but also if you have other dilemmas. For example, containers save kneeling and bending, which is great for anyone with back or knee afflictions. If too much shade or scorching heat is your challenge, you can wheel pots to follow the sunshine or, contrariwise, the shifting shade.

As many of you will agree, indoor gardening is a legitimate option—not just one for wimps—when the weather is daunting (to the plants or to you), be it constant drizzle, howling winds, sultry humidity, or subzero snow. In summer our potted plants go outside. In winter, when everything feels bleak and gloomy, they stay indoors for mutual comfort: We pay the electric bill; they add humidity to the indoor environment, bestow green grace, and reassure me that Mother Nature hasn't abandoned us after all. Whatever your motives for container gardening, the tips in this chapter will help you keep your plants healthy and luxurious. I hope they also help increase your satisfaction and fun. You will read ideas on potting, watering, cleaning, feeding, lighting, and propagating. You'll welcome hints that will help your plants adapt to seasonal changes and enhance the healthy growth of African violets, ferns, and exotic plants such as orchids and dates.

Recipe for a Green Thumb

Whether you're growing bonsai or doing any other kind of gardening, don't be so focused on the results that you forget to enjoy each element as it develops. After all, you're not creating an aircraft. You have to enjoy the process at each stage.

—JOE RUSK, HEAD ANIMAL KEEPER, SAN FRANCISCO ZOO

Houseplants Are Good for You

We generally think of outdoor food crops as the ones conferring health benefits, while houseplants, with the exception of potted herbs, are usually thought of as merely ornamental. But houseplants also make fine air purifiers, say the researchers at the Environmental Research Office of the Science and Technology Lab at NASA's John C. Stennis Space Center in

Bay Saint Louis, Mississippi. Plants can remove a wide range of pollutant chemicals that may contribute to respiratory complaints and fatigue.

"Some of the best purifiers," says NASA microbiologist Anne Johnson, "are peace lily, spider plant, English ivy, Chinese evergreen, and mother-in-law's tongue."

Some houseplants purify air not just through their leaves; roots and soil microbes also cleanse the air. To let them do their job most efficiently, leave the soil uncovered and remove low-hanging leaves, NASA's Science and Technology Lab scientists suggest.

Potting

It's a common fallacy that we're supposed to put gravel or broken pottery on the bottom of flower pots to improve drainage. "Studies have shown it actually hinders drainage," says Kathleen Halloran, associate editor of the Loveland, Colorado–based magazine *Herb Companion*. In such instances water clings to the small particles of the soil and fills the spaces, rather than moving into the gravel and out of the pot. Then it can't drain unless you pour in way too much water.

"Covering the hole up also restricts drainage," adds Kathleen. "When potting, put your soil in damp, instead of dry, and it won't fall out the hole."

✳

"The first thing I do when I buy plants in plastic pots is to transfer them to clay ones," says gardener Dick Gagne of La Crescent, Minnesota. "Clay containers minimize the damage of overwatering because they're porous; in plastic pots, on the other hand, surplus water doesn't evaporate, so if you overwater, the roots may rot."

✳

"Soak clay pots for a day before using them for potting," advises Olga French, formerly a horticulturist for Olbrich Botanical Gardens in Madison, Wisconsin. "If you start with dry pots, they will suck all the moisture out of your potting soil."

✸

"Even when they're clean, clay pots tend to look discolored from soil and water impurities. This stain is virtually impossible to remove," notes garden writer Pat Shedesky of La Crosse, Wisconsin, whose feature articles have appeared in leading garden magazines. "Set the pots inside a basket to hide the discoloration."

When plants outgrow their containers, it's tempting to transplant them into much larger pots to provide lots of growth room and to avoid having to repot as soon. "But don't," Pat Shedesky warns. "Never transplant into a pot more than 2 inches larger than its present diameter. If the pot is too big," Pat explains, "it holds moisture too long as there are not enough roots to take up the extra moisture."

Potting Soil

"No matter how well it performs in the ground during the growing season, in pots normal garden soil will soon form a compacted, heavy mass that prevents root respiration and fertilizer absorption. The result is stressed and hungry plants," says Renee Shepherd of Shepherd's Garden Seeds in Felton, California.

"To help prevent root rot, compaction, and sour soil, start with a good quality commercial container mix from a reliable nursery or garden center. As added insurance, thoroughly mix in about 25 percent perlite or gritty builder's sand. Do not use beach sand!"

✸

When potting container plants, beware of inexpensive, prepackaged soil, cautions nurseryman John Zoerb, owner of La Crosse Floral in La Crosse, Wisconsin. "Generally, it's too fine and it packs too much. Because it lacks pores in between the grains, it never dries out."

✸

Watering Guidelines

Do the leaves of your container plants turn yellow and drop off? "The most common reason," says Dick Gagne, "is overwatering. Most plants do best when their soil gets completely dry between watering."

One reason plants with long vines are prone to problems, notes Dick, is that the farther their tendrils grow from the roots, the harder it is for them to take in water. To provide extra moisture, Dick keeps a spray bottle to mist such plants. "Philodendrons and ferns benefit from misting, too," he says, "but it's detrimental to violets."

✳

"If your home environment is too dry for your container plants to thrive, or if they go downhill when you bring them inside in the fall from a more humid environment, put the pots in shallow pans of water," suggests garden writer Pat Shedesky. "To avoid root rot, raise the pots with river stones or crushed rock so their bottoms aren't sitting directly in the water."

To keep her hibiscus and geraniums loaded with blooms, Pat puts her pots on 12- to 14-inch plastic trays filled with shallow water. "Buy cheap ones from the discount store, the biggest possible," she says.

✳

If you fertilize your container plants regularly, soluble salts will build up unless you water amply, advises commercial grower Lori Bauer of Bauer Nursery, La Crescent, Minnesota. She learned this lesson the hard way. "One year I didn't want the mums to grow too much, so I watered them only lightly. But all the fertilizer built up in them, and they turned yellow and started wilting. If this happens to your plants, you can break up that excess soluble salts level by leaching the plant with clear water. Run water until it's running out the sides and bottom of the pot. Repeat again the same day, leaving at least an hour between waterings," she says.

"If you water your container plants from the top, use tepid water and keep them out of the sun for a while," advises Lori. "Cold water combined with bright sun will burn the leaves.

"If the water from your faucet is cold, let it sit a few hours until it comes to room temperature. If your hot water doesn't go though a softener, you can save time and simply use warm water from the tap."

✻

Sometimes your room feels warm, and yet you have houseplants that falter. "Could your ailing plant be situated near an uninsulated outside wall or over a cold floor?" asks Wisconsin nurseryman John Zoerb. "If the soil temperature of your pot is too low," he says, "the roots can't take up water." John also offers these considerations on watering:

- Tap water often comes out at about fifty-five degrees Fahrenheit, the point at which such plants as Chinese evergreen, diffenbachia, and ficus rebel. If the leaves on your plant yellow or drop off, your tap water may be too cold.

- Roots need air as well as water. If your water has a high mineral salts content, salt deposits will eventually clog the soil. Clay pots can also become clogged by the salt deposits. In such cases it's best to water container plants from the top to flush the salts through the drainage holes.

- Bottom-watering, on the other hand, floats the salts to the top. As the surface soil dries out, a crust of salt deposits will form; remove the crusted soil and replace it periodically.

- "If you repot every year and a half to two years, it's okay to water plants with softened water; if your water has a lot of minerals, it's wise to repot whether or not the supply is softened," concludes John.

✻

To water indoor plants while you're on vacation, use a heavy cotton cord and a glass of water. Put the glass of water next to your plant. Bury one end of the cord in the soil and put the other end in the glass of water, counsels Mark Rogers of La Crosse, Wisconsin.

Feeding Container Plants

Commercial potting soil mixtures may furnish the extra aeration and drainage container plants need. "However, since they may only contain 25 percent soil, they usually lack natural fertility," notes nurseryman Randy Baier of Baier Nursery in La Crosse, Wisconsin. He suggests that you use these soils along with fertilizers, such as Miracid or Rapid-Gro, that have secondary and trace elements.

✳

Many gardeners know that if you give outdoor plants too much nitrogen, they grow lush leaves at the expense of fruit and flower production. But folks aren't always aware that this also holds true for flowering houseplants. A high nitrogen fertilizer will give you lots of foliage but fewer blooms.

✳

"My grandmother, Fanya Metrick, put her used tea bags in the dirt of her potted plants and they flourished. She had a real green thumb," recalls pediatric neurologist Michelle Metrick of Chicago, Illinois.

AUTHOR'S NOTE: *The tannin in the tea makes the soil a little more acidic, which many plants prefer.*

Adapting to Change

Most potted plants from nurseries are potted in black or dark green plastic containers. "These dark pots absorb a tremendous amount of heat in the summer if they're on the side of the house with a sunny exposure," cautions garden writer Pat Shedesky of La Crosse, Wisconsin. "To shade and insulate the roots, insert them inside larger decorative pots," Pat advises.

✳

"All my houseplants go outside in the summer, and I always put them under a bush for shade," says Tatiana K. Bodine of Sioux City, Iowa. "Plants sunburn, so they should be protected."

✳

"Many gardeners know that they must acclimate indoor plants to outdoor conditions slowly. You have to expose them gradually—a few hours each day in a sheltered spot; then bring them back indoors until they adapt and harden off," says award-winning garden writer Tovah Martin, author of *Well-Clad Windowsills* (Macmillan).

"Make sure you use the same gradual process in reverse when it's time to bring container plants back onto the windowsill in the fall. Bring the plants back inside for an hour or more for a few days before resettling them permanently on the windowsill. It takes a little planning to acclimate plants properly in the fall, especially when frosts are threatening, but it's worth the effort," Tovah says.

✳

Unfortunately, it's not always possible to acclimate your plants gradually. Should your plants suffer from a sudden move, be patient and don't despair, counsels Bea Sperling of Vancouver, British Columbia.

"When I brought my gorgeous hibiscus tree indoors, all the flowers and leaves dropped off completely. It looked dead," Bea recalls. "In the hope that it would revive, I put it in a cool room by a window without direct sunshine. After it started to grow tiny leaves and buds, I moved it to a warmer room with a sunny, eastern exposure. Within six weeks, the hibiscus once again was filled with buds and bursting into bloom."

✳

"A greenhouse freeze-up is any indoor gardener's worst nightmare. But, you can actually revive frosted plants if you give them some fast first-aid," reassures garden writer Tovah Martin, who is also staff horticulturist at Logee's Greenhouses in Danielson, Connecticut.

"Don't put them in a sunny, toasty spot," cautions Tovah. "Instead, first run cool water over the frosted growth, and then cut off any severely damaged branches and leaves. Put the plants in a cool, dark cellar for a day or two. You might save their lives."

Problems and Solutions

"Soap and water sprays are a good, nontoxic way to rid container plants of insects. Some plants are sensitive to soaps, though, so be careful. If you buy commercial insecticidal soaps, you have the guidance of the label; with dishwashing soap, you don't. So in the latter case, it may be better to spot-spray only, and see how the plant reacts," advises Beth Weidner, assistant park manager for Alfred B. Maclay Gardens in Tallahassee, Florida.

✳

AUTHOR'S NOTE: *Most houseplants don't seem stressed when you go into a furniture-rearranging frenzy and move their location, so we were caught off guard when our two big figs (Ficus benjaminus) reacted by dropping all their leaves. Fig trees often go into shock when moved. If you must move them and they go bald, mist them frequently with a water-filled spray bottle, fertilize them regularly, and within a few weeks you'll see new foliage.*

Polishing

Shear Perfection hair salon in Westby, Wisconsin, doesn't just beautify people. The leaves of the salon's potted plants stay clean and polished, and perhaps even gain some nourishment, thanks to Miracle Whip salad dressing. "This is suitable for any smooth-leaved plant, and lasts a good month or so," says co-owner Carol Ignasik. "Rub it in with your finger, or apply it with a piece of absorbent cotton."

✳

Spray leaf polishes should be avoided, maintains Minnesota commercial grower Lori Bauer. "Your plant has to breathe, and besides, they make the plants look fake. If it's a good, healthy plant, it's shiny anyway," she says. "I dust the leaves of my plants with my son's old soft cotton diapers and damp water."

Lighting

It can be discouraging to grow houseplants if you've had little success, especially if your home has low light conditions. For increased luck Minnesota gardener Dick Gagne offers two suggestions. "African violets, ivy, fern, and gloxinia are low care and don't really want a lot of light," says Dick. "To compensate for short winter days if you live in the North, try forty-watt fluorescent lighting set with an automatic timer."

Propagating

Have you ever bought a beautiful potted ivy plant and then watched it shrivel and dwindle over time?

If you're reluctant to fuss with repotting and nursing it along but feel guilty throwing it out, Dick suggests an alternative. "Just cut off some of the

AUTHOR'S NOTE: *An interesting and economical gift to perk up a sick youngster (or even a grown-up) is a sweet potato water jungle. It gives cheer to bedridden folks because it grows by leaps and bounds and looks different every day. Take a firm sweet potato, stick three toothpicks about halfway between the two ends of the potato, and dangle the lower half in a jar of water. Within a few days the top will sprout leaves.*

Change the water every day, and run the roots under the faucet too, to prevent rotting.

good remaining sprigs, stick their ends in water, and when they root, repot them," he says.

African Violets

"Water African violets with warm water about the temperature you use for a baby's bath," advises Ruby Nicks of Onalaska, Wisconsin.

Keep African violets in a small pot, as they need to be rootbound to blossom, Ruby adds.

✳

When watering African violets and gloxinias, don't let water touch the leaves, advises Lori Bauer of Bauers Nursery in La Crescent, Minnesota.

Once African violets grow 4 to 6 inches in diameter, new plants appear off the sides once or twice a year, Lori says. If you wish, gently take the plant out of the pot with your fingers, and carefully separate the small ones. Replant, but not too deeply; don't cover the heart (crown). The violets with white blooms may give only two or three babies at a time, whereas the purple flowering plants are more fertile and might give you sextuplets or even eight at once.

How do you get African violets to bloom? The trick is to fertilize often and regularly, insists Lori Bauer. "I never fertilized a plant till I started working here, and mine didn't seem to grow at all. Now I fertilize every week, and they look nice and shiny and healthy—and they bloom," she says.

✳

Ask a bunch of good cooks how much salt you should put in the soup, and chances are few will agree. The same goes for successful gardeners. Violet fancier Dick Gagne (who lives scarcely a stone's throw from Bauers Nursery) credits his own lush and prolific African violets, some of which are ten years old, to restraint in fertilizing.

"After they finish their winter blooming period, I fertilize maybe once a week. While they're blooming, however, I feed them only once every two months," he says.

"You only need one leaf to restart a new African violet plant," Dick notes. "Break off a leaf from the parent plant, and put in a pot. If you wish, first dip the broken end in just a dusting of growth hormone powder. You can buy this inexpensive substance from a florist; a one-ounce package will serve many plantings for years and years to come."

Ferns

"If you want your ferns to grow long, luxuriant fronds, hang them from ceiling hooks or place them on fern stands. Ferns hate to be touched," advises Jeanette Manske of Stoddard, Wisconsin.

"As long as your fern is dark green, it doesn't need water. When it starts turning light in color, it's asking for a drink," says Jeanette.

Poinsettias

"You can make poinsettia blooms last up to a month longer if you clip the little yellow flowers from their centers," advises Pam Olson of Verona, Wisconsin. "This doesn't change the look of the plant noticeably."

✻

Many folks save holiday poinsettia to plant in the garden the next summer. The plant grows prolifically and looks beautiful. Unfortunately, when they bring the plant indoors in the fall, it won't flower and they wonder what they did wrong. The answer, according to Minnesota grower Eugene Bauer, is "nothing."

"Only 1 percent of poinsettias will bloom again—the owners of the other 99 percent feel like failures," Eugene says. In order to flower, poinsettias need days of ever-decreasing daylight and nights of total darkness. To make a pointsettia bloom, you will need a room that never has any unnatural light. "Street or car lights shining in the window or the light of a TV screen are enough to upset its balance," Eugene warns.

Exotic Houseplants

"I have a huge date palm that grew from a pit," says Hilda First of Edgewood, Maryland. "Dates take a long time, and then they'll shoot up about 6 inches overnight. When you want to germinate pits from dates, peaches, oranges, or grapefruit, put them in with a potted plant that you'll be watering anyway. Then you don't have to remember to keep them watered. Otherwise, you forget, and it dries out just before they get ready to sprout."

❋

In tropical Florida, where retired dentist Marvin Sperling lives for six months of the year, bromiliads grow abundantly in the wild. "But these exotic relatives of the pineapple make fine houseplants up North, as well. They need no coddling," says Marvin, who also raises them in his White Meadow Lake, New Jersey, home. "Bromiliads have very small root systems and do best without much water. Just put a little in the cupped depression in the center of their leaves. You can keep them going for generations, because just before the parent plant dies, 'pups' come up on the sides," he says.

❋

Amaryllis doesn't like to be repotted, so Wisconsin garden writer Pat Shedesky, who grows fifty-five amaryllis varieties, lets hers become so rootbound that you can hardly see soil. "If the pot is too large," she cautions, "instead of growing bigger, they go backwards—and get smaller. If you want to raise amaryllis, read a good houseplant book," Pat urges. "Their culture is very exacting, and unless you follow specific guidelines, they won't bloom."

Orchids

"I honestly believe that anyone can grow orchids," assures Wayne A. King, past president of the Orchid Growers' Guild. Wayne, who grows 250 orchid plants on the windowsills of his Cottage Grove, Wisconsin, home, offers these guidelines:

- Buy locally grown plants. Many people buy their first orchids while on vacation and quickly get discouraged when the plants don't respond to their local growing conditions. Of the various orchid groups, Phalaenopsis, or Moth Orchids, and Cattleya Hybrids are among the easiest to grow. (A lavender Cattleya hybrid such as LC Drumbeat is a good beginner's orchid.)

- Most orchids like an abundance of light, but be careful not to overdo it. In summer, direct sun can actually raise the leaf temperature high enough to cause tissue damage. Leaves that look bleached from the sun or blackened from heat are getting too much light.

- Too much shade, however, can reduce needed growth. If light is limited, supplement daylight with cool white fluorescent lights placed as close as possible to the plants.

- Because most tropical and subtropical species grow on trees or rocks, not in soil, orchids need more air at their roots than most other plants. Run a small fan for air circulation near the plant (twenty-four hours a day, if you can).

- Orchid plants, especially Cattleya types, need to be anchored solidly in their pots so that the plants can anchor their new roots. If your orchids are anchored adequately, you should be able to grip the plants and lift them, pots and all. Special wire clips and bamboo stakes are available to help anchor the plants.

- A good growing medium for orchids must be coarse enough to let air pass freely between the particles. If the particles are too large, the medium dries out too quickly. Fir or redwood bark is ideal for orchids, and a small amount of sphagnum moss will help to retain moisture.

- After a year or two, the bark decomposes to a soil-like consistency that holds water and reduces air at the roots. The water ought to pass freely through, so that the pot feels heavier after watering than before but not too much heavier. If the water soaks up like a sponge, repotting is probably in order. The bark in the growing medium supplies nutrition, so orchids don't need heavy feeding. Bacteria and fungi also feed on the bark, however, so an occasional feeding is helpful.

- Most Cattleya hybrids form buds in sheaths that dry up and lead a new grower to worry that the plant won't flower. On some varieties, these sheaths form up to six months before flowering and may turn brown— this is normal. Their stems (Pseudobulbs) also may dry up and this too is normal. Generally, the longer it takes orchid buds to open, the longer you can expect the flower to last—this is your reward for patience.

- "One of the very best tools for growing orchids is an orchid book that outlines these methods," says Wayne A. King. "And don't miss the chance to join a local orchid society. Members are always ready to help with growing problems, and many are generous in sharing plants as well as advice."

  The American Orchid Society (6000 South Olive Avenue, West Palm Beach, FL 33405–4159) publishes a monthly bulletin with valuable tips. The organization can also tell you the names of any local orchid societies and help you locate commercial orchid growers nearest to you.

States of Mind

Don't think it's your failure when your hanging Mother's Day basket peters out and looks like hell. Many holiday gift plants are forced into bloom under artificial conditions and so your chance that they'll come back as a normal perennial are very, very little.

When it looks ratty, don't try to stick it in the garden. It made you happy for a few weeks and that's enough; like a box of chocolates or a bottle of wine, you got the enjoyment, and now it's gone—that's enough satisfaction, isn't it?

—EUGENE BAUER, LA CRESCENT, MINNESOTA, NURSERYMAN

For More Cultured Plants

Do plants respond to music? Some folks feel they do. Music lover Ruth Simons loves experimenting with a wide repertoire to see which music her potted plants like best.

"Schubert's *Unfinished Symphony* really helped my droopy plants perk up," claims the New York native. "On the other hand, they didn't like Wagner."

States of Mind

As far as I'm concerned, if you throw a plant in the garbage, you should be reported for plant abuse.

—ANNIE GARDENER, LOUISVILLE, KENTUCKY

CHAPTER TWENTY-TWO

Reaping the Rewards: Harvesting

Just be patient.
—HELEN HALVERSON

One September afternoon a weather report predicted frost just as I was leaving for an appointment. Frantically, I grabbed an old bedspread and dashed out to the garden. Snatching bushels of ripening tomatoes from the vines, I dragged the heavily laden bedspread into the garage and rushed off, figuring the tomatoes would be temporarily safe.

Unfortunately, my husband returned home from work in my absence, pushed the automatic garage door opener, and drove into the garage as usual, never dreaming he should be on the lookout for a floorful of tomatoes.

All the tender care I had taken in growing my garden of plump treasures was wasted in a cruel twist of harvesttime fate.

Whether you are grappling with sudden frosts or the questions of when to pick and how to store your produce, unless you know how to avoid or anticipate the difficult issues of harvesting, you won't be able to enjoy your fruits and vegetables.

This chapter offers tips to help you through harvesttime, relieving some of the more common frustrations of harvesting peas, peppers, tomatoes, squash, corn, popcorn, potatoes, and melons. Crop storage hints and jelly-making and canning tips will help you enjoy the bounty of your garden.

One more common harvest problem may still perplex you, however: How do you cope with bumper crops? When you have too much of a good thing, try to share the surplus with your local emergency shelter or food pantry. On rare occasions, though, there's such a glut that even the soup kitchens are up to their ears in produce. If you've ever grown zucchini, you probably know what I mean.

Gardener Donna Fuss of Bloomfield, Connecticut, offers this sly solution for dealing with the surplus that challenges the imagination of virtually every zucchini gardener sooner or later:

"If you have mailboxes on your street, as we do on our Rural Delivery, go around in the dead of night and stuff the zucchini in the boxes. I've done that," confesses Donna.

"You can also hang them in plastic grocery bags on railings. The purpose," she explains, "is not to decorate your neighborhood, but to find homes for orphaned zucchinis."

You're at your own risk, though—it's a federal offense to cram boxes designated for the U.S. Mail with unstamped zucchinis.

Hindsight is 20/20 Vision

A garden journal is like a family album of your garden. In a spiral notebook I keep a record of everything I've planted and what has bloomed. I record three years together in columns, with one page per month. That makes it easy to keep track of what I've ordered without flipping pages. If I had bad luck last year, I can see what worked a long time ago, or I can try new things.

—JENNIFER COHN, SYRACUSE, NEW YORK

Peas

"Because snow peas are best when eaten freshly picked," advises Will Vultaggio of Bethlehem, Pennsylvania, "plant only three or four seeds a day if you have a small family. This way, you can enjoy the harvest over a few weeks, and won't have to eat them all at once by yourself."

✳

Luther Shaffer of Kutztown, Pennsylvania, suggests that you use a microwave oven for blanching edible pea pods. "It's quicker and doesn't heat up the kitchen," Luther says. "Because you're not blanching the peas in boiling water, they retain nutrients better. They keep their color much better, too—they're really a brilliant green. Months later, they are still nice and crisp."

To try Luther's method, wash the pea pods and put about one and a half cups of them in an uncovered microwave bowl or Pyrex pie pan for about one minute. Remove them from the microwave, and let them cool off.

Spread the pods on a cookie sheet so that they will freeze individually. Bag the frozen pods. "This allows you to reach in and take just what you need," says Luther. "You can also do green beans the same way."

Peppers

"Don't pull sweet peppers off, or you risk tearing the plant apart. Cut them, leaving one-half inch of stem on the pepper," says garden writer Jan Riggenbach of Glenwood, Iowa.

✳

Raymond Rice of Kutztown, Pennsylvania, discovered an easy way to prepare peppers for freezing: "There's no need to blanch peppers before freezing for later use in soups, stews, and sauces," maintains Raymond. "Simply cut them in strips or small pieces, and lay them on a baking sheet and freeze. Then seal in plastic bags and store in your freezer. This method is also great for chopped onions," he adds.

Tomatoes

If you have a bumper crop of very ripe tomatoes demanding immediate attention, buy yourself some time: If you can't process them immediately, simply quarter the tomatoes, seal them in plastic bags, and pop them into the freezer. "They're handy for such dishes as spaghetti sauce, chili, or soup," says Irene Wojahn of Onalaska, Wisconsin. (Pennsylvania gardener Raymond Rice suggests freezing the tomato wedges on a cookie sheet before bagging them. Once they're individually frozen, you can take out just what you need.)

✳

"For canning, select tomatoes ripened on healthy vines. Dead or frost-killed vines may be too low in acid or cause spoilage," cautions Carol Hacker, home economist for Kerr Group, Inc. in Jackson, Tennessee.

✳

AUTHOR'S NOTE: *Of course, vine-ripened tomatoes are the most delicious. Unfortunately, tomatoes touching the ground are subject to rot before they ripen. If you have this problem, pick those low-growing, immature tomatoes before they go bad, and seal them in a plastic bag with a couple of ripe apples or a banana. The fruit releases ethylene gas, which promotes ripening.*

✳

"Tomatoes taste best if you don't refrigerate them. Ripe tomatoes will keep three days or more in a cool place," advises mail-order seed merchant Renee Shepherd of Shepherd's Garden Seeds in Felton, California.

If your tomatoes are nearly ripe when Jack Frost comes, don't put them on a sunny window, counsels Renee. "Instead," she says, "let them ripen wrapped individually in newspaper, so they aren't touching each other."

❋

When your tomato plants are still laden with green fruit and you're in for a killing frost, Utah gardener Richard Bunker advises that you pick every green tomato left on the vines. Store them unwrapped in cardboard boxes in a cool, dark, humid place. The Bunkers have a basement with a dirt floor, ideal for this purpose. "Generally they'll last until Christmas this way," he says. "Roma tomatoes last the longest of every variety I've tried so far, keeping until February without spoiling."

❋

AUTHOR'S NOTE: *A quick and easy way to ripen your end-of-the-season tomato crop is simply to pluck the entire tomato plants out of the garden, roots and all, and hang them upside down in the garage, suspended from nails.*

Cabbages

Unless you're a restaurant owner or a sauerkraut maker, there's nothing quite as appalling as having all your huge heads of cabbages maturing at once. According to the methods of Bangor, Wisconsin, farmer Bill Hansen, you can hold off harvesting a couple of extra weeks.

Here's how: When the mature head is solid but has not started to split, pull it up a bit, while leaving it in the ground; twist the head a half-turn; then let it settle back.

"This breaks many of the cabbage's roots so that the plant takes up less water, and the head stays intact. Once the head splits, insects get in, and you get much waste," Bill says.

❋

"Cabbages can be harvested in an especially rewarding way," says syndicated garden columnist Jan Riggenbach of Glenwood, Iowa. "When the head is large and compact, cut it off with a knife, but leave the stalk in the ground. Use the knife to slit the remaining stalk into quarters with slashes about 1½ inches deep. Four new cabbages will form from the old stalk. They'll be smaller, but they'll have nice, compact heads. Because cabbage is a heavy eater, add some compost," Jan adds, "and break off any extra shoots."

"If any worms are hiding in your cabbage, they'll float out if you soak the head for five minutes in a gallon of water with one tablespoon of salt," advises Jan.

AUTHOR'S NOTE: *I find that it's especially helpful to do this with broccoli, because the little green worms are so well camouflaged among the dark green florets.*

"When preparing cabbage, grate the core along with the head since the core is highest in vitamins," advises Jan Riggenbach.

Baby Cabbages

Brussels sprouts are extremely nutritious, but many folks find their taste unappealingly strong. Try leaving them in the garden a bit longer than usual. "This vegetable gets much milder and better tasting after the frost," notes retired veterinarian Ken Johnston of West Salem, Wisconsin. "They withstand even a good, heavy freeze."

Leeks

To provide delicious, fresh leeks late in the year, advises Ken Johnston, harvest them in the fall, keeping as much of the root as possible intact.

Put eight or ten leeks upright in a five-gallon pail toward the outer edge of the pail. Cover them with moist garden dirt. Leave some green tops exposed, but pile the dirt up around each plant high enough to keep it blanched (it's the mild white part that's the most desirable).

"You can store them this way in a cool place (such as a garage or basement) for most of the winter," says Ken. "If the soil dries out, add a pint or so of water to keep it moistened."

Greens

"Leafy kale lacks the strong flavor of broccoli, cabbage, or cauliflower that some folks find objectionable," says Ruth Ann Davis of Tucson, Arizona, "and is good finely shredded in raw salads, cooked, or added to soup. Yet kale is a vegetable that home gardeners often overlook."

"The more mature the plant, the sweeter it gets. Keep picking the bigger leaves, and the plant keeps producing. Your kale will even stay green in the winter, with snowbanks over it," Ruth Ann says.

AUTHOR'S NOTE: *If your spinach or other strong-flavored greens develop a bitter aftertaste when boiled or steamed, the American Institute for Cancer Research suggests that you try cooking them in a microwave. With less cooking time and less water, they'll have a milder flavor, less bitterness, and more nutrients. Leafy greens are an excellent source of beta-carotene, a substance related to vitamin A that has been found to lower the risk of some cancers.*

✳

For years Lee Rodman, a native of Syracuse, New York, spent lots of time weeding the garden, yet one of her leisure-time interests was foraging for edible plants in the wild.

When Lee, a nurse, and her husband, a physician, investigated the nutritional benefits of the traditional vegetables they cultivated and the weeds they gathered, they discovered that some weeds actually had more nutrition than the vegetables. So why not grow wild plants, they reasoned, and save the effort of all that weeding?

"We originally sowed lamb's-quarters (*Chenopodium album*), a mild, wild spinach. We don't even plant them anymore—they just come up," says Lee.

Another edible wild crop in Lee's garden is amaranth. "It's very high in protein and other nutrients," says Lee, "and like lamb's-quarters, it's good raw in salad, steamed, or briefly stir-fried."

Edible Flower Blossoms and Seeds

"When nasturtium seeds are still green, they taste like watercress or radish, and they are good in salads and stir-fried dishes," observes Danny O'Deay of San Francisco, California. "You can also use them as a substitute for capers. Fill a small bottle with green nasturtium seeds. Boil vinegar and fill up the bottle, covering the seeds."

✳

Bored with the same old salads? Toss flowers with your salad greens. "The orange and yellow petals of pot marigolds (*Calendulas*) are edible and really cheery," notes herb grower and floral designer Terry Kemp, owner of God's Green Acres in Onalaska, Wisconsin. Violets are another edible, nutritious, and beautiful salad ingredient, adds Terry. "You can also make tea with their leaves."

In Victorian times, says Terry, sugared flowers such as violets, pansies, nasturtiums, rose petals, mint, anise, and hyssop were popular confections, and they are still wonderful for special, original cake decorations. "Kids love them," says the mother of two.

Squash

How do you know when squash is ready to pick? Winter squashes such as butternut and acorn are ready to harvest when their vines die back and/or their rinds are tough and cannot be pierced with your thumbnail, counsels Renee Shepherd of Shepherd's Garden Seeds in Felton, California.

Leave 1 or 2 inches of stem and cure in the sun for about ten days before storing in a dry place at room temperature.

✳

Most garden vegetables must be blanched in boiling water or steam before they are frozen. Blanching stops any further enzyme action that would cause them to develop an "off" flavor in the freezer.

If you want to make fresh zucchini bread in winter, though, you can freeze grated zucchini without blanching it first. "Just defrost twice as much as you need, and squeeze out the water or the excess moisture will make the bread yukky," says Donna Fuss of Bloomfield, Connecticut.

Corn

Many folks will tell you ruefully that they know their corn is ripe when the raccoons devour it. For more helpful signals, pick your corn when the corn silk looks very dark brown and damp and the kernels are milky when pressed with a thumbnail, advises Renee Shepherd of Shepherd's Garden Seeds in Felton, California.

Popcorn

AUTHOR'S NOTE: *It's fun to produce your own homegrown popcorn—you can peel back the shucks and air-dry whole cobs on an old window screen in a well-ventilated place protected from birds and mice. Then remove the kernels from the cobs, and store them. For gift giving leave the kernels on the cobs and use a pretty bow to tie a few cobs together by their shucks.*

✸

"To get big, fluffy popcorn kernels with fewer non-popping duds, store the popcorn in the freezer in a closed jar until you're ready to pop it," advises Hilda First of Edgewood, Maryland. "After the jar has been opened a lot, it tends to dehydrate and lose some of its explosive power, so it's a good idea to add a teaspoon of water to each quart of popcorn," says Hilda.

Potatoes

Potatoes are mature when the tops of the plants become withered and yellow. "I was sure my first potato crop was dying from disease when I saw this happen," Iowa garden writer Jan Riggenbach confides.

✸

If anything's more frustrating than growing a crop and getting awful results, it's getting a fabulous yield and then ruining it. Every year, all across the land, thousands and thousands of gardeners can be heard cursing as they inadvertently spear the potatoes they're trying to harvest.

How to prevent impaling the spuds with your digging tools? "They don't tell you in the book," Wisconsin farmer Bill Hansen counsels, "so experiment. Some varieties of potatoes grow all in one clutch; others try to get as far away as possible, all-which-ways-as-you-can. You have to adjust to their whereabouts, so know your varieties. They tend to be the same in a row, so try to remember the layout of the first potato plant when you're digging, and dig accordingly."

Melons

"Muskmelons will turn from green to yellow, and the melon will fall off with a gentle tug when it's ripe," Iowa garden writer Jan Riggenbach advises. "A further test, before you slice it open, is to press your fingernail into a seam. If you hear a crunch, give it another day on the kitchen counter," she adds.

✳

One of America's most generous couples, Helen and Bill Halverson of Onalaska, Wisconsin, grow four or five truckloads of watermelon and cantaloupe to share with others.

"The very first cantaloupe of the season are extra delicious," Helen believes. To determine when a cantaloupe is ripe, put a little pressure on the stem end. If it's hanging on securely, leave it; if the stem loosens readily and pops off, the melon is ripe, she advises.

"Unlike cantaloupe," notes Helen, "the first watermelon out of the garden tend to be pale and tasteless. Because watermelon take a long time to ripen, most people tend to cut them open too soon. Just be patient," she cautions.

Do you have trouble thunking watermelons like drums, trying to identify the ripe ones by their hollow resonance?

The melon is likely to be ripe when the little curl that grows about 3 or 4 inches away from the melon on the feeding stem has dried into a hard, stiff little filament, notes Helen. "We've decided this is much more effective than relying on our hearing."

AUTHOR'S NOTE: *Watermelons won't ripen after they're severed from the vine, so pick only absolutely ripe ones. Unfortunately, it's impossible to keep a bunch in your refrigerator after harvest because they take up so much space. But you can extend their shelf life the early pioneer way by storing the melons in a cool place, buried in sawdust (old-time farmers also buried them in hay or grain).*

❋

Storing Root Crops

Norma Roggensack of La Crosse, Wisconsin, has had good luck keeping her carrots fresh and readily available during the winter by leaving them right in her garden, buried under a big pile of leaves 2 to 3 feet deep. Even in subzero temperatures, they won't freeze as long as you have piled on enough leaves, Norma assures. "On a mild day," says Norma, "I go out and dig a new bunch."

❋

Missouri native Joe Borntreger has learned how to store vegetable crops with as little spoilage as possible. Joe and his wife, Mattie, have raised ten children on a farm that has no refrigeration, because in keeping with their Amish faith, they use no electricity.

"You can store carrots without sand or any other covering," Joe advises. Just keep them in a plastic pail in a cool, dark place (so they won't sprout) and don't wash them until use. "Store potatoes the same way, with the same conditions," Joe adds.

❋

Here's the lowdown: To enjoy fresh homegrown produce even in midwinter, you can rig up a substitute for an old-fashioned root cellar even on a small city lot, says retired University of Wisconsin Extension agricultural agent Jim Ness.

Simply dig a hole in the ground about 3 feet deep. ("Unless your winters are very severe, this depth is generally adequate," Jim says.) Fill the

AUTHOR'S NOTE: *The frost line may be a few inches deep or it may be 6 feet deep; it varies geographically, and it fluctuates from year to year. To learn your frost line, ask the same folks who supply data to the USDA for its crop reports—your local grave diggers.*

hole with straw, sandwiching your root crops between straw layers below the frost line.

✻

"To store sweet potatoes, harvest them in the late fall just before frost. But keep in mind that a sweet potato freezes very easily," cautions Ruth Switzer of Nehawka, Nebraska.

✻

Sweet potatoes keep best after harvest when stored at room temperature, not in a cool place as with regular potatoes, advises Bee Whirley of Keysville, Virginia.

✻

"When you harvest potatoes and onions, don't wash the garden soil off before storage—they'll spoil sooner if you wash them," warns longtime Wisconsin seed dealer Donna Schultz.

✻

Fruit

Traditionally, fruit was canned in heavy sugar syrup. Most canning directions still call for heavy syrup, but it's possible to have success with low sugar and even sugarless processing.

"We used to use syrup," says Utah gardener Richard Bunker, who raises late-variety Hale peaches for canning. "We finally decided it's not necessary. We found adding just one tablespoon of sugar per quart was ample. Peel the peaches, pit and halve them, then process according to the directions for your altitude. Last year we tried processing the peaches with no sugar at all, and liked them as well," he adds. "After you go awhile, you really acquire a taste for it."

You can also can apricots and cherries without sugar, the Bunkers discovered. Plums, on the other hand, are too tart to can totally sugar-free, Richard believes, so he adds a tablespoon of sugar per quart canning jar.

"Pears are a wonderful fruit to grow if you like eating them fresh, but they are a lot of trouble for home canning," Richard concludes. "They fall off the tree or birds get them before they're ready to pick. You have to pick them green, and let them ripen on the cellar floor. But they don't all turn yellow at one time, so if you can, you'll have to do a batch every other day for two weeks," he warns.

✳

AUTHOR'S NOTE: *Processing the magnificent yield from our apple trees used to be an onerous chore for me because I believed that homemade applesauce had to look like the store-bought variety. One day I got impatient with the fuss and mess of peeling apples and straining sauce and decided to dispense with both. The result was a much tastier, more colorful, creamier sauce with more fiber and higher nutrition. Since we don't spray our fruit, chemical residue on the peel is never a concern.*

AUTHOR'S NOTE: *For berries with good texture, gently spread a single layer on a tray or cookie sheet. Sprinkle with a modest amount of sugar, if desired, and pop them into the freezer. Once they are frozen, bag them. This method avoids bruising, allows the berries to hold their original shape, and lets you unthaw a few without having to take out the whole amount. The berries also thaw out quickly because they aren't squeezed together as they would be if they were bagged before freezing.*

Jams and Jellies

Prickly pear cactus (*Opuntia*) are interesting, virtually care-free plants.

Many folks who grow them for ornamental purposes don't realize they are also edible. Former New Mexico resident Ingrid McKenna Goldbloom recalls, "When the pears ripen, they make a delicate, rich ruby-red jelly. But watch out! Wear tough gloves when picking and peeling, and be very careful about sampling the fruit while you're working—they're covered with fine, barbed hairs."

✳

If you've ever made jelly, you know what a messy business it is. Perhaps like most of us, you simply assumed that the splashes, drips, and sticky puddles were inevitable. Not so!

"Most jelly bags are way too small," holds Richard Bunker of Salt Lake City. To avoid the mess, he advises that you let your boiled fruit drain overnight in a flour sack in your bathtub.

AUTHOR'S NOTE: *When Richard recommended his "Swedish juicer," he graciously offered to mail a picture to help me describe it. So when the juicer's picture arrived, I was tickled to read the words emblazoned upon it:* MADE IN KOREA.

Even less messy is a stainless steel Steam Juicer, which steams the washed fruit and collects the juice in a separate compartment. "It's easy and efficient," says Richard. "For making any jelly, this is the best way."

Home Canning: You Can Do It!

A couple of generations ago, home canning skills weren't a hobby—they were a necessity. Today fewer folks know how to can, and many are leery of undertaking the seemingly complicated and demanding task.

"If you want to get all the basics succinctly," declares Utah gardener Richard Bunker, who cans at least 150 quarts of produce a year, "the best canning guide is The Kerr Kitchen Cookbook." This canning and freezing guide, newly revised and updated with more low-sugar recipes, is available where Kerr jars are sold, or by writing Kerr Group, Inc., P.O. Box 76961, Los Angeles, CA 90076. Please include a check for $4.00 to cover postage and handling.

States of Mind

Be optimistic and be prepared. Buy all your canning supplies as soon as you have the garden planted. It gives you incentive to tend the garden and also saves a trip to the store when you're busy picking the produce.

—LEEANNE BULMAN, FARMER, WISCONSIN

CHAPTER TWENTY-THREE

Moonlight and Squirrels' Ears: Garden Folklore

Never prune a tree in a full moon . . . you bleed out its strength, and the tree will lose power.
—RICARDO BORRERO

For many thousands of years, people have been cultivating gardens without the benefit of an understanding of soil science, chemistry, plant physiology, meteorology, or genetics. In ancient times the wondrous phenomenon of tiny dry seeds transforming into growing plants must have seemed like magic. Indeed, many civilizations relied upon the mercy of their gods and the vagaries of charms and incantations to bring them a bountiful harvest.

In ancient Egypt, for instance, farmers molded effigies of the god Osiris out of earth and corn and buried these in their fields as a fertility charm.

Today we don't go this far, but many colorful folk practices are still with us. As long as the miracle of life remains a mystery and we remain at the mercy of powerful forces we cannot control—storms and droughts, for instance—folk rituals will remain a part of the gardening tradition.

Beyond that, many gardeners simply enjoy approaching the task in the time-honored ways of their forebears.

No doubt many of these folk customs really are valid, though as of yet not fully understood. One of the most widely followed is the ritual of regulating activities such as planting, pruning, and harvesting according to the phases of the moon.

This chapter explores the customs, taboos, superstitions, portents, and folklore that pepper the language and practice of planting, tending, and harvesting a garden. You'll enjoy a mixture of luck charms, myths, omens, and even a dash of voodoo. Make sure you read the sections on nature's signs and weather portents. Over the ages astute folk have grown skilled at reading natural signals and synchronizing seasonal garden chores with their appearance. Even today many of nature's cues can provide us with valuable information.

Because they're fun to read and because they have historical interest, the chapter includes recipes for remedies using plants once commonly believed to possess great curative power. One or two of these are tempting to try, but be forewarned—while most are harmless, at least one (the rabies "cure") is clearly deadly!

When you read the advice and precautions of this chapter, I hope they will bring a smile to your face. But keep in mind that some, like the following planting tip from my husband, should be taken with a grain of salt: "If you lie in bed and cover your face with a pillow during any phase of the moon," he says, "but especially on a weekend, beautiful flowers will grow in your garden, because other members of your household will do the work!"

Good Luck, Bad Luck

If you can't find the rue you planted in your herb garden, you might logically wonder if insects, disease, or climate is the culprit. Consider this, though—it could be black magic!

"Rue is often stolen in big city gardens because it's used in voodoo rituals," says Sarah Price, curator for New York City's Central Park Conservatory Garden. "Folk wisdom has it that rue stolen from someone else's garden is the most potent."

✳

Organic gardeners beware: "It's terribly unlucky to leave a wagonload of manure overnight," insists Maria Daily of El Paso, Texas. Get out there and spread it right away.

✳

AUTHOR'S NOTE: *Do you have a plant that refuses to thrive despite your best efforts? Maybe you made the mistake of being too polite. According to an old superstition that a West Virginia friend of mine recalls from childhood days, you should never say "thank you" when folks share plants, tubers, or cuttings from their gardens. If you say thanks, the plant won't grow. This belief doesn't seem to be confined to the hills of West Virginia; I've heard it echoed by folks from all over the land.*

Planting Lore

Iona Wabaunsee (now of North Bend, Washington) learned this common piece of folklore while growing up in the Ozark Mountains: Plant three grains of corn to a hill: one for the bugs, one for the crow, and one to grow.

"The Indians have a similar saying in their language," says Iona, whose late husband, Albert, was a member of the Potawatomi tribe.

✳

Lyda Lanier, who farms in Tomah, Wisconsin, and writes feature articles about rural life for numerous publications, has a variation: one for the crow, one for the cutworm, and one to grow.

"And if all three come up, I just enjoy them—I don't sucker (thin) them," Lyda says.

✳

"Where I live, in Kutztown, Pennsylvania, a common belief in the Pennsylvania Dutch country is that you must plant your peas and your onions by St. Patrick's Day," says Luther Shaffer.

✳

Sometimes it's hard to remember ideal planting dates. For turnips, though, there's an old rhyme to keep you from forgetting: "Plant on the tenth of July, wet or dry," reminds Mary Dempster of Garnivillo, Iowa.

✳

Iowan Monica Lazere shares this bit of folk medicine for the rose garden. "If your soil isn't rich in copper, bury three or four copper pennies in the soil alongside the roots of your rosebushes. It increases the strength of the stems and the beauty of the flowers. I used to do this with Peace roses," she says. "But with inflation, today you'd better put in a few more," she adds.

AUTHOR'S NOTE: *If you use U.S. pennies minted since 1982, you'll need a whole lot of them, because they are now mainly zinc, with only a 2.6 percent copper coating. So if you want to enrich your soil's copper content, bury only pennies dated 1981 or earlier.*

Moonstruck

Many gardeners, like Mary Dempster of Garnivillo, Iowa, hold to the widespread custom of planting potatoes on Good Friday. Ask any of its practitioners why they do this, and they'll tell you it's tradition—their parents and grandparents always planted on that day.

"I never heard of any religious significance," says Sister Arita Dopkins, retired chair of religious studies at Viterbo College. Sister Arita suspects the custom has links to moon-phase planting traditions. "Easter is always the first Sunday after the first full moon of the spring—two days following Good Friday. Therefore, your potatoes just get settled in when the moon starts to decrease," the theologian notes. "My dad did it, too. He even dug under the snow to plant. You plant root crops in the dark of the moon, when it's decreasing. You plant above-ground crops when the moon is increasing," she says.

✷

Plant all underground root crops (like potatoes) on a dark night when there's no moon, advocates one of Keysville, Virginia's most fabulous gardeners, Manuel Lacks.

AUTHOR'S NOTE: *Scientists have documented that some flowering plants, such as sweet peas, need a period of total darkness to blossom. If they start setting buds during the lunar dark phase, the moonless nights trigger the hormones needed to bloom. But if the plants mature during the full moon, the moonlight delays flowering. Potatoes and other vegetable crops may respond similarly to the influence of moonlight.*

✷

Many folks hold that the moon phase influences harvesting as well as planting: If you want your potatoes to keep well, dig them only when the moon phase is on the decrease, Manuel recommends.

As a matter of fact, the Virginia gardener plants his whole vegetable garden strictly by the moon. He sows corn only after the full moon, when it's on the wane. Green beans go in right after the change to the new moon in the waxing phase.

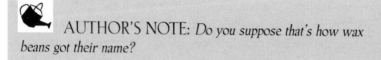 AUTHOR'S NOTE: *Do you suppose that's how wax beans got their name?*

✳

"Never, never prune a tree in a full moon or even when it's three-quarters full," admonishes Ricardo Borrero, a San Francisco, California, resident originally from Colombia, South America.

"At home," Ricardo says, "people believe that the sap is all through the tree at that time. If you trim, you bleed out its strength, and the tree will lose power. You should cut in the new moon or when the moon is in the decline. In Colombia, wood for timber, furniture-making, and export is never cut in a full moon. Because the fibers are open, the timber is more susceptible to termites, and insects can enter the tree."

AUTHOR'S NOTE: *I'm told that commercial walnut growers in Iowa prefer to cut their timber in winter before the sap has risen, believing that the wood is of better quality at that time.*

Reading Nature's Signals

The word phenology sounds like something one might study as a philosophy or theology major, but it's only the scientific word for the common homespun practice of using natural signals for planting, pruning, and harvesting.

Though Jennifer Cohn of Syracuse, New York, has a degree in natural resources and has worked in horticulture and botany, she still relies upon some old-time gardening lore learned from her mom and grandma: "When forsythia blooms, that's the time to prune your roses," she says. "When lilacs are blooming," adds Jennifer, "it's time to fertilize the lawn, and when oak leaves are the size of a mouse's ear, it's time to sow your corn," Jennifer concludes.

✳

Similarly, retired University of Wisconsin Extension agricultural agent Jim Ness of Onalaska, Wisconsin, recalls that "the old-time farmers used to believe that the proper time to plant corn is when the leaves of the white oak are as large as a squirrel's ear."

AUTHOR'S NOTE: *Where I live, the time to plant corn is when the dogs start scratching their fleas.*

Ice Men and Other Weather Portents

Nearly every child knows who Jack Frost is, but many a person grows up without ever having heard of the "Ice Men." For Jeanette Manske the "Ice Men" are as real as old Jack. The isolated farm in Chipmunk Coulee, Stoddard, Wisconsin, that Jeanette has lived on all her life had no electricity or even any road in her childhood sixty years ago. Although much has changed over the years, Jeanette believes that the old garden wisdom she learned long ago still holds true.

"Be alert for the Ice Men," says Jeanette. "They like to visit in the spring, around the time of the full moon in May. So listen to the weather forecasts, and be prepared to cover vulnerable plants such as tulips and bleeding hearts, which may be blooming then."

AUTHOR'S NOTE: *Folklore can also help you predict the arrival of Jack Frost in fall, according to my farmer neighbors. At the first thunderstorm of the year, count six months ahead. You can expect frost at the full moon following that date.*

✳

It's helpful to be forewarned when you're in for a shorter than usual growing season, so watch for the signals your plants send out.

"Be acquainted with their normal blooming schedule. If they respond quicker than usual, winter will come early," observes retired nurseryman Cy Klinkner of La Crosse, Wisconsin. "Funkia normally bloom the third week in August. When they bloom in June, expect a short summer—fall will set in early," he predicts.

It's also a common folk belief that you can predict a severe winter when the evergreens produce more seed than usual. Cy Klinkner swears that this is no mere superstition. "Look at the pine cones, juniper berries, or arborvitae seed clusters in mid-July to see how abundant they are. If it's a big crop, then make the woodpile bigger, and caulk and insulate the house, because you're gonna need it," prophesies the nurseryman. "My wife and I kept a log for years; another nurseryman I know kept track for sixty years, and he was able to forecast with better accuracy than the weather bureau. Incidentally, this predicts cold, but not snow," Cy adds.

✳

Have you been afraid to keep poinsettias for fear they'd poison children and pets? Well, put your fears aside. Folklorist Jan Harold Brunvand of the University of Utah in Salt Lake City, who is an authority on urban legends, assures us that this long-held belief is false. Professor Brunvand cites research at Ohio State University that concluded a fifty-pound child could eat more than 500 poinsettia leaves without serious ill effect.

He points out that the American Medical Association's *AMA Handbook of Poisonous and Injurious Plants* declares poinsettia produces either no effect or occasional cases of vomiting, and the Consumer Product Safety Commission describes it as a "non-food substance which if eaten could cause some discomfort."

"We've been brainwashed by this piece of seasonal folklore. It may have evolved because the name `poinsettia' sounds slightly like the word 'poison,'" says the Utah folklorist.

Tree Doctoring

Ricardo Borrero of San Francisco, California, cut back his persimmon too severely one season, and it didn't produce for the next two years. Finally, Ricardo resorted to an old folk practice from his native Bogota, Colombia.

"To make a fruit tree bear, hammer a large nail [such as a tenpenny size] at a 45-degree angle into the trunk just at ground level. It turns the tree into a female!" insists Ricardo.

Remedies

A few years ago bandage manufacturers began marketing brightly colored bandages for children. Many years ago, however, folks used green bandages of another sort. "Wounds packed with leafy greens were less likely to turn gangrenous, and soldiers injured on Civil War battlefields were often treated with this remedy," says Joan Dolbier of Winona, Minnesota, a regional historian and registered nurse.

Today the wild herb plantain is usually regarded as a nuisance in our lawns and gardens. But in the days before antibiotics, small injuries were often complicated by infection. "A poultice made with a big wad of plantain leaves and warm milk was a popular treatment for such wounds," notes Joan. In fact, when livestock were injured, whole gunnysacks of leaves were packed into the gaping hole. "Plantain compresses allegedly drew out the pus from infected wounds and helped them heal cleanly," she says.

✳

Deer's ears, or mullein, another common weed often found in fallow garden beds, was also valued by pioneers for its healing properties. Some country folk still treat infection and promote healing in injured animals with a solution of mullein leaves steeped in hot water, notes herb grower Terry Kemp of Onalaska, Wisconsin.

✳

One popular old-time remedy still enjoys a good reputation as a cure for warts. A slice of raw potato rubbed over the affected area is said to make the wart disappear. (Some folks believed you had to bury the potato afterward, being careful not to reveal its location to anyone; some buried the potato in a cemetery, while others completed the task by the light of the full moon.)

"When our son was a toddler, he had itty bitty warts all over his hand," recalls Meredyth Lillejord of La Crosse, Wisconsin. "I know they're viral, but I'd heard that if you rub them with a raw potato, it's supposed to get rid of the warts. We tried it, and the warts disappeared."

AUTHOR'S NOTE: *Although modern medical research finds no potent ingredient in potatoes, it's been reported that sometimes this cure works, notes dermatologist Stephen B. Webster, M.D., of La Crosse, Wisconsin.*

"In such instances the cure probably works by suggestive therapy," speculates Dr. Webster. The patient's state of mind triggers the body's own immunologic mechanism to manufacture lymphocytes, and it's these lymphocytes, rather than anything in the potato, that make the wart vanish, he explains.

✽

Many gardeners grow horseradish for the tang it adds to bland foods. But in the nineteenth century, folks also grew horseradish for use as a beauty treatment.

This facial recipe comes from a compendium of helpful hints published in 1890 by Lyman C. Draper and William A. Croffut: "To remove freckles, scrape horseradish into a cup of cold sour milk; let it stand twelve hours; strain, and apply two or three times a day."

✽

To prevent hydrophobia (rabies), Draper and Croffut recommend a risky cure we'd never try today. In their above-mentioned book, *A Helping Hand for Town and Country: An American Home Book of Practical and Scientific Information Concerning House and Lawn, Garden and Orchard, Field, Barn and Stable, Apiary and Fish Pond, Workshop and Dairy, and the Many Important Interests pertaining to Domestic Economy and Family Health,* they advise, "Take a white onion, cut it across the grain into four equal slices, sprinkle fine salt on them and apply to the wound, bandaged on, as soon as possible after the bite, when the onion will extract the poison; repeating every half hour with fresh slices until the onion ceases to show any discoloration."

After you finish reading that title, there's hardly time left to take this cure!

Recipe for a Greener Thumb

Gardening is like raising kids. Methods change constantly. What's right today isn't necessarily right tomorrow, but we all made it through! If you're having success, keep it up.

—DONNA FUSS, CONSULTING ROSARIAN, AMERICAN ROSE SOCIETY

If you want to be happy for an hour, drink wine.
If you want to be happy for three days, kill your pig
    and eat it.
If you want to be happy for nine months, get married.
If you want to be happy forever, become a gardener.

—OLD FOLK SAYING

Index

About the Author

Starting at the age of five in her folks' World War II Victory Garden, Shelley Goldbloom has gardened in New York, British Columbia, North Carolina, New Mexico, Oregon, Wisconsin, and Kentucky, where she and her husband now live.

Shelley has been a garden consultant to Minnesota Public Radio and garden columnist, and a radio host and producer. An award-winning freelance journalist, she writes for *Better Homes & Gardens* Special Interest Publications and is the author of four books: *Garden Smarts, The Unofficial Gardener's Handbook, Just Say "No Car Keys" and Other Survival Tactics for Parents of Teenagers,* and *A Zillion and One Things That Drive Moms Crazy.*

Also of Interest from
THE GLOBE PEQUOT PRESS

BEAUTIFUL EASY LAWNS & LANDSCAPES $16.95
Unintimidating advice for a great lawn with no fuss

**LANDSCAPING THAT SAVES ENERGY
AND DOLLARS** $17.95
A guide to conserving energy through landscape design

WINDOWBOX GARDENING $22.95
A wonderful array of ideas and plantings for windows

THE VICTORY GARDEN KIDS' BOOK $15.95
A fun guide to growing vegetables, fruits, and flowers

PERENNIAL GARDENS $18.95
A practical guide to home landscaping

BEAUTIFUL EASY GARDENS $15.95
A guide to planting and enjoying ten great gardens

THE NATURALIST'S GARDEN $16.95
How to garden with plants that attract birds and wildlife

EFFICIENT VEGETABLE GARDENING $15.95
Getting more out of your garden in less time

SIMPLE GARDEN PROJECTS $19.95
A collection of original designs to build in your garden

Available from your bookstore or directly from the publisher. For a free cat-
alogue or to place an order, call toll-free 24 hours a day 1-800-243-0495
or write the Globe Pequot Press, P.O. Box 833, Old Saybrook, Connecticut
06475-0833.